COMPUTER-MEDIATED
COMMUNICATION

COMPUTER-MEDIATED COMMUNICATION

Approaches and Perspectives

SECOND EDITION

John C. Sherblom and Judith E. Rosenbaum

University of Maine

cognella® | ACADEMIC PUBLISHING
320 South Cedros Ave., Ste. 400, Solana Beach, CA 92075

Brief Contents

Contents

Chapter 12   Communities   191

Preface

Computer-mediated communication (CMC) is one of the most exciting areas of study in the communication discipline today. Technology is rapidly changing the way we communicate, allowing us to be simultaneously more mobile and more connected. This connected mobility changes not only our communication ability but our relational expectations and experiences as well.

When John has a phone conversation with his brother while sitting on top of a mountain overlooking the ocean hundreds of miles away from where his brother is located, it changes the conversation and their relationship. Judith's spouse never used to text her from the grocery store. Now he does, involving her in the real-time decision-making processes of shopping for food, even when she is not physically present.

The advent of personal computers, the Internet, cell phone towers, and mobile phones has changed the way we communicate in our relationships and in society. Numerous scholars study the implications of this CMC, including the use of cell phones, text messages, computer videoconferencing, social media, and hybrid forms of computer-mediated and face-to-face conversations. In this book, we review five approaches and multiple perspectives to CMC and analyze their implications for our interpersonal and societal relationships.

New to This Edition

This second edition substantially updates and revises our review of these approaches and perspectives. The five approaches now more directly focus on the relational experience of CMC as reflected in the current research literature. These approaches describe the constraints, experience, relationships, interactions, and implications of CMC.

The second edition also includes several new perspectives within these approaches. Media synchronicity (Chapter 3) provides a discussion of information conveyance and meaning convergence through the media capacities of CMC. Person (Chapter 5) presents a communication perspective on the expression of a virtual identity in a CMC environment. Individuals (Chapter 10) describes the presentation of self in CMC relationships, with a focus on the implications for participant interaction and privacy management.

The chapters on affordances (Chapter 4), propinquity (Chapter 7), groups (Chapter 11), communities (Chapter 12), and actor-networks (Chapter 14) have been revised extensively. Each of these chapters includes new literature on the implications for CMC. These revisions both update and provide a fuller discussion of the constraints, experiences, and interactions that shape CMC.

In addition, each chapter has been updated to include a practical application of the perspective. These applications are drawn from recently published journal articles. Each generates insight into the applicability of the perspective to current CMC issues and enlivens the applicability of the perspective.

Finally, an updated communication ethics challenge and a set of discussion questions at the end of every chapter reflect current CMC concerns and practices. Further reading provides a list of current as well as foundational literature for each of the perspectives. These lists offer additional available resources for independent research into each of the perspectives.

Approaches

The book begins with a brief introduction that overviews the multiple approaches and perspectives to CMC. A short transition page at the beginning of each approach summarizes the approach and describes the perspectives within it. The book concludes with a discussion of the implications of CMC in ongoing relational and societal communication.

Computer-Mediated Communication: Approaches and Perspectives describes five approaches to the study of CMC. These approaches look at the constraints, experience, relationships, interactions, and implications of CMC. Each of the five sections of the book describes one of these approaches with chapters that provide multiple, alternative perspectives on it.

Perspectives

In Approach I, the perspectives of media richness (Chapter 1), media naturalness (Chapter 2), media synchronicity (Chapter 3), and affordances (Chapter 4) represent four perspectives on the constraints of CMC. In Approach II, person (Chapter 5), presence, (Chapter 6), and propinquity (Chapter 7) describe the experience of CMC. In Approach III, the social information processing theory and hyperpersonal perspective (Chapter 8) and the social identity model of deindividuation effects (Chapter 9) show how relationships form through CMC. In Approach IV, multiple perspectives on individuals (Chapter 10), groups (Chapter 11), and communities (Chapter 12) explain how CMC shapes interactions. In Approach V the Proteus effect (Chapter 13) describes the personal implications of CMC participation. The actor-networks perspective (Chapter 14) develops the implications of the multiple CMC influences for relationships. Together these perspectives identify important CMC issues for interpersonal communication and for society at large.

Chapters

Each chapter provides a theoretical background, description, and discussion of the perspective. One or more practical applications follow the discussion of that perspective.

A "Perspective in Context" section at the end of every chapter provides an analysis and critique, an in-practice application, illustration, and connection to the next perspective. A communication ethics question, list of keywords and phrases, discussion questions, and selected references follow.

Acknowledgments

We would like to thank the scholars who generously spent their time and energy reviewing the first edition of this book and making extensive comments and suggestions for the second. Their reviews helped shape this book and the ideas within it by challenging the perspectives included and providing insights that pushed the ideas further. Communication is an interactive process rather than directional expression, and a book often is shaped as much by engaging the reviewer comments as by an author's original presentation of ideas. We greatly appreciate the time, energy, and thoughtful contributions of the following reviewers to this book.

Reviewers of the first edition:
    Scott W. Campbell (University of Michigan)
    Amber Walker Jackson (Penn State University)
    Diane Karol Nagy (University of Florida)
    Erin K. Ruppel (University of Wisconsin–Milwaukee)
    Zuoming Wang (University of North Texas)
    Lesley A. Withers (Central Michigan University)
    Jason S. Wrench (SUNY New Platz)

Reviewers for the second edition:
    Traci L. Anderson (St. Cloud State University)
    Jakob E. Barnard (University of Jamestown)
    Scott Christen (Tennessee Tech University)
    Scott Haden Church (Brigham Young University)
    John W. Howard III (East Carolina University)
    Jeremy Harris Lipschultz (University of Nebraska at Omaha)

Finally, on a personal note, we would like to thank our respective spouses for their support during the writing and revising of this book. John would like to thank Liz. Judith would like to say thank you to Dennis.

Introduction

C omputer-mediated communication (CMC) is one of the most exciting areas of study in the communication discipline today. Technology is rapidly changing the way we communicate, allowing us to be both more mobile and more connected at the same time. This connected mobility changes not only what CMC looks like and how we engage with it, but our expectations of relational communication as well. The ubiquitous use of the Internet, personal computers, tablets, and smartphones changes the way we communicate in our relationships, communities, and society. Figure 0.1 shows CMC as both affecting and affected by our relational communication. The constraints, experience, relationships, interactions, and implications of CMC influence our everyday lives.

Communication is more than the exchange of content information from one person to another. "Communication has [both] a content and a relationship aspect" (Watzlawick et al. 1967, p. 54). Every message carries relational and social cues along with the informational content. Communication is the symbolic system of human expression through which individuals share information, create personal identities, connect with others, develop relationships, participate in groups, and construct communities. Relational cues reside in the language, style, and nonverbal expressions. They communicate our perceptions of personal identity, interpersonal relationships, social roles, and cultural expectations (Ruesch & Bateson, 1968). Using the relational cues embedded in that communication,

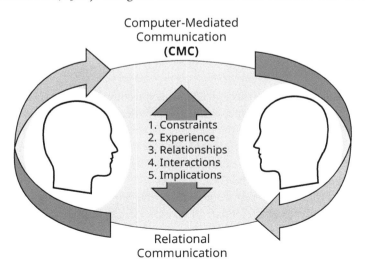

FIGURE 0.1 Computer-Mediated Communication.

individuals come to simultaneously understand the message content, their relationship to each other, and the social world within which they exist. When computer hardware, software, and networks mediate the expression, exchange, and interpretation of the informational content and relational cues, the communication is computer-mediated.

CMC

Computer-mediated communication (CMC) describes communication expressed and interpreted using a technological medium. We use the term CMC to describe any communication that is technologically mediated, in part, in whole, or across multiple platforms. This includes, but is not limited to, the use of texting, email, social media, audio- and videoconferencing, or the use of any digital platform to communicate. Whether you text, tweet, share a TikTok video, email, Snapchat, FaceTime, or Zoom, we call that CMC. The study of CMC analyzes the implications of this technological mediation on our communication, including both the informational content of the messages shared and the embedded relational cues that affect both on- and offline communication.

CMC Is Relational Communication

People use CMC for many of the same reasons they communicate face-to-face: to express themselves and to understand others. They use CMC to develop their personal, inter-personal, and social relationships. In this book, we limit our discussion of CMC to these personal, interpersonal, and social forms of relational communication. We do not include mass media presentations within our definition. CMC describes an interpersonal process in which individuals use a technological medium to develop meaningful understandings of themselves and their interpersonal, group, and community relationships with others. Movie streaming, television watching, news feeds, and other forms of one-way or one-to-many communication are not included in our discussion, even when they occur on a cell phone or a computer. In other words, watching a movie by yourself does not count as CMC, but using a cell phone or laptop to text or talk with someone about a movie, show, or newsfeed does.

Constraints, Experience, Relationships, Interactions, and Implications of CMC

Whether meeting face-to-face or through CMC, people communicate to create a common understanding in their relationships within the broader social context. A big question for communication scholars is how people co-construct a common meaning within the social context of a CMC medium. Some scholars focus on the communication constraints. Others describe the communicator experience. Still others investigate the relationships, interactions, and implications of the CMC process.

Each section of the book presents one of these five approaches to the study of CMC, described here in analyses of the constraints, experience, relationships, interactions, and implications. The chapters in each section present one or more analytic perspectives within that approach. Figure 0.2 summarizes the five approaches we use in the present analysis of CMC.

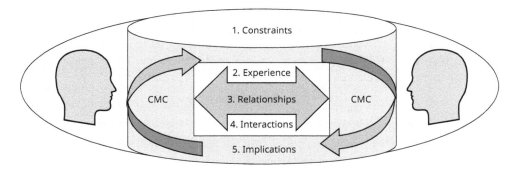

FIGURE 0.2 CMC Relationship Cycle.

Five Approaches to CMC

The analysis of constraints, experience, relationships, interactions, and implications provides useful approaches to understanding each aspect of CMC. The perspectives presented in each chapter describe the multiple influences and implications of each approach. Taken together, these approaches and perspectives describe the multiple influences of CMC in the construction of personal self-identity, interpersonal relationships, work group dynamics, and social communities. Paying attention to these multiple, interacting influences can help us develop competence and expertise in our relational communication using a technological medium (Sherblom, 2010).

Constraints

Approach I focuses on the constraints of the media used for CMC. Many CMC platforms, such as texting and email, provide asynchronous, visually anonymous, written forms of communication. This can create constraints on the ability to express and interpret the content information and relational cues. This approach often highlights these constraints by contrasting this type of CMC with the fully embodied, synchronous verbal communication and nonverbal expression available in a face-to-face conversation. Using this contrast, the perspectives within this approach analyze the effect of the reduced social cues of a visually anonymous, asynchronous, text-based CMC medium on the ability to communicate (Walther & Parks, 2002).

Each perspective within this first approach makes a different assumption about the nature of CMC, and each draws a different conclusion about how that nature impacts the communication. The media richness perspective locates the constraints in the technological characteristics of the medium. It views the asynchronous, visually anonymous, text-based characteristics of the medium as technological constraints on the ability to express nonverbal emotional-relational communication (Daft & Lengel, 1986). The media naturalness perspective places the constraints in the human mind and argues that this constraint is a consequence of human evolution (Kock, 2004, 2005). Media synchronicity redefines the constraints as capabilities of a medium and examines how they affect the transmission of information and co-construction of meaning in a variety of communication contexts (Dennis et al., 2008). The affordances perspective does not view the technological characteristics of the medium as constraints but as potentials perceived and used by participants to accomplish communication goals (Gibson, 1986). Each of these perspectives provides some insight into the potential constraints of CMC and the possibilities for managing them. Understanding these multiple perspectives can facilitate more effective communication and better CMC experiences.

Experience

Approach II describes the experience of CMC. It provides three perspectives on that experience. The first perspective holds that individuals develop online identities through their engagement with CMC. These identities grow out of online presentations of the self, which are carried out in the social environments that characterize CMC and that shape an individual's experience with others online (Koles & Nagy, 2012). Second, CMC users experience a presence within the medium and a social presence with others. Presence means being immersed in the mediated environment (Lee, 2004). Social presence is the feeling of closeness and connectedness to another person in that environment (Short et al., 1976). This sense of presence and social presence further shapes a person's online experience with CMC. Third, people can also generate or lose a sense of relational closeness and emotional intimacy with others through their participation in CMC. Propinquity describes this sense of relational closeness and examines how people's use of CMC can affect more than their online social presence, but their offline relationships as well (Korzenny, 1978). Person, presence, and propinquity describe the multiple influences and implications of a CMC experience. Examining these experiences provides insight into how people use CMC to develop effective and satisfying relationships.

Relationships

Approach III looks at how people use the text-based language of CMC in their relationships. The social information processing perspective describes how communicators strategically substitute verbal messages for the missing nonverbal cues, interpret the stylistic cues available in the text, and use the existing contextual information to reduce their interpersonal uncertainty and develop relationships in CMC (Tidwell & Walther, 2002). The hyperpersonal perspective discusses the relationship implications of being able to edit a text-based presentation of self to create a positive image (Walther, 1996). The social identity model of de-individuation effects (SIDE) describes the tendency of people, particularly in text-based CMC to identify strongly with a group and show a bias toward those who use language differently (Postmes et al., 1998). Each of these perspectives describes different implications of the influence of language use on relational communication.

Interactions

Approach IV focuses on the influence of CMC on individual, group, and community interactions. Individuals must develop communication strategies for their self-presentation, personal authenticity, identity shift, information warranting, and privacy management in their CMC interactions. The CMC context offers challenges to how individuals do each of these (Abidin, 2017; Carr et al., 2021; Trepte, 2021; Walther & Parks, 2002). Groups form networks of relationships through CMC that provide informational and emotional social capital (Lin, 1999). Participants in these groups must activate and mobilize that social capital to make it useful (Cao & Smith, 2021). Online communities offer communication spaces in which participants can connect to others, find information, and elicit emotional support. Participants in these communities continually shape and transform their own and each other's identities and relationships (Willson, 2006). The interactions of individuals, groups, and communities online describe some of the increasingly pervasive implications of CMC for our personal and relational communication.

Implications

Approach V examines some of the implications of participating in a CMC environment. The perspective of the Proteus effect describes how changes in virtual self-presentation affect a person's cognitions and behavior in physical world relationships (Yee & Bailenson, 2007). The actor network perspective analyzes the combined influence and implications of the technological, social, and cultural use of CMC and how it affects our worldview and understanding of each other (Latour, 2011). Participating in CMC, whether on social media platforms such as Facebook, Snapchat, and Twitter, or through texting and email, can have potentially positive or negative effects on our relationships. These effects extend beyond CMC to implications for our personal, relational, group, and societal futures (Baym, 2015).

Relational Communication, Constraints, and CMC

During his senior year in high school, John had to attend a funeral for one of his best friends. The friend had been drinking, was driving too fast, missed a curve, and drove his car into a tree on his way home from a party one night. Outside the church at the funeral the following week, John hugged his friend's girlfriend, talked softly, and cried with her. When he entered the church, he saw his friend's mother and took her hand, but had no words. The pain on her face left him speechless.

There are times in life when we find ourselves speechless. We can be inarticulate in our communication ability in any medium, especially in a new situation when we lack the interpersonal skill and relational competence to cope. Communicating through a CMC medium can complicate this sense of inarticulateness.

Differences with the constraints, experience, relationships, interactions, and implications of the medium can make CMC more challenging. Experience and skill with the medium, and the relationship history, social context, and community norms, affect the success of that CMC. Understanding the potential constraints, experiences, relationships, interactions, and implications, can facilitate the communication. In this book, we provide multiple approaches and perspectives to that understanding.

Perspectives in Context

Each chapter provides a clear, detailed description of one or more perspectives on CMC. Practical applications, analysis and critique, and a communication ethics challenge follow these descriptions. In addition, one or more of six characters illustrate the use of the perspective described in the chapter.

Illustration of Concepts

Cheryl, Darius, Alex, Pam, Sean, and Jasmine are the characters who illustrate each of the perspectives in the chapters. Cheryl is the regional vice president of Commercial and Residential Furniture Product Sales. She supervises the work of two sales representatives, Darius and Alex, who spend most of their time on the road visiting retail furniture businesses or working on installation job sites. Cheryl, Darius, and Alex communicate daily through email, texting, phone calls, and videoconferencing.

Pam is the owner and manager of the Home Products Store. She has two full-time employees, Sean and Jasmine, who split their time between working in the retail store, managing the growing volume of online sales, and traveling to professional job sites to take measurements, make recommendations, provide competitive bids, and oversee the installation of residential and office furniture. Pam regularly uses CMC to communicate with them and with her suppliers and customers. Pam, Sean, and Jasmine also frequently communicate with Cheryl, Darius, and Alex, from whom they purchase much of their furniture, and upon whom they rely for product information. Figure 0.3 shows their roles and relationships.

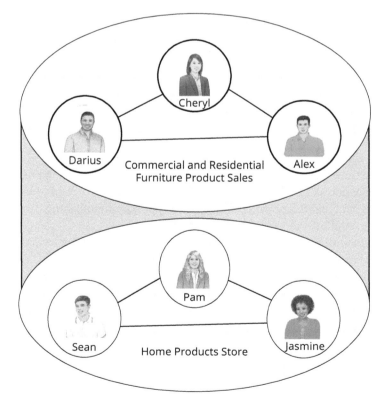

FIGURE 0.3 Character Roles and Relationships.

Looking Forward to Media Richness

In the next chapter we discuss media richness. Media richness describes the technological constraints of a CMC medium on the efficient and effective use of CMC to accomplish a person's communication goals. For example, Cheryl chooses text messaging to efficiently deliver straightforward sales information to Darius and Alex. She uses weekly sales meetings for face-to-face discussions of more complex customer issues. Knowing when and how to use CMC efficiently and effectively is an important communication consideration.

COMMUNICATION ETHICS CHALLENGE

What Are Communication Ethics?

In each chapter we explore a specific ethical communication question. These questions are based on the assumption that the purpose of communication is to express an authentic personal presentation of self, develop a close social presence with others, create relationships, and establish communities in an honest and open way. Our perspective is that ethical communication promotes personal authenticity, relational trust, honest conversation, participative decision-making, and community building. Defining less than ethical communication can be a bit complicated, but less ethical communication might, for example, try to disguise a personal agenda, deceive others, manipulate a relationship, or take unfair advantage of a group or community. Each question raises a practical issue. How do I communicate in an authentic, trustworthy, participatory, positive, community-building way?

- Do I have an ethical responsibility to communicate openly and non-strategically within the constraints of a medium, even if these constraints make it difficult for me to do so?

- Is it ethical to choose a medium and communication style that will benefit me personally, perhaps disadvantaging the other person? Why (not)?

- Do I have a communication responsibility to connect with other people, or can I ethically use CMC to preserve my privacy, to deceive, or to keep others at a distance?

- Does engaging in a personal relationship with someone create any additional ethical communication responsibilities? What are these additional responsibilities?

- What are my ethical communication responsibilities when engaging in an individual identity, group network, or online community?

KEYWORDS AND PHRASES

Communication is the symbolic system of human expression through which individuals share information, create personal identities, connect with others, develop relationships, participate in groups, and construct communities. It has both a content and a relational aspect.

Computer-mediated communication (**CMC**) describes communication expressed and inter-preted using a technological medium. We use the term to describe any communication that is technologically mediated, in part, in whole, or across multiple platforms.

QUESTIONS FOR FURTHER DISCUSSION

1. Are you always effective at communicating through CMC? Do you think you could find more effective and productive ways to communicate with friends, family, and professional people through CMC? Why?

2. What do you think are the most important approaches of CMC to know about: the constraints, experience, language, opportunities, or effects of participation?

3. Ethical communication is based on the assumption that the purpose of communication is to express an authentic personal agency, promote honest dialogue, develop relation-ships, encourage participative decision-making, and establish communities. Less ethical communication might be used to disguise a personal agenda, deceive others, manipulate a relationship, or take unfair advantage of a community. Do you think people are more likely to be unethical in CMC than face-to-face communication? Why?

Image Credits

Constraints

Goal of this approach: To compare and contrast the media richness, media naturalness, media synchronicity, and affordances perspectives on CMC. Approach I focuses on the constraints of CMC. Each chapter presents a perspective that describes the influence of CMC constraints on everyday human communication practices.

Media Richness: describes how the characteristics of CMC media can serve as constraints on human communication. This chapter examines how the immediacy of feedback, availability of nonverbal cues, use of language variety, and personal focus of various CMC media shape communication practices.

Media Naturalness: examines how the human mind's preference for face-to-face conversation constrains people's ability to communicate using a CMC medium.

Media Synchronicity: analyzes how communicators appropriate the transmission velocity, parallelism, symbol sets, rehearsability, and reprocessability constraints of a CMC medium to achieve information conveyance and meaning convergence.

Affordances: provides a perspective that recognizes the interaction between the participant perception of and characteristics inherent in a CMC medium. These characteristics form both the constraints and potential for CMC. The affordances perspective describes how it is not the constraints of the medium, mind, or communication context that matter, but the perception of how to use these as potentials for communication.

1

Media Richness

C heryl is the regional vice president of a commercial and residential furniture sales company. Her job is challenging. It requires that she engage in multiple forms of CMC on a daily basis. Cheryl supervises the work of two sales representatives, Alex and Darius, who spend most of their time on the road visiting retail furniture businesses. She also spends a large amount of her time reading product reviews, regional sales figures, and quarterly reports. Cheryl communicates with Alex and Darius through email, text messages, phone calls, videoconferences, and weekly office meetings. She is aware of the communication constraints that come with these platforms and tries to use each medium strategically to accomplish her goals.

FIGURE 1.1 Cheryl.

Defining Media Richness

Media richness refers to the extent to which a CMC medium allows people to communicate effectively, sharing both content and relational information. All communication messages contain both content and relational information (Ruesch & Bateson, 1968; Turner & Foss, 2018; Watzlawick et al., 1967). Content refers to the information contained within the message. Relational information describes the interpersonal meaning of the message, including the reason it was sent and how it is worded. "The relationship classifies, or subsumes, the content aspect, although ... the content aspect [equally] can be said to define the relationship" (Watzlawick et al. 1967, p. 54).

The media richness perspective begins by recognizing that "human social systems [are] ... more complex than [computer-mediated] machine systems" (Daft et al., 1987,

p. 356). The complexity of human systems creates relational ambiguity and "the existence of multiple, and conflicting interpretations," which constrain the ability to communicate efficiently and effectively through a computer-mediated system (Daft & Lengel, 1986, p. 556). To understand a CMC message, a recipient must reduce the ambiguity of both the content and the relational information.

Four Constraints of a Medium

Four characteristics of a CMC medium create constraints on the ability to resolve this content and relational ambiguity: (a) the ability to provide feedback, (b) the ability to use multiple nonverbal cues, (c) language variety, and (d) personal focus. Each of these constraints affects the ability to communicate efficiently and effectively through CMC (Daft et al., 1987; Lengel & Daft, 1988).

Feedback describes the immediacy of response to a communicated message. In a synchronous medium, such as face-to-face conversation, participants can simultaneously speak, listen, provide verbal and nonverbal feedback, and respond to questions and comments. Participants can seek clarification, show agreement, contradict, talk over, interrupt, and negotiate a common understanding. These communication abilities facilitate coming to a common understanding. Feedback in an asynchronous medium, like an online forum, is slower and less facilitative of producing that understanding.

Nonverbal cues are the vocal inflection, facial expressions, hand gestures, and bodily movements that facilitate the interpretation of verbal information. The ability to communicate using multiple nonverbal cues helps people convey their meaning. Communicating through a text-based medium such as Facebook messenger or Google Chats provides fewer nonverbal cues than talking face-to-face.

Language variety describes the range of meaning that can be conveyed through a medium using the linguistic symbols available in and appropriate to that medium. The greater the variety and appropriateness of the linguistic symbols available in a medium to convey that meaning, the easier it is to express, interpret, and understand concepts and ideas. Using the appropriate symbolic expression, whether the right word, numerical equation, picture, or graph, facilitates a clearer and more nuanced expression of the information. Face-to-face communication allows a wide variety of symbolic expression, including tone of voice, facial expression, and shoulder shrugs along with the verbal content. Communicating through a phone conversation or texting constrains some of these varieties of expression. Spoken language has rules but allows for a variety of informal expression, slang, vocal emphasis, purposeful mispronunciation, and verbal play. Written language is more formal in its rules for grammar, punctuation, and sentence structure. These formal rules constrain the variety of expression possible. In CMC, participants often use misspelled words, emojis, and a variety of other symbolic features to facilitate the expression and interpretation of their communication.

Personal focus is the extent to which a message conveys personal feelings and emotions. A personal focus establishes a connection and relationship and shares feelings, emotional support, trust, and friendship. The close, physical presence of a private face-to-face conversation between two close friends facilitates a personal focus. The face-to-face

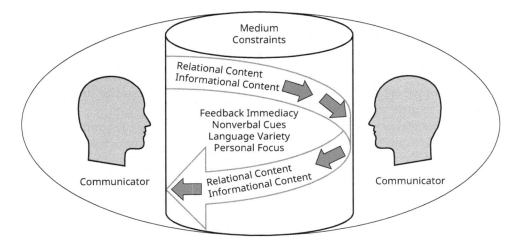

FIGURE 1.2 The four constraints on media richness.

conversation allows for the socio-emotional expression of feelings and perspectives that can contextualize the shared information. Leaning forward with a lowered voice and hushed expression suggests the sharing of a personal confidence. A pause and change in facial expression may indicate sadness, joy, or excitement about a bit of personal news. Written communication can express personal feelings as well, but the medium can make this more difficult (Daft et al., 1987).

Media richness focuses attention on how these four characteristics of a medium constrain the informational and relational content of a message expressed through CMC. Even in videoconferencing, because people are not sitting together face-to-face in the same physical space, they can experience a change in the feedback, nonverbal cues, language variety, and personal focus of the conversation. Other forms of CMC provide even less immediacy in feedback, nonverbal cues, language variety, and personal focus.

Figure 1.2 illustrates these four medium constraints. Compared to a face-to-face conversation, a CMC medium constrains the immediacy of feedback, nonverbal cues, language variety, and personal focus. These constraints reduce the ability to communicate informational and relational content in a message.

A Continuum of Lean to Rich Communication

The degree to which these four characteristics constrain communication describes the richness of a medium. That is, the extent to which immediate feedback, nonverbal cues, language variety, and personal focus are available in a medium place it along a continuum that runs from lean to rich. Face-to-face conversation provides the richest medium, with the fewest constraints. An audio medium, such as a phone call or audioconferencing, is next. Texting, email, and written memos each provide an increasingly leaner medium. Media that combine audio or video, with added written communication (e.g., using the chat function during a Zoom meeting) exist somewhere in between (Daft et al., 1987; Lengel & Daft, 1988).

In face-to-face conversation, we can see each other and adjust our communication as we speak. I may try to soften my words, clarify my expression, or change what I am saying before I even complete my sentence, depending on my interpretation of your simultaneous nonverbal response. In a phone conversation, you can object midsentence. We can talk over each other, argue, interrupt, agree, dispute facts, or laugh together before anyone completes an utterance.

An audio medium, such as the phone, carries nonverbal vocal cues, immediate feedback, and the expression of personal emotions. It, however, constrains the transmission of nonverbal gestures, so provides a leaner medium than face-to-face conversation. No matter how much I gesture, shrug my shoulders, or pace around while talking on the telephone, the person on the other end of the phone conversation only hears my words and tone of voice.

Texting provides a leaner medium. I can compose, review, and edit a text message before sending it. I might anticipate an immediate response and phrase the message accordingly, but texting allows a less synchronous response to that message. The receiver can think about the content before responding, and people often delay their responses to text messages.

Email generally provides fewer nonverbal cues and less synchronous responses than texting. It typically uses language that is more formal, provides less immediate feedback, and is less expressive of personal emotion. These characteristics make even a personal email leaner in its communication. Standardized emails sent to a large group of people, such as an office memo, meeting announcement, or report, are leaner still. Impersonal memos and written reports sent to a group, whether on paper or electronically, provide the leanest form of relational communication. Table 1.1 places these types of CMC along a media richness continuum.

TABLE 1.1 **Media Richness Continuum**

	Communication Medium	Feedback Immediacy	Nonverbal Cues	Language Variety	Personal Focus
RICH	Face-to-face communication	Available	Available	Available	Available
	Videoconference	Available, more formal	Reduced facial expression, physical gestures	Available	Available
	Telephone conversation	Available	Lacks facial expression, physical gestures	Available	Available
	Text message	Available	Specialized, limited	Specialized, limited	Stylized, available
	Email	Less immediate	Limited	More formal	less common
LEAN	Memo, written report	Unavailable	Unavailable	Unavailable	Unavailable

Fit the Communication to the Medium

People desire to use the medium that is most efficient and effective to achieve their communication goal. To do this, they fit their communication to the medium. There are three methods for fitting communication to the constraints of the medium. The first is to consider the language requirements of a communication message and select an appropriate medium. The second is to match the richness of the medium to the communication task. The third is to match the medium to the communication function.

Language–Medium Fit

The language–medium fit method considers the verbal, visual, and numeric information demands of a communication task. Not every medium handles every language demand equally well. This approach proposes using a medium with the capacity to meet the language demands of intended communication (Farmer & Hyatt, 1994). Table 1.2 illustrates the language demands.

Verbal information can convey a broad range of abstract ideas and concepts, as well as concrete meanings. The meaning of these words is often ambiguous. The synchronous interaction of a face-to-face conversation, however, allows questions, interruptions, rephrasing, discussions, and reinterpretations of an initial message. This can facilitate a more nuanced understanding of the meaning expressed through both verbal and nonverbal language.

The vocal inflection, facial expression, and body language enhance the verbal expression to enhance a sense of shared meaning. The synchronous verbal and nonverbal communication expressed in the form of questions, critical comments, sarcastic remarks, and humor contextualize the message and help clarify each person's understanding of the meaning. In CMC, using a synchronous videoconferencing medium, such as Zoom, FaceTime, or Skype, best facilitates this type of verbal communication.

TABLE 1.2 **Language–Medium Fit**

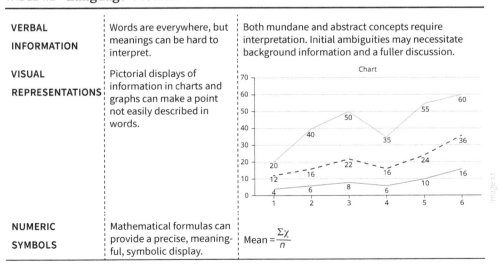

VERBAL INFORMATION	Words are everywhere, but meanings can be hard to interpret.	Both mundane and abstract concepts require interpretation. Initial ambiguities may necessitate background information and a fuller discussion.
VISUAL REPRESENTATIONS	Pictorial displays of information in charts and graphs can make a point not easily described in words.	
NUMERIC SYMBOLS	Mathematical formulas can provide a precise, meaningful, symbolic display.	Mean $=\dfrac{\Sigma\chi}{n}$

Visual representations can show spatial relationships and geometric information in a picture, chart, graph, map, or diagram. This representation may show a spatial relationship in two or three dimensions or a sequence through time. These visual representations have a holistic quality that can be difficult to express verbally and often require specialized software to produce. A medium that allows some combination of verbal and visual communication, such as face-to-face discussion with paper handouts, texting with pictures, email with attachments, or videoconferencing with document sharing, may be required for this kind of visual communication.

Numeric symbols can express formulas to communicate important information about budgets, program costs, sales commissions, profit sharing, pay increases, retirement benefits, or other types of statistical relationships. Not every communication medium can convey a mathematical formula easily, clearly, and succinctly. The formula in Table 1.2 provides an example. The verbal statement of this formula that the mean equals the sum of x divided by n takes more effort to state and to interpret than the numeric expression. Placing the formula into numeric language provides a succinct, unambiguous expression. Neither face-to-face communication nor texting is particularly well suited to conveying this type of mathematical expression. If we meet face-to-face, we will probably want to share the formula in writing and then discuss it. An audio- or videoconferencing system may require document sharing to meet the language demand of sharing this formula. Email may require an attachment to carry the numeric information in written form. To communicate effectively and efficiently, a person must fit the communication medium to the verbal, visual, and numeric language demands.

Communication Task Efficiency–Medium Fit

The **communication task efficiency–medium fit** method strives to balance the efficiency of transmitting the message content with the effective interpretation of its meaning. This can be challenging. There are three important considerations for achieving this balance between efficiency and effectiveness. First, efficient communicators often strive to handle routine communication matters as quickly and efficiently as possible. They do not let the richness of a medium reduce the efficiency of handling routine issues. Second, they do not let the lack of media richness restrict their communication or implicitly censor discussion of important content information. Finally, when unsure, effective communicators generally choose a rich communication medium. A loss in efficiency is better than inadvertently curtailing the communication needed to accomplish a task effectively (Lengel & Daft, 1988). Figure 1.3 shows the need for achieving an efficiency–effectiveness balance within the constraints of a medium.

A lean medium is the most efficient means for an exchange of everyday content information. It is preferred for communicating straightforward, non-ambiguous

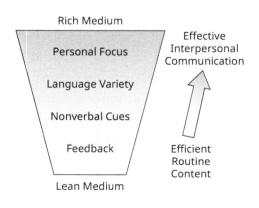

FIGURE 1.3 Task Medium Fit.

TABLE 1.3 **Communication Task–Medium Fit**

Effective: Requires more time, energy	Implement new plan or strategy that requires commitment	Rich medium
	Build interpersonal trust, relationship	Rich medium
	Show personal interest, caring	Rich medium
	Non-routine, controversial issue, or difficult conversation	Rich medium
Efficient: Quick	Routine information exchange	Lean medium

content. A lean medium is efficient for making simple requests, exchanges of routine information, official documents, and noncontroversial directives. Non-routine communication requires a richer medium for discussion.

A rich medium is more effective for (a) relaying non-routine, complex, or controversial content information; (b) showing a personal interest or concern; (c) building trust in an interpersonal relationship; and/or (d) implementing a new plan or strategy that requires commitment and involvement of participants. A rich medium allows participants to express emotion, demonstrate personal interest, show interpersonal caring, and build relationships. It is necessary for more demanding relational communication tasks. A rich medium allows the shared meaning and development of a common understanding among participants. A rich medium is better for handling controversial decision-making and problem-solving tasks and for implementing new plans or strategies that require participant involvement. Table 1.3 shows this communication task-medium fit.

Communication Function–Medium Fit

The communication function–medium fit method works to align the purpose of a communication to the richness of a medium. McGrath and Hollingshead (1994) describe eight communication functions. These eight functions are creativity, planning, decision-making, problem solving, task implementation, performance evaluation, negotiation, and conflict resolution. Each function places a communication demand on the richness of the medium. To be effective a communicator must choose an appropriate medium to fit the communication function. Table 1.4 shows these eight communication functions and the recommended choice of medium richness.

Use a Lean Medium for Creative and Planning Functions

Groups can accomplish creative and planning functions effectively through a lean medium. Text-based CMC groups often perform better than face-to-face groups in generating a larger number of more diverse and more creative ideas. Participants communicating through a text-based computer medium often feel less inhibited and are more willing to express their ideas. Using a leaner medium can facilitate equality in participation of group members and generate a more diverse and creative set of ideas. Planning functions are often routine and do not require much discussion or negotiation of roles or functions (McGrath & Hollingshead, 1994).

TABLE 1.4 **Communication Function–Medium Fit**

Communication Function	Communication Issue	Medium Richness Choice
Conflict resolution	Discuss and resolve conflicting reasons, viewpoints	Rich
Negotiation	Resolve multiple interests, mixed motives	Rich
Performance evaluation	Address power, status issues	Rich
Task implementation	Implement and evaluate project	Rich
Problem solving	Discuss issues and solutions	Rich
Decision-making	Achieve consensus or agreement	Rich
Planning	Address routine objectives and agenda	Lean
Creativity	Have a less inhibited generation of ideas, more equal participation	Lean

Use a Rich Medium for Understanding, Involvement, and Commitment

Decision-making and problem-solving functions require more communication richness. For a group to arrive at a decision or to solve a problem, participants must be able to achieve a common understanding. This understanding comes through discussion of the underlying causes, contextual influences, and likely consequences of any decision or solution. A rich medium, such as face-to-face discussion, generally works better for this communication function, but a synchronous video or audio conference may provide enough richness to achieve the goal as well. Groups who are experienced in their discussion with each other and have the expertise in using the medium sometimes find that synchronous forms of CMC outperform face-to-face interactions in efficiently and effectively accomplishing these decision-making problem-solving functions.

Task implementation and performance evaluation also require a rich medium. Participant involvement is necessary to achieve commitment to the long-term, successful implementation of a project. Without participant commitment, the project is likely to fail in meeting objectives. Performance evaluation of an individual, group, or task accomplishment requires a rich medium. To be successful, the communication medium must facilitate questions, discussion, and a common understanding of goals, objectives, and the ongoing areas that need more development.

Negotiation and conflict resolution represent competitive issues and are complex. They involve issues of status, power, multiple perspectives, personal interests, mixed motives, and sometimes hidden agendas. Resolving these communication functions requires a rich medium, such as a one-on-one, face-to-face conversation, and full discussion of the issues. Face-to-face groups generally perform better for functions that require negotiation.

Use a Multistep Communication Function Approach for Complex Functions

Some groups use a multistep approach, combining lean and rich media to accomplish a complex function efficiently and effectively. For example, a group might use a lean

CMC medium to initially generate ideas and involve members in more equal participation during the early creative and planning phases of a project. Once they generate the ideas, the group can meet face-to-face to critically review, discuss, and evaluate them. Following this discussion, the group may use a lean medium again to gather more information before they meet once again to make a decision. Using a lean CMC medium to share information and ideas can enhance both the group creativity and efficiency in decision-making. Following that with a face-to-face meeting facilitates discussion of the contextual issues, problem solving, and resolution of conflicts. A CMC group may generate more potential ideas and solutions through a lean medium, but they may need a face-to-face discussion to evaluate those ideas, maintain relationships, and get commitment to the project (McGrath & Hollingshead, 1994).

Figure 1.4 illustrates fitting the CMC medium to the communication function. Creativity and planning are best accomplished efficiently and effectively through a lean medium. The media richness needed for decision-making and planning functions depends on group experience and expertise. Task implementation and performance evaluation need a medium rich enough to facilitate discussion. Negotiation and conflict resolution are challenging communication functions that require a rich medium, such as face-to-face negotiation, to achieve a successful outcome.

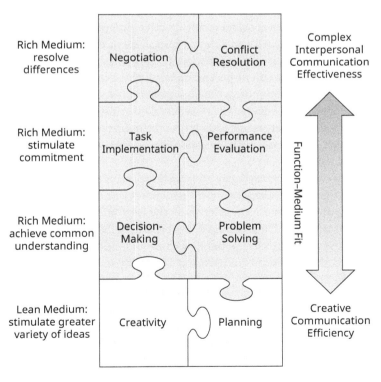

FIGURE 1.4 Function–Medium Fit.

Applying Media Richness

Media Richness in Supervisor Communication

To understand how technology affects the relationships between supervisors and their employees, Fairweather (2022) examined the richness of communication in the texting, email, and phone conversations that 186 employees had with their supervisors. Respondents perceive each medium as presenting some communication constraints that affect the quality of their relationship with their supervisor. They express concern for the effect of these constraints on their supervisor's approachability, supportiveness, and help with professional development.

Employees rated the telephone as the medium most effective in fostering a positive relationship with their supervisor. Phone conversations rated the highest for increasing approachability (82% of respondents), supportiveness (71%), and professional development (72%). These results suggest that phone conversations offer a rich-enough medium for building a relationship with a supervisor. Respondent comments indicate that being able to hear the vocal tone and inflection, and engaging in a conversational discussion of issues, helps avoid miscommunication with their supervisor. In addition, they perceive phone conversations as more private and secure. Their communication privacy and security are concerns for employees, especially when discussing sensitive issues with their supervisors.

Other media also appear effective in fostering positive supervisor–employee relationships. Many participants consider email effective. Some respondents, however, think that the asynchronous nature and delayed responses of email make it an ineffective medium that can lead to miscommunication. Others think videoconferencing is effective as well, as it is closer to an in-person meeting that provides vocal tones and body language useful for understanding the supervisor's response. However, this is only the case when videoconferencing is not used as a substitute for face-to-face meetings. The overuse of videoconferencing adds stress to their workplace relationships. They also complain that phone conversations and videoconferencing are often scheduled at inconvenient times.

Some respondents prefer texting for shorter, more casual messages. They indicate that it helps foster a friendly relationship with their supervisor. Most respondents, however, perceive texting and chat message systems as the least effective medium for fostering a positive relationship with a supervisor. Several describe texting as unprofessional, and many express a concern in its inability to provide full communication of a message. In addition, the missing vocal tone and body language increases the opportunity for miscommunication.

Overall, respondents perceive the benefits of the media richness in their phone conversations with supervisors but also note that communication in any medium that is friendly and personalized bolsters their perceptions of supervisor approachability and supportiveness. Some, however, indicate a preference for receiving performance feedback communication, particularly of any deficiencies, in a leaner medium. An asynchronous medium, such as in a text or email, allows an employee time to think and respond.

Customer Loyalty to Messaging Apps

Tseng et al. (2017) analyzed customer loyalty to cell phone messaging apps. They found that the media richness constraints affect how users perceive an app and their loyalty in using it. The ability of an app to provide interactive feedback, plus the use of multiple nonverbal cues, language variety, and a personal focus, affected the user loyalty. First, participants who received feedback from others using the app ascribed more social-relational usefulness to it in terms of the app helping them maintain their personal connections, business relationships, and social activities and in presenting them with collaboration opportunities. They expressed a sense of belonging to a community and overall feeling of psychological well-being while using the app. Second, the availability of multiple nonverbal cues contributed to user perceptions of an app's reliability and functionality. This increased their general satisfaction, use, and ongoing loyalty. Third, the variety of available language symbols, such as emojis, and an efficient tool for locating and using them effectively, facilitated user ability to create a personal focus in a variety of communication contexts. Fourth, an app that allowed users to personalize a message, and to share their beliefs and values in a wide variety of different relationships, groups, and contexts, builds customer loyalty.

Perceived Media Richness

The media richness perspective has grown from its original premise of choosing a CMC medium for efficient and effective communication. More recent studies conceptualize media richness as a subjective perception of the participants who use the medium rather than as the objective characteristics of a technology. Participant communication habits in providing feedback, nonverbal cues, language variety, and a personal focus all carry important relational information. The more participants provide immediate feedback, supportive nonverbal cues, a variety of relationship-tailored language, and a personal focus, a medium, regardless of its leanness, appears richer (Ishii et al., 2019).

This places media richness in the perceptions of interpersonal relationships and social practices of participants rather than in the technology. The media richness perspective recognizes that participants often find ways to use a medium for relationally rich communication. This richness, expressed through participant use, builds and maintains the relationships through their communication habits rather than an objectively defined set of characteristics embedded in the technology of a medium. Three studies describe the implications of perception of media richness.

The Perceived Media Richness of Instagram

Lee and Borah (2020) surveyed 671 young adults about their perceptions of the media richness of Instagram. They found that participants who perceive Instagram to be a rich medium are more likely to use the medium for self-presentation and developing new relationships. Higher perceptions of richness are associated with stronger participant agreement to statements such as "Instagram allows me to express my feelings more fully" (p. 60). This indicates a participant–platform interaction in the perception of media richness. Participants who used Instagram for personal communication perceived it to be a richer medium to the extent that it fulfilled their personal self-expression and social interaction needs.

Media Richness of Streaming Services

Hsu et al. (2020) analyzed user perceptions of streaming services that provide real-time audio and video coverage of events. These services allow interaction between the streamer and the user of the service during that coverage. The researchers found that providing immediate personalized feedback to users during the streaming event affects user perceptions of media richness, which in turn has a positive impact on loyalty to the streaming service. They conclude the streaming services can enhance their media richness by providing immediate feedback, with nonverbal cues, language variety, and a personal focus in their verbal and nonverbal responses to user questions and requests during the event. This enhances the interaction and increases the perceived friendliness. Second, responding in real time to user requests with a rich verbal and nonverbal language variety gives users a sense of being in a closer, more intimate relationship and increases sociability. This builds a collective sense of an online community, which creates loyalty to the service by providing a relationship between the streamer and the participants. Streamers can build on this by encouraging users to share their interests with others as a way of increasing the size and perception of community cohesion and richness.

Negative Implications of Media Richness

In contrast, Xiao et al. (2021) find that participants can be overwhelmed by a rich medium if it continually presents negative information. They examined the media richness implications of using a WeChat messaging system as a primary source of information during a life-disrupting event, in this case the COVID-19 pandemic. WeChat is a rich medium that provides users with a variety of information, from videos to news, to purchasing opportunities. Participants using the WeChat messaging system during the COVID-19 pandemic complained that the large amount of negative information provided by the medium triggered increases in personal stress, anxiety, and social media fatigue. In addition, the perceived richness of the medium led to communication overload, decreased decision-making quality, and reduced personal coping strategies. Xiao et al. (2021) describe this as a potential dark side of participation in a medium that relays largely negative information.

Summary: Media Richness

Media richness originally views the four constraints of feedback, nonverbal cues, language variety, and personal focus as characteristics of the medium. Users can select a medium that best fits their concerns for communication efficiency and effectiveness based on these qualities. Perceived media richness moves these qualities to the interaction between the constraints inherent in the medium and the participant.

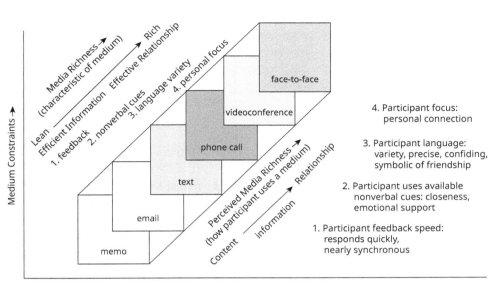

FIGURE 1.5 Perceived Media Richness.

Participants who are experienced in using a particular medium can provide richness in their feedback immediacy, use of nonverbal cues, language variety, and personal focus. A quick response makes texting or email more synchronous, building a sense of relationship. Slow responses have the opposite effect. Participant choice in the use of formal or informal language both represents and defines the relationship more than the content information in the message. A personal focus can develop a deeper connection between two people. Each of these qualities works within the constraints of the medium, but the relational style of the participant establishes the richness of the communication. Figure 1.5 illustrates this conception of perceived media richness as an interaction of participant communication style and medium constraints.

Perspective in Context

Analysis and Critique

Media richness focuses attention on the constraints of the medium. The goal is to fit the language, task, and function fit to the medium for efficient and effective communication. Lean media are best used for routine communication. Rich media, on the other hand, are most effective for decision-making, problem solving, task implementation, performance evaluation, negotiation, and conflict resolution. Four critiques of media richness are worth considering (Kock, 2005).

The first critique is that the tenets of media richness are vague. Media richness identifies four constraints but does not specify the degree of their relative importance. If a medium facilitates feedback but restricts some nonverbal cues, such as a personal phone call, is it richer, leaner, or about the same as a medium, such as a videoconference lecture, that allows more nonverbal cues but does not facilitate immediate feedback? Are personal nonverbal cues more or less important than the availability of immediate feedback, language variety, or personal focus? Does one combination of these characteristics influence the richness of communication more than another? The media richness perspective is not very helpful in answering these questions.

A second critique is that media richness reduces human communication to the efficient and effective transmission of information, which could be said to present a form of technological determinism. According to the media richness perspective, human agency exists in selecting the appropriate medium. Users choose a lean medium for efficient information transmission and a rich one for an effective understanding of more complex topics. Yet humans find ways of communicating effectively through a variety of media. There is a long history of developing and maintaining intimate relationships through letter writing. People do more than choose the appropriate medium. They actively engage in relational communication (Kock, 2005).

A third critique is that empirical research results do not always support the predictions of media richness. Kock (2005) reviews several studies that contradict media richness assertions. Dennis and Kinney (1998) also find no support for the media richness assertion that feedback immediacy and availability of nonverbal cues improves the task performance of groups. Both indicate that people can learn to use a lean medium, such as email, to accomplish a complex communication task.

A fourth critique is that media richness misplaces where the constraints are located. The perceived media richness perspective responds by moving the constraints to the interaction of the participant and medium. In their review of the literature, Ishii et al. (2019) conclude that "media richness is subjectively based ... and we expect that ... as more communication technologies continue to advance [it will] continue to propel future research" (pp. 129–129).

Media Richness in Practice: Advertising on Cell Phones

Tseng and Wei (2020) examined the constraints of media richness in advertising aimed at cell phone users. They explored the effect of media richness on each of the five advertising stages: Gaining the consumer's attention, interest, search, action, and sharing with friends. Their results show that rich media ads have a greater effect on consumer decision-making than other forms of advertising. The richness of the medium in which the ad is placed positively influences customer decision-making behavior in the three early stages (stimulating attention, interest, and search behaviors) but has little effect on the latter two stages of user action and sharing. At the same time, creating and using these kinds of ads also has higher costs for both the marketer and audience, so may be less efficient. Therefore, the authors recommend that marketers place mobile ads only in the three early stages to improve marketing success and reduce advertising costs.

FIGURE 1.6 Efficient, Effective Uses of CMC.

Illustration of Concepts

Cheryl uses a combination of email, text messages, and phone calls to communicate efficiently and effectively with Alex, Darius, and their customers. Cheryl communicates with Alex and Darius several times a day to confirm product availability, pricing, special offers, and appropriate customer discounts. She also provides customers with up-to-date product information and approves all large furniture sales, quantity discounts, and credit application requests. She uses different media for different purposes.

Cheryl uses email to send technical specifications and detailed product information. She usually attaches this information, containing lists, charts, and graphs, and then summarizes it in more personal natural language in the body of the email itself. She also exchanges text messages with Alex and Darius multiple times a day to deal with time-sensitive issues, such as specific customer product questions. For issues that require more privacy or fuller discussion, she uses the phone or, occasionally, if it includes the customer, a short videoconference.

Once a week, Cheryl, Alex, and Darius meet face-to-face as a sales team, usually in the office on Monday mornings. These informal meetings help them maintain their relationships as a team and provide an opportunity to discuss any issues that may have arisen during the week. When it is not possible to meet in person, they videoconference or schedule another time to meet later in the week.

Cheryl works hard to communicate efficiently and effectively, paying attention to her nonverbal cues, feedback, language, and personal focus within the constraints of each medium. She strives to provide the nonverbal cues, quick feedback, natural language, symbolic expression, and personal focus to increase the perception of richness in her communication in every medium. Her strategic use of CMC, based on the richness of the media, facilitates that efficient and effective team communication, providing the information and guidance needed to keep customers happy and achieve the team's regional sales objectives. Figure 1.6 illustrates the team's strategic use of multiple forms of CMC for efficient and effective communication.

Choosing a Lean Medium: For Whose Benefit?

Media richness assumes that a communicator will choose an appropriate medium to be effective and efficient. This assumption ignores the question of ethical communication. Does being effective mean choosing a communication medium through which you can construct relational understanding and consensus, or is the purpose to achieve a strategic personal advantage in expression and persuasion? Choosing a lean medium to achieve a personal goal can become an ethical concern.

For example, I may wish to achieve a group goal about which I feel strongly. However, I anticipate negative feedback from members of my work group. Instead of discussing the controversial issue face-to-face during our monthly work group meeting I might decide to communicate strategically with the group through a lean, text-based medium. After the face-to-face meeting, I send the necessary information to the group in a short email. Email allows me to edit the text so that it conveys only the necessary information, not my emotion, so there is an advantage to using email. Sending the information through email also does not allow others to engage in a lengthy discussion of the issues. I can strategically achieve my goal without having to negotiate with others, respond to negative feedback, or attempt to achieve a group consensus on a controversial topic.

Is my communication strategy ethical? Should CMC always be used to facilitate discussion, understanding, and consensus, or is it ethical to use it more efficiently to achieve a personal communication goal?

Looking Forward to Media Naturalness

In the next chapter, we review media naturalness, which presents a different perspective on the constraints to human communication. To misquote a famous line from Shakespeare, "The fault, dear Brutus, is not in the communication medium, but in ourselves." Media naturalness places constraints in the biological evolution of human communication systems. Human evolution has shaped our communication abilities and constrains them today.

KEYWORDS AND PHRASES

Communication function–medium fit aligns the purpose of a communication to the richness of a medium.

Communication task efficiency–medium fit balances the efficiency of transmitting the message content with the effective interpretation of its meaning.

Feedback describes the immediacy of response to a communicated message. In a synchronous medium, such as face-to-face conversation, participants can simultaneously speak, listen, provide verbal and nonverbal feedback, and respond to questions and comments.

Language–medium fit describes the extent to which the medium's capacity meets the language demands of intended communication. This method considers the verbal, visual, and numeric information demands of a communication task and the ability of a medium to meet those demands.

Language variety describes the range of meaning that can be conveyed through a medium using the linguistic symbols available in and appropriate for that medium.

Lean medium is a medium that is efficient for making simple requests, exchanges of routine information, official documents, and noncontroversial directives.

Media richness refers to the extent to which a CMC medium allows people to communicate effectively, sharing both content and relational information.

Nonverbal cues are the vocal inflection, facial expressions, hand gestures, and bodily movements that facilitate the interpretation of verbal information.

Numeric symbols use formulas to communicate important information about budgets, program costs, sales commissions, profit sharing, pay increases, retirement benefits, or other types of statistical relationships.

Personal focus is the extent to which a message conveys personal feelings and emotions. A personal focus establishes a connection and relationship, shares feelings, emotional support, trust, and friendship.

Rich medium is a medium that is more effective for (a) relaying non-routine, complex, or controversial content information; (b) showing a personal interest or concern; (c) building trust in an interpersonal relationship; and/or (d) implementing a new plan or strategy that requires commitment and involvement of participants.

Verbal information refers to the use of words. This kind of information can convey a broad range of abstract ideas and concepts, as well as concrete meanings.

Visual representations show spatial relationships and geometric information in a picture, chart, graph, map, or diagram. These representations may show a spatial relationship in two or three dimensions, or a sequence through time.

QUESTIONS FOR FURTHER DISCUSSION

1. Choose a social media platform (e.g., Facebook, Instagram, TikTok, a dating site). Do the characteristics of the medium affect the communication that takes place there? How?

2. Compare two or three different social media platforms. Discuss the differences in communication on each. Do you think that those communication differences are influenced by the medium?

3. What kind of medium is best for an in-depth discussion about politics, a richer or leaner medium? Why? What about a conversation with a friend in need of support? A job interview?

Image Credit

Fig. 1.2a: Copyright © 2016 Depositphotos/StudioIcon.

2

Media Naturalness

A lex is outgoing and self-confident. He likes engaging people in conversation, especially when he can help them out. He is currently a regional sales representative for Commercial and Residential Furniture Products. He is particularly knowledgeable and successful in selling commercial lighting solutions. He enjoys his job and likes developing long-term relationships with his customers. Alex makes most of his money through repeat sales to satisfied customers.

FIGURE 2.1 Alex.

The Naturalness of Face-to-Face Conversation

The media naturalness perspective builds on the scientific theory of human evolution. It views the processes of human communication as resulting from natural selection. This focus on natural selection offers a different explanation of the constraints on human communication than the media richness perspective suggests (Kock, 2005).

The media naturalness perspective holds that the more CMC reflects face-to-face communication, the more "natural" it feels and the less effort it requires. This is seen as the result of the natural selection and adaptation processes of evolution which have defined the physical, emotional, cognitive, and social constraints of human communication. This evolutionary process, occurring across multiple generations, endowed modern humans with a brain optimally designed for face-to-face conversation. Any medium that suppresses the qualities of that face-to-face conversation reduces the naturalness and makes communication more challenging (Kock, 2004).

The Evolution of Human Communication

Human evolution occurs through the processes of inheritance, mutation, and natural selection. Children inherit most of their genetic attributes from their parents. Occasional genetic mutations produce attributes that are different from those of parents. Beneficial mutations tend to survive and pass from one generation to the next through procreation, producing more children who are more likely to have that attribute.

TABLE 2.1 **Three Influential Processes of Evolution**

1. **INHERITANCE**	Children inherit most of their genetic attributes from their parents.
2. **MUTATION**	Occasional genetic mutations produce attributes that are different from those of parents. Some are beneficial to survival and mating.
3. **NATURAL SELECTION**	Beneficial mutations pass from one generation to the next through procreation, producing more children having that attribute.

These evolutionary processes of inheritance, mutation, and natural selection affect the development of human communication skills. Individuals who possess good relational communication skills are more likely to find an intimate partner, reproduce, and generate offspring. Hence, having good communication skills is beneficial not only to personal survival, but to the prospect of mating and the procreation of children.

From one generation to the next, human sensory organs and brain functions become increasingly efficient and effective in expressing and interpreting the meaning of verbal and nonverbal cues in intimate face-to-face contexts, creating a cross-generational evolutionary drift toward a species with enhanced relational communication skills. Hence, people today have become skilled at interpreting the meaning present in the verbal, nonverbal, auditory, and visual cues of face-to-face conversation. These nonverbal cues enhance and add subtlety, nuance, and context to the verbal content of a message, making understanding its meaning a relatively automatic, efficient, and effective process. A medium that reduces the ability to express or interpret these multiple verbal and nonverbal cues will feel less natural and be a more difficult context in which to communicate (Kock, 2004, 2005). Table 2.1 shows the three evolutionary processes that affect the development of human communication.

Face-to-Face: Colocation and Connection

The extent to which communication feels natural in face-to-face conversation depends on two dimensions. One is the space-time dimension represented in the physical colocation. The other is the expressive-perceptual connection dimension of participants in the conversation.

The space-time dimension identifies the importance of being together in the same space at the same time. There are two aspects of this dimension: colocation and synchronous conversation. Colocation permits participants to see and hear each other within the same communication context and environment. This facilitates a mutual communication experience that fosters a common understanding. Synchronous conversation assumes that participants are in the same space at the same time. This allows an interaction with turn taking, interruptions, feedback, talk-overs, redirections, verbal tangents, asides, nonverbal head nods, and collaborative expressions for arriving at that a common understanding (Kock, 2004, 2005).

The expressive–perceptual dimension builds on the space-time dimension and argues that the ability to observe vocal inflections of speech, facial expressions, and

TABLE 2.2 **Two Dimensions and Five Qualities of Media Naturalness**

1. Space-Time Dimension	Presence	
Colocated communication	Same place	Share a common communication context
Synchronous communication	Same time	Engage in an interactive communication exchange
2. Expressive-Perceptual Dimension	Nonverbal Communication	
Speech	Share vocal energy	Speak, listen/Convey vocal content, relational message
Facial expression	Share emotion	Observe/Convey facial expression
Body language	Share context	Observe/Convey gestures, bodily stance

physical body cues facilitates the expression and interpretation of meaning. In addition to being colocated in a synchronous exchange of conversational information, the ability for each person to hear the other's spoken word, see facial expressions, and assess physical cues enhances the naturalness of communication. Speech conveys the vocal qualities of anxiety, excitement, hesitation, qualification, and overall expressiveness. These qualify and amplify the verbal meaning. Facial expressions show frustration, distaste, enthusiasm, fear, and excitement, adding to the emotional content of the voice and words. Physical body cues, in gestures and bodily stance, further contextualize the meaning. These dimensions of time-space synchronous colocation and expressive-perceptual connection facilitate the coordination of a common meaning among participants (Kock, 2004). Table 2.2 summarizes these dimensions and their qualities.

The Natural Effects of Colocation and Connection

Physiological Arousal

Sharing time and space, and an expressive-perceptual dimension stimulates physiological arousal among participants. Physiological arousal is a heightened state of attention and emotion, whether happy, sad, angry, or joyous, that participants experience when together in face-to-face conversation. People laugh and cry together, share joy, get excited, and become angry in emotionally synchronous conversations. When one participant becomes animated, other conversational participants join in the enthusiasm. Face-to-face conversations are full of interpersonal excitement, anger, resentment, and pleasure. Conversations stimulate emotional responses that often appear contagious.

In face-to-face conversation, participants experience each other's speech rate, vocal tone, facial expressions, hand gestures, physical stances, and body postures. They listen to the auditory expression of excitement, nervousness, intensity, sincerity, and intimacy in the spoken word. Biological and cognitive coevolution facilitate the expression and interpretation of this shared emotional energy (Kock, 2004).

Colocation and an expressive–perceptual connection help people understand, empathize, and learn from each other. Mirror neurons in the brain facilitate this process. They help us not just hear but feel what the other person is saying. They synchronize our emotional attunement to the other person, linking our brains together, building social cohesion, and facilitating a common understanding (Cozolino, 2006).

In face-to-face conversation, the mirror neurons in our brains become activated, providing a link between the spoken language and gestures we observe and our internal experience. Through these mirror neurons we internally replicate the sensation of the words and behaviors, making connections in our brains between the language, physical movements, and experience. The internal mirror neuron networks link our brains together in a synchronization of emotional attunement. They connect our internal perception to the language and physical act of expression, vocalization, and hand movements being used to communicate. The spoken language and nonverbal gestures of face-to-face conversation work together to build social cohesion and understanding. Mirror neurons are thus an important part of the social brain, facilitating relational communication. It makes a difference whether I say "fire" in a hushed, intimate whisper or yell it with a panicked facial expression and a quick, agitated body movement, gesturing behind me (Cozolino, 2006; Presti, 2016).

Figure 2.2 places the physical presence and synchronous conversation qualities of colocation and the nonverbal expression, emotional experience, and cognitive connection of the expressive-perceptual dimension on a plot. Face-to-face conversation provides a natural medium for communication through its space-time colocation and expressive-perceptual connection. The physical colocation allows the experience of a common communication context and synchronous conversation. The expressive-perceptual dimension facilitates a shared nonverbal expression, emotional experience, and cognitive connection. Any medium that increases the distance in the space-time colocation and expressive-perceptual dimensions separates the participants and makes the communication less natural and more difficult. Figure 2.2 illustrates this effect of increasing distance along the space-time dimension of colocation and the expressive-perceptual connection of conversational speech and nonverbal emotional expression on the naturalness of a communication medium.

Speech Imperative

Of all the cues present in face-to-face conversation, the most important to the feeling of naturalness is speech. The degree to which a medium supports the ability to produce and listen to speech influences its naturalness more than the use of facial expressions or body language. People naturally attune to the subtleties of emotion and meaning of speech intonation, pitch, pauses, and rate (Kock, 2004).

Speech plays an important role in human evolution. It uses the mouth, nose, and lungs originally designed for eating and breathing to produce meaningful patterns of sound. The human brain interprets these sound patterns and automatically turns them into electrical impulses and chemical activities that stimulate both personal and social

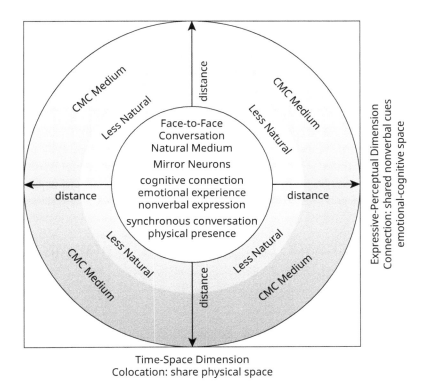

FIGURE 2.2 Time-Space Colocation and Expressive-Perceptual Connection.

meaning. We do not have to think about it. For most of us, the conversion of acoustic speech patterns to thought just happens.

Patterns of sound become symbolic meaning through a set of sensory and cognitive processes optimized by natural selection for speech. A medium that facilitates speech enhances the efficiency and effectiveness of our communication. A medium that constrains the ability to speak adds a degree of ambiguity to the message, which means that people must work harder to express and interpret its meaning (Kock, 2004).

Communication Ambiguity

Communication ambiguity is the degree to which the meaning of a message can be misinterpreted. As the nonverbal cues available in a medium decrease, communication ambiguity, and the probability of misinterpretation, increase. The spoken language available in synchronous, face-to-face communication relies on the automatic circuits of the brain to interpret the meaning of a message. To the extent that a medium differs from this spoken communication context, the less participants can rely on these automatic brain circuits to interpret the meaning and the more ambiguous the communication becomes (Kock, 2004).

The Naturalness of CMC

CMC provides a less-natural medium than face-to-face conversation. Videoconferencing loses the sense of colocation while maintaining some interpersonal synchronicity in vocal cues, facial expressions, and other physical cues such as leaning into or away from the camera. A phone conversation or audioconference maintains speech and synchronous conversation but loses the facial and physical cues. Texting is less synchronous and provides less expressive–perceptual nonverbal communication, except for stylized emojis. Vocal cues are missing, but some nonverbal cues, such as the opportunity for nearly synchronous response and use of informal language, remain. Email lacks colocation, vocal quality, facial expression, and physical body cues; and is often more formal and less synchronous than texting.

Cognitive Schema, Learning, Effort, Adaptation, and Alignment

Cognitive Schema

Through evolution, our brains have developed specialized brain circuits designed for information processing. Over millions of years, these brain circuits have developed into increasingly automatic and unconscious cognitive schema that process the speech patterns, vocal tones, facial expressions, and body language of conversational communication. Today they provide interpretive cognitive schema for many common relational communication scenarios. These default cognitive schema help us efficiently interpret the meaning of a message by simultaneously evaluating the patterns of verbal, vocal, facial, and physical body cues. They provide efficient cognitive short-cuts for quickly interpreting the most likely meaning of a message.

Face-to-face conversation relies on these built-in, automatic, cognitive schema to quickly assess the meaning of a message. The schema provide readily accessible information that is easily retrievable and relatively common in meaning across people. They represent people's first impression or understanding of something.

Communication through a medium that reduces the available colocation and expressive-perceptual connection cues available in face-to-face conversation cannot rely on these schema. This means that participants must make more effort to express and interpret the meaning of a message. The more a medium restricts or modifies the available nonverbal cues, the more cognitive effort it requires and the slower the communication process becomes. A word spoken in face-to-face conversation transmits information from one person to another about 18 times faster than the same word typed and sent through email. This means, as Kock (2005) points out, that exchanging 600 words in face-to-face conversation takes about 6 minutes. Typing and transmitting the same information in an email can take much longer. Face-to-face conversation is a highly efficient communication medium (DeRosa et al., 2004; Kock, 2004, 2005).

Learning and Cognitive Effort

In addition to the hardwired information-processing cognitive schema, evolution also provides the ability to learn new things. This learning induces changes in the brain, creating new cognitive circuits. Our brains have many of these learned circuits, but we cannot access them as efficiently as the automatic ones. Retrieving learned information requires more cognitive effort. In addition, the learned circuits must be refreshed and partially relearned from time to time. Hence, learning, relearning, and exchanging the meaning stored in these circuits requires more cognitive effort (Kock et al., 2007).

In addition, these learned circuits reflect individual experience, education, and expertise in a particular area of interest. That experience, education, and expertise differs from person to person. This can lead to more potential for misunderstanding among people.

As the naturalness of a medium decreases, the cognitive effort required to communicate increases. In a less natural medium, participants must rely on their learned, rather than automatic, cognitive schema. Reliance on this type of cognitive circuit requires more effort in learning and relearning the schema and increases the communication ambiguity, which requires effort to resolve (Kock et al., 2007).

Cognitive effort describes the amount of time and energy needed to transfer information from one person to another through a communication medium. By making this cognitive effort, participants can learn to communicate efficiently and effectively in a less natural medium, but that requires cognitive adaptation and alignment.

Cognitive Adaptation and Alignment

Initially, people must make a cognitive effort to overcome the communication ambiguity associated with a less natural medium. As participants become familiar with the use of the medium, they generate new cognitive schema, social behaviors, and communication habits that require less effort. These new schema, behaviors, and habits facilitate the coordination of interpersonal meaning and mutual understanding, making communication more efficient and effective for participants experienced in a medium (Kock, 2004).

Cognitive adaptation describes a person's ability to learn through experience, develop expertise, and adopt new cognitive schema to communicate effectively in a medium (Kock, 2004). As people gain experience with the medium, they develop new cognitive schema to adapt to it. This cognitive adaptation reduces the effort needed to use a medium to communicate effectively. It also decreases the amount of communication ambiguity in the medium. As cognitive effort and communication ambiguity decrease, the experience of communication naturalness within the medium increases (DeRosa et al., 2004).

As multiple participants gain experience with a medium, they can align their learned cognitive schema to each other and become more effective communicators even in a less natural medium. Schema alignment identifies achieving a relative sameness between the cognitive schema of two or more people, who, over time, reduce their communication ambiguity and develop a common way of thinking about a problem or issue. Schema alignment among participants reduces cognitive effort and facilitates communication. As participants get to know each other and align their schema, they find it easier to communicate, regardless of the medium (DeRosa et al., 2004; Kock, 2004).

Placing the constraints in the human mind and body rather than in the medium explains how people are able to learn to communicate more efficiently and effectively through CMC over time. It takes cognitive effort to learn and to renew that learning, but once achieved, schema adaptation and alignment facilitate effective and efficient

TABLE 2.3 Cognitive Schema, Effort, Learning, Adaptation, and Alignment

COGNITIVE SCHEMA	Built-in, routine cognitive schema to reduce communication expressive and interpretive effort in a face-to-face medium.
COGNITIVE EFFORT	Cognitive effort needed to develop new schema to adapt to communication in a less natural medium.
LEARNING	Routine schema no longer adequate. Must learn new schema. New cognitive schema learning requires effort.
COGNITIVE ADAPTATION	A new, less natural, medium requires cognitive adaptation. With adaptation, effort decreases in any medium.
SCHEMA ALIGNMENT	Schema alignment among participants requires more effort. With experience, effort decreases, regardless of medium.

communication among participants even in a less natural medium. Table 2.3 lists the media naturalness concepts of cognitive schema, effort, learning, adaptation, and alignment.

Compensatory Adaptation: Cognitive Schema, Effort, Alignment in CMC

Figure 2.3 illustrates these concepts as they apply to CMC. Face-to-face communication is synchronous along the dimensions of time-space colocation and expressive-perceptual connection. Speech, facial expressions, physical posture, and other nonverbal cues stimulate physiological arousal and orient participant attention, reducing the communication ambiguity of face-to-face conversation. As CMC moves from synchronous communication,

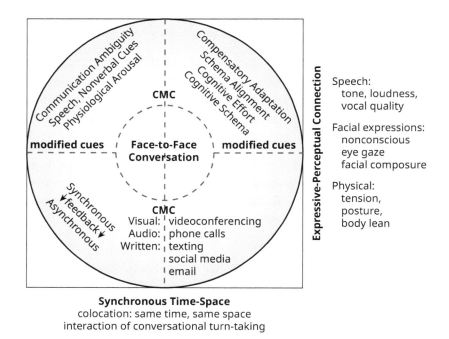

FIGURE 2.3 Cognitive Schema and Compensatory Adaptation to CMC.

such as videoconferencing and phone calls, to asynchronous communication, such as texting, social media, and email, the loss of speech, facial, and physical cues makes the medium less natural. Participants must engage in compensatory adaptation by learning new cognitive schema to communicate effectively. These new schema take cognitive effort to learn and practice, but with experience participants can adapt to the medium and engage in schema alignment with other participants, increasing the effectiveness and efficiency of their communication.

Applying Media Naturalness

Videoconferencing Exhaustion

Karl et al. (2022) investigated why people find videoconferencing so exhausting. After surveying 549 videoconference users, they identified six common complaints about the videoconference experience. Three of these complaints center on the lack of professional meeting management, the difficulty of working from home, and the perceived violation of social etiquette when other people eat lunch during a meeting. The other three complaints refer to the media naturalness of videoconferencing, in particular issues of colocation, nonverbal cues, and speech.

Colocation

Videoconference participants complained about not being able to see others adequately due to background lighting and odd camera angles or only being able to see the top of heads. Complaints also mentioned participants having their faces too close to the camera, participants not looking at the camera, walking around in a distracting manner, perpetually staring into the camera, or not having the camera on at all. Many participants felt that all participants should leave their cameras on during a meeting. Having cameras turned off gives the impression that a participant is lurking or multitasking and not fully engaged in the meeting.

In face-to-face conversation, participants can usually see the other people to whom they are speaking. They can see a person's face and make eye contact. Being able to see their facial expressions and other nonverbal cues improves the communication effectiveness. Seeing others on screen during videoconferencing can improve the quality of the interaction and facilitate coworker relationships. Done poorly, it can be a distraction.

Nonverbal Cues

Synchronous nonverbal cues are also important to communication, in particular in videoconferencing calls. Participants find the nonverbal cues of others who sit too close to the camera and stare into the screen disconcerting and disruptive to the conversational flow. In face-to-face meetings, participants don't usually stare into each other's eyes, and a prolonged direct gaze into the camera can create a sense of discomfort among the other participants. Many find this unnatural, distracting, uncomfortable, and disturbing. In addition, participants often see their own face on the computer screen. Some participants become self-conscious about their physical appearance. Watching their own repetitive nonverbal gestures or trying to stop fidgeting disrupts their focus and takes their attention away from the conversation.

Speech

Being able to hear others easily, without background noise, is also important. This requires the effective use of participant microphones. When individuals do not turn off their microphones, background noises from their various locations can interfere with a meeting. Participants may lose their ability to hear the speaker. When participants forget to turn on their microphones before speaking it can cause an interruption and interfere with the meeting flow. Inadequate bandwidth also can interfere with videoconferencing transmission and disrupt the conversational interaction.

These videoconference-based differences in the experience of having a synchronous, colocated face-to-face conversation reduce the communication naturalness and require more cognitive effort of the participants to align their cognitive schema and meaning structures during the meeting. This cognitive effort produces videoconferencing fatigue. However, the media naturalness perspective predicts that, over time, with practice, learning, and alignment, videoconference participants will engage in compensatory adaptation and experience less exhaustion.

Perspective in Context

Analysis and Critique

The media naturalness perspective makes some of the same assertions as media richness about the importance of feedback immediacy, nonverbal cues, language variety, and personal focus to effective communication. It also places media on a continuum with face-to-face conversation being the most natural, followed by media that include voice, such as videoconferencing and phone calls, then more nearly synchronous interactions, such as texting, finally followed by email. The media naturalness perspective, however, differs from richness in several ways.

First, media naturalness places the constraints on communication in the adaptation of the human mind and body to a particular medium instead in the characteristics of the medium itself. This has the advantage of explaining how humans can learn to communicate efficiently and effectively within a CMC medium. With cognitive effort and practice, participants can engage in a compensatory adaptation to the medium, learn to overcome the ambiguity, and align cognitive schema. It takes cognitive effort, and participants find communicating in a less natural medium challenging at first.

Second, media naturalness includes being colocated in space and time and cognitively connected through physiological arousal and the sharing of human emotion as important to a shared understanding. Genetically programmed neural networks recognize common patterns of vocal and nonverbal cues that help reduce communication ambiguity and increase cognitive schema alignment. Over time, with practice, participants can become proficient and will begin to perceive the medium as a more natural place for communication.

Third, media naturalness places communication agency in the person. The media richness perspective assigns a person the task of selecting an appropriate medium, with the best fit, through which to communicate. Naturalness assigns a person the responsibility of making a cognitive effort, while communicating, to learn, adapt, and align to the cognitive schema of other participants. This defines effective communication not as a selection process, but as an ongoing cognitive activity of engagement with both the medium and other participants.

Fourth, media naturalness is an evolutionary theory. Human communication is a highly evolved system that functions naturally in a face-to-face medium. The evolutionary development of the neural networks in the human brain underlie the cognitive alignment needed for communicating meaning. To be effective in another medium, an individual must make the cognitive effort necessary to organize thoughts, avoid ambiguity, and communicate with the intent of aligning cognitive schema with another person.

If the naturalness of face-to-face conversation evolved over millions of years and many human generations, how does a single generation of participants learn to communicate effectively in a relatively new CMC medium that is different from face-to-face? This is not a question of evolution but a matter of learning. Media naturalness alludes to learning but does not develop it. A learning theory might provide a better explanation of this generational shift in CMC ability than biological evolution.

In addition, the speech imperative indicates that people naturally prefer to talk rather than text. Speaking relies on automatic cognitive processes; writing invokes learned schema. Yet, many people prefer to text rather than talk on their phones. This suggests that there are other influences, such as social environment, that shape people's comfort with a communication medium. Texting provides short, asynchronous messages without the verbal communication available in a phone call. There are no vocal subtleties, intonation, pitch, pause, or rate of speech relational cues available, only the informational content of the text. Yet, it is convenient, allows editing before sending, and often receives a quick response. These relational communication advantages appear to offset the speech imperative.

Still, considering the media naturalness perspective when discussing how people use different media to communicate has advantages. Showing how both biological evolution and learning affect communication provides a place for human efficacy and responsibility. Effective use of the various media can vary with participant, experience, and expertise. We can learn to communicate through any medium. With enough experience and expertise, we may become proficient.

Media Naturalness in Practice: Interpreting User Software Agreements

Why do we find software agreements so annoying and difficult to read? Kock et al. (2015) explored whether watching short video presentations of those annoying agreements, instead of the traditional written ones, would help users make better decisions. The media richness perspective anticipates that shifting to a richer medium, such as video, will increase communication effectiveness. This should improve a user's ability to make a good decision. Media naturalness suggests that the extra cognitive effort associated with having to read the document will stimulate a compensatory adaptation in the user's cognitive schema. Users will make an extra effort to align their cognitive schema with the intent and meaning of the document clause. This extra effort should facilitate understanding the contract better and making good decisions about accepting or rejecting specific clauses.

To test these ideas Kock et al. presented 339 participants with 20 software agreement clauses, each of which could be accepted or rejected independently in the process of installing a desired software purchase. Six deceitfully worded clauses were interspersed among the 14 non-deceitful ones.

They found that participants who viewed the contract clauses in video clips reported make less cognitive effort and experienced less communication ambiguity than those who read the clauses as text. Correct rejection of deceitful clauses, however, was associated with greater cognitive effort and recognition of more communication ambiguity in the wording of the contract. The people who watched the videos were thus less effective at rejecting deceitful clauses. Making that cognitive effort and perceiving the communication ambiguity in the contract wording helps participants successfully identify and reject the deceitful clauses.

This finding is consistent with the media naturalness proposition of compensatory adaptation and inconsistent with the media richness expectation. Presenting contract information in video format provides an easier experience but does not improve decision-making.

Illustration of Concepts

Alex works hard and is continuing to learn how to best use CMC to maintain his customer relationships. He makes note of his customer preferences in their initial interactions with him. Some call him on the phone, others text, and a few stay in touch through email. Alex accommodates these preferences by responding in the customer medium of choice.

Alex always follows up initial customer interactions with a face-to-face conversation. These conversations allow him to better evaluate the level of enthusiasm for a product, suggest alternatives if necessary, stimulate interest in the purchase, and reduce any communication ambiguity. The conversational interactions are important, but once customers have placed their orders, Alex stays in contact with them during the ordering and installation processes through the customer medium of choice. He believes that represents the medium in which the customer is the most experienced and feels the most comfortable communicating, in other words, the one that feels most natural to them. He reduces their cognitive effort in communicating with him by learning their preference and aligning his schema to theirs. He believes this contributes to his success in maintaining long-term relationships and generates repeat sales.

Alex recognizes the influence of media naturalness in his communication with customers. Face-to-face conversations about products and lighting solutions stimulate a sense of presence and physiological arousal through synchronous speech and nonverbal cues that can mitigate the relational communication ambiguity. In addition, Alex adapts and makes the cognitive effort to align his thinking with his customer preferences for a communication medium, choosing the one that appears more natural for them. Figure 2.4 summarizes and illustrates the considerations.

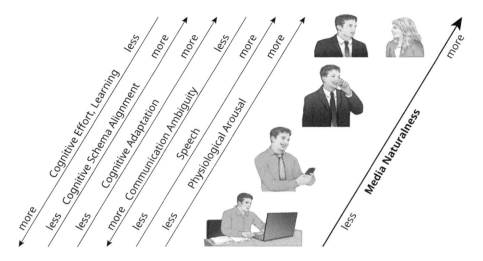

FIGURE 2.4 Media Naturalness and Cognitive Effort.

Looking Forward to Media Synchronicity

The media richness and naturalness perspectives both describe constraints. Media richness places these constraints in the medium. Media naturalness places them in the human communicators. In the next chapter, we describe the media synchronicity perspective. Media synchronicity builds on the principles of richness and naturalness to describe the multiple influences of medium and human interaction within a broader relational communication context.

COMMUNICATION ETHICS CHALLENGE

Whose Cognitive Effort Is Required?

The manager of a small technical work team is experienced and expert at reading long technical reports and often shares these with the work team. Reading these reports requires a great deal of cognitive effort. The written communication is often ambiguous in meaning and dry in content. The manager could provide much of this information in short informal presentations and answer any questions afterward. However, the manager is busy and thinks the team members should learn to read and understand this material on their own. With enough time and effort, they can learn to read these technical reports and eventually will understand the information in this written medium, but they will need to develop the cognitive schema first. Mentoring is important. Is there an ethical balance of responsibility for communicating complex technical information to the less experienced members of a work team?

1. Is it the manager's responsibility to provide the information in as simple, clear, and effective manner as possible?

2. Does the team have an ethical responsibility to make a cognitive effort to read the technical reports and develop their own understanding of the material?

3. How do we ethically balance the cognitive effort needed by various team members to understand this important information?

KEYWORDS AND PHRASES

Cognitive adaptation describes a person's ability to learn through experience, develop expertise, and adopt new cognitive schema to communicate effectively in a medium.

Cognitive effort describes the amount of time and energy needed transfer information from one person to another through a communication medium.

Cognitive schema help us efficiently interpret the meaning of a message by simultaneously evaluating the patterns of verbal, vocal, facial, and physical body cues. They provide efficient cognitive short cuts for quickly interpreting the most likely meaning of a message.

Colocation permits participants to see and hear each other within the same communication context and environment.

Communication ambiguity is the degree to which the meaning of a message can be misinterpreted. As the nonverbal cues available in a medium decrease, communication ambiguity, and that probability of misinterpretation, increase.

Expressive–perceptual dimension builds on the space-time dimension and argues that the ability to observe vocal inflections of speech, facial expressions, and physical body cues facilitates the expression and interpretation of meaning.

Facial expressions show frustration, distaste, enthusiasm, fear, and excitement, adding to the emotional content of the voice and words.

Media naturalness is a perspective holds that the more CMC reflects face-to-face communication, or the more "natural" this communication is, the less effort it requires from its participants to engage in collaborative activities.

Physical body cues in the gestures and bodily stance further contextualize the meaning of a particular communication.

Physiological arousal is a heightened state of attention and emotion, whether happy, sad, angry, or joyous, that participants experience when together in face-to-face conversation.

Schema alignment identifies achieving a relative sameness between the cognitive schema of two or more people who, over time, reduce their communication ambiguity and develop a common way of thinking about a problem or issue.

Space-time dimension identifies the importance of being together in the same space at the same time. There are two aspects of this dimension: colocation and synchronous conversation.

Speech conveys the vocal qualities of anxiety, excitement, hesitation, qualification, and overall expressiveness.

Synchronous conversation assumes that participants are in the same space at the same time.

QUESTIONS FOR FURTHER DISCUSSION

1. Which medium do you find the most natural medium for communication with professional colleagues? Family members? Friends? Why?

   - Do you find texting a friend more or less natural than talking on the phone?

   - Do you find it easier to text a friend you know and get along well with than to text a stranger?

   - Do you find it easier to email or call a potential employer?

   - Is any of this evidence of cognitive schema alignment?

2. The media naturalness perspective argues that any medium that suppresses the advantages of face-to-face communication makes communication harder. Is this true for you: Do you prefer talking to someone face-to-face than texting? Does this differ for different topics? How can this be explained by the media naturalness perspective?

3. Do you see a difference in what kinds of media you prefer versus those preferred by your parents or even grandparents? How is this evidence of the "evolutionary use of communication"?

3

Media Synchronicity

D arius is 26 years old and works as a regional sales representative for Commercial and Residential Furniture Products. Darius's father is a carpenter who specializes in furniture repair. When he was young, Darius worked with his father after school and on weekends. Darius learned a lot about furniture construction from his father. He can look at a piece of furniture and know how well made it is. He can make durability comparisons between different lines of furniture, estimate how long each item will last with rough use in a commercial setting, and predict how satisfied a customer will be long-term. Darius is good at communicating with people; he is able to explain things, answer questions, and respond appropriately to customer concerns.

FIGURE 3.1 Darius.

Information Conveyance, Meaning Convergence

The media synchronicity perspective builds on both the richness and naturalness perspectives, but it shifts attention from the constraints of the medium and the effects of human cognitive schema to the fundamental processes of communication. The media synchronicity perspective identifies these processes as information conveyance and meaning convergence. Conveyance describes the transmission of information through one or more messages to accomplish a communication task. Convergence is the process through which people achieve a common understanding of the meaning of that transmitted information. These two processes define communication as the transmission of information through a medium, much like described in media richness, and the achievement of a common understanding, much like the cognitive schema alignment as indicated by media naturalness (Dennis et al., 2008).

Converging on a common meaning of information requires the conveyance of that information. A sender must prepare and send the message. An individual or group of participants must not only receive but also interpret and understand that message to converge on a common meaning. Each CMC medium has a set of capabilities that affect these conveyance and convergence processes of communication. Participants use these

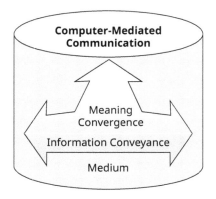

FIGURE 3.2 Information Conveyance and Meaning Convergence in CMC.

media capabilities to accomplish their communication goals (Dennis et al., 2008).

Figure 3.2 illustrates the conveyance and convergence processes of CMC. Convergence on a common meaning among participants builds on the conveyance of information. The efficient and effective conveyance of the information, however, is necessary but not sufficient for participants to arrive at that common meaning.

Synchronicity

The ability of a medium to support synchronous communication facilitates meaning convergence. When participants are able to work together at the same time, they can more easily coordinate their communication behavior. This facilitates the ability to share information, opinions, and perspectives and arrive at a common understanding.

Synchronous communication, however, is necessary but not sufficient for synchronicity. Participants often communicate synchronously but process information asynchronously. Synchronicity describes a pattern of coordinated communication among participants who share a common focus. It is this common focus that facilitates the meaning convergence of these participants, working together at the same time (Dennis et al., 2008; Ishii et al., 2019).

Media Capabilities

Each CMC medium has a set of technological characteristics. These characteristics provide the media capabilities that participants may use. Five media capabilities interact with synchronicity to influence the information conveyance and meaning convergence processes. These are transmission velocity, parallelism, symbol sets, rehearsability, and reprocessability of a medium (Dennis et al., 2008). Figure 3.3 lists the five media capabilities that influence information conveyance and meaning convergence in CMC.

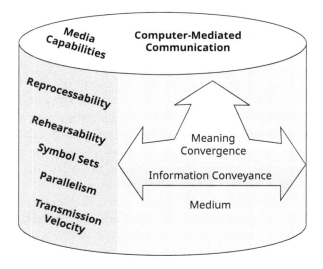

FIGURE 3.3 Five Media Capabilities influence Conveyance and Convergence.

Transmission Velocity

Transmission velocity is the speed at which a medium transmits information. This refers to more than just passing on information, though. It includes the rapidity of transmission, immediacy of feedback, and synchronicity of turn taking in communication. This capability varies with the medium as well as with the user. Paper letters have a lower transmission velocity than an email because of the nature of the medium. However, a delayed response to a text, email, or voice message; a dropped cell phone signal; video-conferencing difficulties; or participants who are late to a face-to-face meeting all reduce transmission velocity and feedback immediacy as well.

In general, increased transmission velocity supports synchronous communication, which facilitates meaning convergence. A high transmission velocity means that messages reach recipients with less transmission time, allowing for faster responses, which means communication can become more of a continuous exchange process, with quicker feedback, more interaction, and improved coordination among participants. This supports synchronous conversational coordination and shared meaning making among participants (Dennis et al., 2008).

Parallelism

Parallelism refers to the number of simultaneous transmissions that a medium allows. It refers to how many people can send and receive multiple messages simultaneously. Some media limit the number of transmissions that can effectively take place at the same time. This reduces the quantity of information transmitted. Many forms of CMC, such as texting, social media, and videoconferences, allow the transmission of multiple, concurrent, relatively simultaneous, or different kinds of messages to the same or different destinations. This capability increases the volume of information a person can transmit to one or more recipients within a given amount of time. This increases transmission velocity and reduces the time needed to send large amounts of information.

This simultaneous sending and receiving of messages, to and from numerous recipients, enables multiple simultaneous conversation threads in a CMC medium. Although this can increase transmission velocity and conveyance of information, it can also reduce the interactional coherence of a discussion and convergence on a common meaning by making it harder for participants to develop a shared focus. Consider a group chat, for instance. It is an excellent medium for parallelism as it enables multiple people to communicate with multiple recipients in the same space. However, conversations here can also become unfocused. One participant may start a discussion about a topic at the same time that another starts a discussion on a different topic, and a third makes comments on a third, unrelated topic. The discussion becomes an interleaving of the messages of these three topics rather than focusing on meaning convergence of one topic at a time (Dennis et al., 2008; Torro et al., 2022).

Symbol Sets

Symbol sets refer to the diverse ways a medium allows people to communicate. When people communicate, they use a variety of symbols, from words to facial expressions, body language, written language, vocal tones, and charts, graphs, and visuals. This media capability refers to the extent to which a medium allows people to use one, some, or all of these symbols. Whether through words, tables, figures, images, video, mathematical equations, models, or other types of digital or written symbols, various forms of CMC allow participants to use multiple symbol sets simultaneously in their expression of ideas.

Appropriately using these multiple symbol sets affects the communication synchronicity in two ways. First, the use of a more natural symbol set, one that is more similar to face-to-face conversation in terms of use of vocal tone, verbal articulation, visual feedback, and physical gestures, supports synchronous communication more than a text-based medium that allows for fewer symbol sets. Second, some information is best conveyed using a specific symbol set. Trying to explain to someone how to change a tire is easier to show visually than write about, for example. This means that a medium that allows participants to use the symbol set that is best suited to expressing a particular kind of message increases synchronicity because it improves information conveyance and meaning convergence (Dennis et al., 2008).

Rehearsability

Rehearsability is the ability to practice and edit a message before sending. A medium that supports rehearsability, such as texting and email, allows the sender to review the message and, if need be, change it to express the intended meaning more precisely before transmission. This can reduce the amount of effort a recipient must make in decoding the message and improves the information conveyance and meaning convergence.

Rehearsability is particularly important for conveying new or complex information. It enables the sender to consider the possibility of multiple interpretations and alternative perspectives. This allows for editing and rewording of the message to more accurately convey the information and reduce potential misinterpretation.

Rehearsability is less important when participants share common experiences, cognitive schema, and/or a discussion approach to a topic, issue, or problem of concern. The shared experience, schema, and approach mean that participants can communicate using a common set of familiar symbols and expectations.

At the same time, rehearsability can have negative effects on the transmission of information. When people take time to review and edit messages, rehearsability can create delays in information conveyance. It does not impede the transmission velocity of a medium but can reduce the functional velocity of information conveyance, as senders take longer to compose and edit messages and responses. This transmission delay can reduce synchronicity and impair the discussion focus. However, because rehearsability allows participants time to carefully edit a message, they can be precise in a statement of issues and integrate and respond to the comments from others, which could increase synchronicity, assuming the receiver, of course, pays attention (Dennis et al., 2008; Torro et al., 2022).

Reprocessability

Reprocessability is the persistence of a message over time. It describes the ability of both sender and receiver to access, reflect on, reprocess, and reinterpret a message after it was

TABLE 3.1 **Media Capabilities**

TRANSMISSION VELOCITY	Immediate, synchronous, or rapid feedback
PARALLELISM	Simultaneous transmissions, large volume of information
SYMBOL SETS	Multiplicity of available symbols, cues, language variety
REHEARSABILITY	Ability to practice and edit a message before sending
REPROCESSABILITY	Persistence, ability to review, reread message at later time

initially sent. Written forms of communication provide more reprocessability than spoken words, unless these have been recorded. Reprocessability allows a recipient to reexamine a message, document, or other form of communication later, after an event has passed. This allows a recipient to spend more time decoding the message; consider it within a broader or different context, such as previous messages; and review its meaning within the background of ongoing events. It also provides a group or organizational memory that can be helpful to new participants.

Reprocessability affects both information conveyance and meaning convergence. It affects the functional transmission velocity in an exchange of information as it enables both sender and receiver to reread and think about a message prior to responding. This is especially important in the review of new, complex, and large quantities of information. It facilitates convergence by supporting information processing, revisiting earlier discussions, and facilitating a common understanding and ongoing mutual construction and adjustment of a shared meaning.

Reprocessability, however, can create delays in message exchange when receivers take time to review and think about issues before responding. This can create a functional impediment to information conveyance. A reprocessability delay in information transmission can reduce synchronicity by slowing the discussion and convergence on a common understanding (Dennis et al., 2008). Table 3.1 lists the five media capabilities.

Communication Context

Most communication progresses through a series of phases involving task inception, problem solving, conflict resolution, and execution. Inception begins the process with the development of an initial approach and understanding of the goals. Problem solving clarifies the goals, criteria, concerns, possible resolutions, and expected participation in a project. Conflict resolution selects among differences in opinion, values, interests, preferences, perspectives, assignments, rewards, and potential consequences. The execution phase coordinates and carries out the activities necessary to accomplish the agreed-on tasks. How participants communicate in each of these phases affects the information conveyance and meaning convergence processes, and some phases are more likely to facilitate each process. Conflict resolution, for instance, may require more convergence than execution, when conveyance is more prominent (Dennis et al., 2008).

Participants use CMC to accomplish the same two general communication functions as in face-to-face conversation. One is a production function that contributes to the accomplishment of the task. This includes exchanging information, finding creative approaches to a problem, designing methods of analysis, and implementing possible solutions. The second function is to build and maintain social relationships. This function is present in the relational content of the messages and patterns of interaction. Through these patterns of communication participants offer support, contribute to participatory discussion, display power, or facilitate decision-making. These patterns of communication strengthen, challenge, or degrade participant relationships. Participants engage in these communication functions simultaneously, and the patterns that develop in the context affect the information conveyance and participants' meaning convergence (Dennis et al., 2008).

Appropriation of Media Capabilities

Participants choose a CMC medium to meet a specific communication goal. However, they do more than learn how to use the medium to accomplish that goal. Participants appropriate the capabilities of a medium and adapt them to their communication goals. They do so in a variety of communication contexts. Successful adaptation increases the likelihood of future appropriation to achieve comparable goals in similar communication contexts and decreases the need for additional cognitive effort and learning (Dennis et al., 2008).

Thus, the communication context, participant familiarity, experience, training, and social norms all affect the appropriation of media capabilities. Participants experienced with a medium, engaged in a routine communication task, and familiar with each other can convey information and converge on a common meaning more easily in any medium because they know how to appropriate the media in ways that align with their intended usage. To the extent that the medium, task, or participants are new to the communication process, both conveyance and convergence become more difficult because the appropriation process does not occur as naturally. The context of the communication, its function, as well as its phase (e.g., task inception or conflict resolution) also affect how people use CMC (Dennis et al., 2001, 2008).

Summary: Media Synchronicity

The media capabilities of transmission velocity, parallelism, symbol sets, rehearsability, and reprocessability affect information conveyance and meaning convergence. This effect, however, depends on how participants use a medium for their communication as much as the technical capability of that medium itself. Participant familiarity with the task and each other, training, experience, and social norms all influence the appropriation of the media capabilities for accomplishing information conveyance and meaning convergence through CMC. The communication context of information production and social function, and the inception, problem solving, conflict management, and execution phases of task, also affect this ongoing CMC. Figure 3.4 summarizes this placement of media capabilities within this broader communication context.

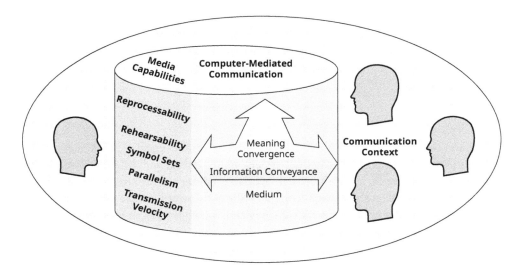

FIGURE 3.4 CMC Occurs Within a Communication Context.

Applying Media Synchronicity

Texting for Business and Personal Use

Park and Lee (2019) investigated the effect of texting for business and personal use on participant feelings of social intimacy and communication fatigue. They rely on the media synchronicity perspective and analyze the impact of transmission velocity, parallelism, symbol sets, reprocessability, and rehearsability in the texts. Park and Lee carried out a survey among 607 users of mobile messenger apps; 245 participants reported on their use of texting for personal use, and 158 reported on their use of texts in a business context.

First, transmission velocity, as measured in the speed with which one provides feedback, is important in both personal and business contexts. A quick response to a message is shown to be essential to maintaining good personal and business relationships. Responding quickly to either a friend or a colleague's message reduces fatigue, suggesting that hesitating in responding creates a sense of continuing obligation to an important communication task left undone.

Second, being able to review and reprocess a message after sending and receiving a response is important in both business and personal contexts. In the personal context, reprocessability increases social intimacy. At the same time, it is a communication task that requires time and energy, increasing communication fatigue, both in the personal and business context.

Third, rehearsability affects fatigue, but only in the business context. This suggests that participants spend more time and energy rehearsing, editing, and revising their business text messages to avoid mistakes. Personal text messages are more spontaneous, and errors more easily forgiven.

Although certain features of the medium lead to fatigue, relational benefits, such as social intimacy in the personal context, make the communication task worth it. Participants indicate that achieving a mutual understanding in the conveyance of information and meaning convergence is important in both their business and personal communication.

Email for Romantic and Utilitarian Use

Wells and Dennis (2016) investigated how media naturalness and media synchronicity predict the use of email and voicemail in personal romantic and utilitarian work communication. The media naturalness perspective predicts a communicator will engage in compensatory adaptation when using a medium to communicate emotional affect. Media synchronicity anticipates that the emotional content of the message will differ depending on the medium.

First, the authors ask participants to compose messages either in an email or as a voicemail. For the utilitarian task, participants compose a message that coordinates a group project or provides feedback on a friend's resume. For the romantic communication task, participants generate a message expressing their feelings for a friend. A pilot study indicated that participants find these tasks equally difficult yet familiar, equivalent in emotional value, and easily recognizable as either utilitarian or romantic.

Results found that romantic emails were perceived as the most positive and emotional, with utilitarian work voicemails coming in second. Romantic voicemails were perceived as least emotionally arousing. In addition, the content of the romantic email is more emotionally positive than the romantic voice messages. The utilitarian email expresses less positive emotion than the voice messages. This suggests a possible interaction between the communication task and the medium. The researchers conclude that participants adapt their language in the romantic emails, using explicit textual statements to compensate for the lack of vocal cues. The voicemail messages convey vocal cues that the emails lack. Even the use of emoji in an email lacks the emotive quality and variety of the vocal cues found in the voicemails. Therefore, when sending romantic messages, participants expend greater cognitive effort to accomplish their communication task in email.

The cognitive effort put into romantic email messages produces more arousing physiological responses than the voicemails. The cognitive effort and resulting physiological response indicate a compensatory adaptation made by email senders to accomplish a communication task in a less natural medium.

Perspective in Context

Analysis and Critique

The media synchronicity perspective conceptualizes CMC as the processes of information conveyance and meaning convergence that occur using media capabilities to accomplish communication. Media capabilities are no longer defined as the technological characteristics of a medium but as the uses that participants are willing to make of them.

However, the media synchronicity perspective still places the capabilities within the medium, limiting them to five pre-specified characteristics that participants can adjust. Although this provides more agency to CMC participants than the media richness perspective suggests, it still centers on the technology rather than the participants. In addition, the separation of information conveyance and meaning convergence is somewhat problematic. One cannot convey information without having some prior agreement on meaning. For example, to tell someone what the temperature feels like, they need to understand what you mean when you say "really cold" or know how to interpret the Fahrenheit (or Celsius) degrees that you mention. Just as meaning convergence is based on information conveyance, information conveyance requires some degree of shared meaning convergence.

Despite this, media synchronicity provides a useful method for examining patterns of communication that occur within a network, group, or community of users. It considers the multiple influences of communication functions, phases, and context. Media synchronicity extends the potential of research examining the global use of CMC for collaboration. Numerous studies demonstrate the usefulness of media synchronicity concepts in their analysis of communication patterns in software development projects and collaboration among participants in multiple large, multinational corporations (Ishii et al., 2019).

Media Synchronicity in Practice: Tweeting Disasters

Son et al. (2019) reviewed how people use Twitter (now known as X) during a major disaster such as a blizzard, earthquake, flood, hurricane, tornado, or wildfire. Each disaster has three identifiable phases: Preparedness, which happens before the disaster, response during, and recovery after the disaster has ended. The preparedness and recovery phases before and after the disaster involve risk communication. The immediate response phase, during the disaster itself, requires crisis communication.

Results show that participants use different strategies for risk and crisis communication tasks. During a disaster, people need accurate, detailed, and specific information in a timely manner. Twitter provides a convenient and powerful tool for communicating with people during a disaster.

In their crisis communication, Twitter users are more likely to rely on hashtags than words. These communication strategies minimize recipient cognitive processing efforts. Including a disaster-related hashtag in a tweet leads to a faster retweet time in the crisis phase compared to the risk communication phase. However, to be retweeted, others must view a tweet as trustworthy and important. Research shows that retweeting "harnesses the power of collective intelligence" (p. 59) A community of people deliberate over sharing and resharing information it considers relevant and important, collectively deciding what matters and what does not. Retweets help build collective knowledge and harness the power of the community in deciding which tweets are vital enough to share. In addition, people's ability to rapidly retweet information creates collaborative communication networks that allow people to post eyewitness accounts that become a primary source of information for first responders.

During the preparation phase, before the disaster strikes, and afterward, when the crisis has abated and been replaced by the recovery phase, risk communication efforts on Twitter look considerably different. Communication centers on conveyance, with people trying to share and gather as much and as detailed information as possible.

When it comes to risk communication, participants often retweet detailed information about how to best prepare for or recover from disaster events. It requires cognitive effort to process this information, but that effort is appropriate to the risk communication task in preparation and recovery. The study also showed that the increasing the number of hashtags, links, or words in a tweet do not slow the average retweet time during risk communication the way that it does during the crisis phase of a disaster.

Overall, the effect of words, hashtags, and link symbols on retweet time depends on the communication task. Fewer words and more easily interpretable hashtags reduce the average retweet time during a disaster. Including a link that is only interpretable after following it increases retweet time. In crisis communication, important hashtags help to disseminate information quickly. A short tweet conveying specific information about hazardous events is, on average, retweeted faster than risk communication that pertains to damage, relief, recovery, and news updates. In short, participants adapt their use, using different strategies and symbol sets (hashtags and links) and shifting their patterns of communication from risk to crisis to risk in the preparedness, response, and recovery phases of the disaster.

Illustration of Concepts

Darius pays attention to the communication function, phase, and familiarity in his customer relationships. His goal is to convey easily understood information through whatever medium is appropriate to converge on a mutual common understanding of the task and potential furniture solutions. He achieves this goal by building relationships with new customers before he provides specific information. This allows him to understand which form of communication will be most effective.

Darius knows that customers often find the technical details and differences among product lines overwhelming at first. He also knows that to make a sale he needs to not just present them with the necessary information, but help them understand why his company's products are good quality. To ensure that he engages in successful conveyance and convergence, he always establishes which CMC formats are easiest and most familiar for his clients to use and tries to adapt to those as much as possible.

Darius also uses strives to use media that are appropriate for the kind of information he needs to convey; when he needs to send specifications of specific pieces of furniture, he attaches drawings of the various pieces to an email. When customers need more information, he offers to meet with them in person so that they can come to a common understanding of the various details.

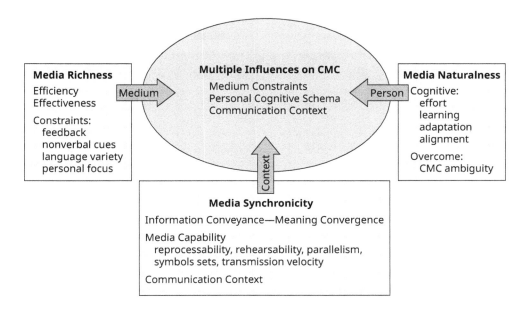

FIGURE 3.5 Media Richness, Naturalness, and Synchronicity Influences on CMC.

Summary: Media Richness, Naturalness, and Synchronicity

Media richness, naturalness, and synchronicity each describe influences on CMC. Media richness focuses attention on the immediacy of feedback, nonverbal cues, language variety, and personal focus available in a medium. Media naturalness describes the cognitive effort, learning, and adaptation alignment needed to overcome the ambiguity of a CMC medium. Media synchronicity describes how participants use the media capabilities of reprocessability, rehearsability, symbol sets, parallelism, and transmission velocity to accomplish their information conveyance and meaning convergence goals. Figure 3.5 illustrates these multiple sources of influence on CMC.

Looking Forward to Affordances

Media richness, naturalness, and synchronicity each recognize participant perceptions and use of a medium as a modifying effect on the medium, person, and context influences. Perceived media richness, the natural ability to learn and form new cognitive schema, and user appropriation of media capabilities all recognize that participant perception and use of a medium influence the CMC. In the next chapter, we describe the affordances perspective. Affordances present the participant perception and use of a medium as a central influence and issue of concern for CMC. Participants strategically use the affordances perceived in a medium to accomplish their CMC tasks. Effective use of these affordances facilitate CMC, often in new and creative ways.

Communication Expertise and Convergence in Group Decision-Making

Media synchronicity describes the influence of familiarity with the CMC medium, communication task, and other participants on the ability to convey information and converge on a common meaning of a project in a work group. Unfortunately, not all participants are equally skilled communicating, engaging with a work task, or interacting with others through a CMC medium. If I am part of a group, and I am more experienced and familiar with the medium than other group participants, I may be tempted to engage in more information conveyance and push a specific meaning forward. But is that the right thing to do? What is my ethical responsibility to communicating in the group?

1. It is more efficient for us as a decision-making group to move forward with meaning convergence based on what I think? I have experience and expertise and know what works best.

2. To what degree does the cohesiveness of the group matter to our success? A newer group member may feel left out of the decision-making process and be less committed to the project if we settle on a decision too quickly and without discussing options, and this may impact meaning convergence. Does this matter to our group's success?

3. To what extent do I have an obligation to the group decision-making process to not hurry the process, let others suggest alternatives, and work at the pace of the newer group member in arriving at a decision?

KEYWORDS AND PHRASES

Appropriation occurs when participants adapt the capabilities of a medium so that they can reach their communication goal.

Communication functions refer to the purposes of communication. There are two general communication functions: a production function that contributes to the accomplishment of a task and building and maintaining social relationships.

Convergence (in media synchronicity) is the process through which people achieve a common understanding of the meaning of transmitted information.

Conveyance (in media synchronicity) describes the transmission of information through one or more messages to accomplish a communication task.

Media synchronicity perspective builds on both the richness and naturalness perspectives, but it shifts attention from the constraints of the medium and the effects of human cognitive schema to the fundamental processes of communication.

Parallelism refers to the number of simultaneous transmissions that a medium allows. It refers to how many people can send and receive multiple messages simultaneously.

Rehearsability is the ability to practice and edit a message before sending. A medium that supports rehearsability, such as texting and email, allows the sender to review the message, and, if need be, change it to express the intended meaning more precisely before transmission.

Reprocessability is the persistence of a message over time. It describes the ability of both sender and receiver to access, reflect on, reprocess, and reinterpret a message after it was initially sent.

Symbol sets refer to the diverse ways a medium allows people to communicate. When people communicate, they use a variety of symbols, from words to facial expressions, body language, written language, vocal tones, and charts, graphs, and visuals.

Synchronicity describes a pattern of coordinated communication among participants who share a common focus.

Transmission velocity is the speed at which a medium transmits information. This refers to more than just passing on information. It includes the rapidity of transmission, immediacy of feedback, and synchronicity of turn taking in communication.

QUESTIONS FOR FURTHER DISCUSSION

1. Are there communication situations when you may not want synchronicity? What are these? Why? How does this speak to importance of convergence?

2. Compare two uses of CMC with which you are familiar in terms of their transmission velocity, parallelism, symbol sets, rehearsability, and reprocessability. Rank these platforms in terms of their ability to facilitate communication synchronicity. How do they compare? Does the platform with more media capabilities facilitate greater synchronicity?

3. Do you experience synchronicity in your CMC use? To what extent does this interact with the five features of the medium (transmission velocity, parallelism, symbol sets, rehearsability, and reprocessability)?

Image Credit
Fig. 3.4a: Copyright © 2016 Depositphotos/StudioIcon.

4

Affordances

Jasmine is a 25-year-old woman who graduated from college 3 years ago. She is smart, talented, creative, and conscientious. She works hard and believes she can be successful in the furniture sales business. She carefully researches her products and puts in the extra time needed to find the products that best meet her customers' needs. She is still early in her career and believes that some customers see her as inexperienced. Jasmine works hard at bolstering her professional identity and relationships with her customers.

FIGURE 4.1 Jasmine.

A Reciprocal Relationship of Participant and Medium

Affordances offers an alternative to the media richness, naturalness, and synchronicity perspectives on the relationship of a person to the CMC medium. Unlike media richness, which emphasizes the constraints of the medium, or media naturalness, which shifts attention to limitations of the human mind, or media synchronicity, which describes media capabilities within the communication context, the affordances approach focuses on the relationship between participant perception and the features of a medium (Gibson, 1986).

Gibson (1986) originally coined the term affordance to describe the relationship of an animal, human or otherwise, to its environment. An affordance describes a feature of the environment that is perceived and used by a participant in that environment to behave in a specific manner. It refers "to both the environment and the animal. ... It implies the complementarity of the animal and the environment" (Gibson, 1986, p. 127).

The perception that people have of the physical, social, and virtual environment around them is the result of their interaction with and understanding of that environment. There is a reciprocity between how people act and their understanding of the environment. They act in accordance with their understanding and develop that understanding in response to the environmental response to their action. This reciprocity of action is central to the idea of affordances as the interaction of "distinguishable yet mutually supportive realities" (Lombardo, 1987, p. 3).

Thus, affordances recognize both the environmental potential and the participant's perception of how to realize that potential. It is not the constraints of medium, mind, or communicative context that matter. It is the interaction of participant perception and action within the medium. That perception guides how a participant engages with the medium and uses it (Gaver, 1991; Gibson, 1986).

Affordances in the Natural Environment

To survive, an animal must perceive the affordances of an environment to make it habitable. An environment provides the potential for safety and food, but the animal must find safe places to hide and locate an adequate food supply. In other words, the animal must actualize the potential of the environment through its behaviors. Actualizing that environmental potential provides the animal an environmental niche within which to build a livable habitat (Gibson, 1986).

Perceiving the potential available within the constraints of the environment creates the affordance. The potential needs to be present in the environment, but the animal must perceive it. The affordance itself exists in the interaction between the features of the environment and the qualities of the individual (Feaster, 2010).

An environment may possess a certain quality (a flat rock). For that quality to become an affordance, the participant must perceive a use for it ("this rock is flat so I can sit on it") and then actualize that use ("I am tired and will use this rock as a seat"). The affordance of a seat is dependent on a person perceiving and using the flat rock for sitting. Until that happens, a rock is just a rock.

In short, affordances describe the relationship between the potentials and constraints of a medium and the perceptual limitations of the person. Affordances exist in a person's ability to combine the perception of the environmental potential with personal goals, competencies, expectations, and experiences to achieve a desired outcome. They allow a person to perceive and interact with an environmental medium in useful ways (Ingold, 2018; Vallverdù & Trovato, 2016).

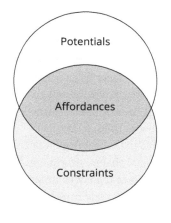

FIGURE 4.2 Affordances: Perceiving Environmental Potentials and Constraints to Communication.

Relationship of Affordances to Medium Potentials and Constraints

This concept of affordances helps explain how different people can use the same CMC medium in different ways to accomplish their communication goals and purposes. Participants use the medium based on their perceptions of its potential. These perceptions interact with the potentials and constraints of a medium to produce the affordances. Differences in experience, expertise, and orientation affect the affordances that arise in this relationship (Leonardi, 2011; Treem & Leonardi, 2013). Figure 4.2 illustrates this concept of affordances as the interaction of perceived potentials and constraints of a medium.

Affordances of CMC

Affordances in a CMC environment are the perceptions of the communication opportunities provided by a medium that, when used by participants, result in specific communicative practices. By recognizing the affordances of a medium, participants can become effective in accomplishing their communication goals.

The media used for CMC differ from that of face-to-face conversation. Hence, the communication affordances differ as well. Each CMC medium provides a different set of communication capabilities. Affordances depend on these potentials and constraints of the medium and the participant experience and expertise with the medium that shape their perceptions and use. Each medium, however, affords a potential pathway for effective communication within its constraints. Participants, however, can choose different paths in each medium to afford effective communication (Dings, 2018). Figure 4.3 shows that the communication path may differ in a face-to-face and a CMC environment.

False Perceptions, Hidden Potential, and the Reciprocity of Affordances

A participant may have a false perception of an affordance or, alternatively, be unaware of a potential use of a medium. Each of these represents "the mismatch between user perception and the [medium's] ... inherent properties" rather than an affordance (Fox & McEwan, 2017, p. 301). Affordances require the "possibilities for action ... that enable or constrain potential behavioral outcomes in a particular context" (Evans et al., 2017, p. 36).

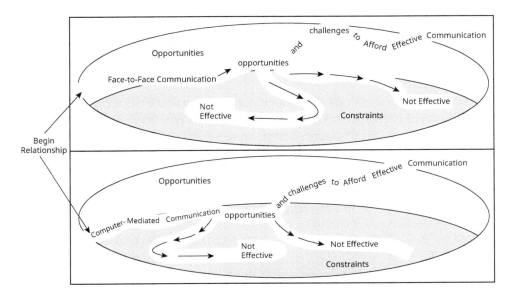

FIGURE 4.3 Face-to-Face and CMC Environments Provide Different Affordance Pathways.

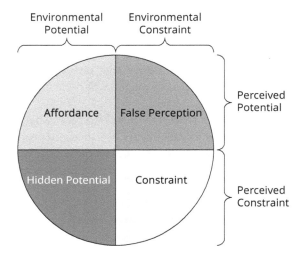

FIGURE 4.4 Affordances Represent Accurate Perceptions of Medium Potential.

A potential that an individual perceives, but which the medium does not provide, is a false perception, not an affordance. For example, some social media platforms allow participants to edit or delete their posts at a later date. Others are more restrictive of this ability. Participants who believe that they can delete a post on a platform that does not allow this have a false perception. They assume that the medium allows something that it does not.

Alternatively, novice users who lack knowledge, expertise, or experience often do not perceive the potential of a medium. For example, participants who have less experience with a videoconferencing platform such as Zoom may not realize that they can send messages to individuals during the group meeting without anyone else seeing them. Until a participant perceives this feature, it is a hidden potential of the medium rather than an affordance (Gaver, 1991).

Neither false perceptions nor hidden potentials capture the reciprocal nature of an affordance in the participant perception and use of a medium. Only the accurate perception and effective use of a medium represents an affordance (Evans et al., 2017). Figure 4.4 contrasts affordances with false perceptions, hidden potentials, and medium constraints.

Criteria for Identifying Affordances

Evans et al. (2017) offer three criteria for identifying affordances. First, an affordance is not a characteristic or feature of the medium. The technological features of a medium do not change. Affordances, however, change with the participant perception and use of the medium. Second, affordances do not describe communication outcomes. An affordance might make an outcome possible, but it is not the same as the outcome and can facilitate a variety of outcomes. Third, an affordance is not a binary opposition but a variable potential. Different people, with different expertise and experience, can use the same affordance with different outcomes. Anonymity, persistence, and visibility provide examples of how these three criteria help define affordances (Evans et al., 2017).

Anonymity is the degree to which a source is unknown or unspecified. Three criteria help identify it as an affordance. First, anonymity is not a feature of a medium. People can decide how anonymous they wish to be. They may decide to use their real name or a pseudonym. They can choose to share a profile picture of themselves or not. Second, it is not an outcome but can lead to a variety of communication outcomes, such as people who are anonymous feeling more emboldened to speak out. Third, it can vary along a continuum from full anonymity to full identity and can change over time.

Persistence describes the extent to which communication remains accessible after its original presentation. It too often is described as an affordance. First, it is not solely a feature of a platform. Tweets, for example, are accessible in their original form any time after creation, unless people delete them or make their account private. Second, it is not an outcome but can produce a variety of communication outcomes, such as social media users presenting themselves more carefully since their posts will remain online to people being cancelled for a post made years ago. Third, persistence is variable. Some social media sites, such as Snapchat, provide ephemeral forms of communication designed to disappear quickly. Others, like Facebook, provide more lasting forms of communication.

Finally, visibility recognizes the ease with which one can find information. Visibility is not a feature of the platform. Many social media platforms aggregate information, making it more visible and easier to find, but users can affect the visibility of their information by changing their privacy settings and making that information less visible. Visibility affects outcomes such as information sharing, and search tools can make information more visible, but the ability to use these tools effectively is what makes that information more readily accessible to some users than to others. Third, visibility is variable. Some information is harder to find or takes more time to locate. Visibility varies with the site and how users of the site handle their data. Hence, visibility is an affordance representing an interaction between user and medium (Evans et al., 2017).

Technological, Communication, and Social Affordances

McVeigh-Schultz and Baym (2015) describe three additional characteristics of CMC affordances. First, CMC affordances do not exist on their own. They *emerge* in communication practice. Second, affordances *interact* across levels of technological, communication, and social influences to affect the participant–medium relationship. Third, CMC participants can use affordances *strategically* to communicate effectively within the constraints of a medium.

Affordances occur at multiple levels in the communication–technology relationship. Some arise in perceptions and use of the CMC technology. Others occur in the communication made possible by that platform. Still others exist in the social context within which an individual engages in CMC. This points to the existence of technological, communication, and social affordances (Bastiaenses et al., 2015; McVeigh-Schultz & Baym, 2015).

A technological affordance emerges through the interaction of technology and sociocultural uses. It refers to an adaptation of the technical characteristics of a medium to a particular communication purpose or goal. For example, a synchronous audioconferencing system may have voice-activated or facilitator-controlled participant microphones that limit interaction to one speaker at a time and reduce the possibility of interruptions, such as you sometimes have in a face-to-face conversation. This feature becomes a technological affordance when a facilitator uses it to guide or limit group discussion (Anders, 2016; Erhardt et al., 2016).

A communication affordance refers to the interaction between a person's perception of the communication potential of a medium and its desired use. Communication affordances describe how people use CMC to achieve a particular communication outcome. A facilitator who strategically turns participant microphones on and off to give priority to a particular point of view or to control the flow of discussion in a decision-making group is using a characteristic of the technology as a communication affordance (Schrock, 2015).

A social affordance describes the relationship between a person and the medium in a way that changes social practice. The increase in videoconferencing over the past few years may ultimately change the social nature of organizational relationships and practices. Some videoconferencing participants comment that the increased use for business meetings is reducing "the hierarchy of the workplace, [making it] ... more human" (Karl et al., 2022, p. 351; see also Wellman et al., 2003).

Affordances in CMC

These multiple levels of affordances influence how people use CMC to communicate. Fox and McEwan (2017) summarize the affordances that affect how people construct messages, engage with others, and engage in group communication through CMC. These occur at the multiple levels of CMC, influencing how participants engage with the content they share through CMC.

Message Construction

Message construction affordances affect how people express themselves through CMC. They make it possible for CMC users to create content. They also shape the communication outcome.

Bandwidth describes the amount and kind of cues that are available in a medium. CMC generally provides fewer nonverbal cues, such as facial expressions and body language. This may afford less potential for participants to resolve misunderstandings or create a set of shared goals than in face-to-face conversation. At the same time, CMC affords the creation of new cues in the form of emojis, acronyms, and other expressions that allow users to express themselves in ways and that sometimes spill over into face-to-face interactions (e.g., OMG, LOL) as well (Fox & McEwan, 2017).

Editability allows a participant to revise or retract a communication message before, and sometimes after, posting or sending. Many forms of CMC, such as social media posts, emails, and messages, afford people this ability. This is more difficult in face-to-face conversation. One can apologize, or try to explain, but cannot un-say something once spoken and heard (Fox & McEwan, 2017).

Rehearsability is the ability to practice and edit a message before sending. Perceiving this affordance allows adjustments to a message that may reflect an initial response from a "test" audience. This ability varies with medium and is more difficult when speaking live to an audience face-to-face (Treem & Leonardi, 2013).

Persistence is the degree of permanence of a message. Message permanence in CMC is variable. Text-based communication does not disappear quickly. Text messages, email, social media comments, and almost anything posted to the internet have persistence. Unless recorded, videoconferences performed through FaceTime, Skype, Zoom, or other software remain only in the memory of participants.

The written messages people send, pictures they post, and electronic documents they create are visible to a network, group, organization, or community of people and persist for a longer period of time than spoken communication does. Others can review these written forms of communication, word for word, after a conversation has ended. People can interact directly with the original text, with or without the knowledge of the original author, long after a text or document is posted (Fox &McEwan, 2017; Leonardi et al., 2013; Treem & Leonardi, 2013).

Privacy, also known as visibility, identifies the control that a person has over who will see a message. Many forms of CMC allow people to send private messages. When these messages are in the form of text, however, others can easily repost using, for instance, a screenshot, making them visible to a wide array of people (Treem & Leonardi, 2013).

Messages posted on a social media and email sent to a workgroup list, or a network, have both more immediate and potential visibility than a personal phone call or private videoconference, unless these are recorded. This affordance describes how many people ultimately have access to the communicated message, which differs with a CMC medium. Like persistence, visibility, or lack privacy, expands the range of people, groups, organizations, networks, and communities that have access to a communication (Leonardi et al., 2013).

Personalization allows users to tailor their messages to a specific audience. People can use specific settings on social media to make posts visible to a specific circle of friends or family members. Videoconference calls often afford the ability to message specific participants (Fox & McEwan, 2017).

Anonymity describes the extent to which people using a CMC medium can conceal their identity. It can also refer to the extent to which people can separate their offline self from their online persona. Email and social media platforms often allow people to use pseudonyms or false names to hide who they are. Anonymity may contribute, at least partially, to the less inhibited communication and social behavior that occurs in some forms of CMC (Fox & Holt, 2018; Fox &McEwan, 2017; Lea & Spears, 1991).

Engaging With Others

CMC affordances also affect how people engage and interact with each other. They influence how participants develop their relationships through CMC. They facilitate conversational flow and control and can affect social movements (Fox & McEwan, 2017).

Social presence is the extent to which CMC participants feel a close relationship to one another. Forms of CMC that are asynchronous, such as email and social media platforms, reduce the sense of social presence. Synchronous forms of CMC, such as videoconferencing and instant messaging, can increase that social presence, but participant use of the medium is an important contributor to this feeling (Fox & McEwan, 2017).

Network association describes the ability to engage in conversations with a broad network of geographically distributed individuals. Through social media, people are able to connect with others, and to the contacts of those others, creating an expanded and diverse network. Through this network, participants can join conversations of interest and gather information from multiple diverse sources (Fox & McEwan, 2017; Majchrzak et al., 2013).

Accessibility describes the ease with which people can communicate across time and space. The use of cell phones, texting, and applications such as WhatsApp, Twitter, and Facebook allow people to communicate and connect with a large group in ways that are not as easy through face-to-face communication. Participants can use this CMC affordance to mobilize large groups of people for mass protests and to facilitate social movements. A lack of technical literacy and limited access to broadband internet in some parts of the world, however, can form a constraint on this affordance (Fox & McEwan, 2017).

Conversational control recognizes how people manage their CMC interactions. It describes how people participate in conversations occurring on a CMC platform. Triggered attending, metavoicing, and generative role taking provide three examples of conversational control behaviors (Majchrzak et al., 2013).

Triggered attending allows a participant to be part of an online conversation but remain relatively uninvolved until alerted to a topic of interest. The visually anonymous, asynchronous nature of some types of CMC allows participants to lurk, appearing to be present, but not actively participating in a conversation. Participants can monitor the evolving content of the conversation while doing other things until a topic of interest enters the discussion. Then they can enter the conversation to share their knowledge and perspective.

Metavoicing describes engaging in the ongoing conversation by commenting on the presence and participation of others. This may include commenting positively about the person's profile, conversational statements, or other contributions. Metavoicing is not simply stating an opinion or making a comment but responding explicitly to something that is already online, such as retweeting a person's message to show support or commenting positively on someone's post. It uses the social media platform to build recognition and support for participant contributions.

Generative role taking is a third form of conversation control. Participants can alternately take on leadership roles and engage in behaviors that sustain productive group dialogue. When a conversation stalls or devolves into divisive dialogue, a participant may step in to offer a potential solution. This can facilitate fuller participation and more creative solutions than often occur in groups whose member roles are more rigidly predefined. Although generative role taking does not necessarily foster productive conversations, these unplanned role-taking steps often evolve into more equitable power sharing among members of a social media group. The flexibility of the medium facilitates participant fluidity, creativity, and the ability to modify group routines, contexts, and communication (Majchrzak et al., 2013).

Group Communication

Leonardi (2013) identifies three additional types of affordances used by some CMC group participants. These are individual, collective, and shared group affordances. Each of these affect the ability to participate in CMC group communication.

An individual affordance represents an ability one member may have due to a particular role in the group or technical expertise. A group facilitator, for example, may be able to activate and deactivate the microphones or texting capabilities of other group members or selectively mute or encourage contributions from particular participants. This ability, facilitated by the medium and members' use of it, can affect the group decisions and discussion outcomes.

Collective affordances allow the members of a specialized work team to use the CMC medium in complementary ways. Group members can divide a topic and simultaneously research multiple aspects of a problem before reporting results to the group as a whole. Group members can more easily multitask in CMC than in face-to-face meetings, conversing through text messages while at the same time researching their part of the problem, analyzing data, and writing results. When done in real time, during a group meeting, this collective effort can expedite the overall group decision-making process.

Shared affordances provide all group members common access to a CMC medium characteristic. For example, when all group members can view and simultaneously edit a document, manipulate a data set, or dynamically view the results of a report, they can discuss issues and reach a group decision more quickly and easily. Members can suggest wording changes, data analysis alternatives, variations in report presentation, and reordering of materials. The ability of multiple members to simultaneously making changes to a shared document can facilitate the discussion of different possibilities to achieve a common understanding.

Each of these group affordances relies on participant use of a technological capability of the CMC medium. Participants recognize and use these capabilities to create the affordance. These affordances influence the member participation, conversational flow, and decision-making in CMC groups (Fox & McEwan, 2017). Table 4.1 Lists message construction, engaging with others, and group communication affordances of CMC.

TABLE 4.1 **CMC Affordances**

Type	Definition
MESSAGE CONSTRUCTION	
Bandwidth	Amount and kind of cues that are available
Editability	Ability to revise one's communication
Rehearsability	Ability to practice and edit a message before sending
Persistence	Permanence of a message across time
Privacy or visibility	Ability to keep a communication private or make visible to particular audiences
Personalization	Ability to tailor messages to a specific audience
Anonymity	Extent to which CMC users feel they can conceal their identity
ENGAGING WITH OTHERS	
Social presence	Sense that participants are close to one another
Network association	Conversations with a geographically distributed network of individuals
Accessibility	Communication across time and space
Conversation control	Ability to manage CMC interaction and flow of information
Triggered attending	Observer of online conversation until alerted to a topic of interest
Metavoicing	Comments made about the presence and participation of others
Generative role taking	Taking on leadership roles that create productive group dialogue
GROUP COMMUNICATION	
Individual	Technological ability available to one group member but not to other participants
Collective	Specialized team member work facilitated by CMC medium
Shared	Common access to a medium characteristic shared by all group members

Applying Affordances: Family Relationships

CMC Affordances for Saving Face

Pearce and Malhotra (2022) analyzed the face maintenance strategies that young people in India use when attempting to correct misinformation and falsehoods shared by their older family members on social media. Losing face means that a person experiences a loss of respect and prestige and suffers embarrassment and humiliation. People negotiate face-saving measures in their communication by expressing a concern for the other person's face, or their sense of self-respect, while simultaneously preserving their own integrity of self-face and retaining the mutual face of the relationship within broader family and social contexts. This face negotiation, however, can become difficult in some situations, and cultural orientations and socialization influence how people respond (Lim et al., 2012; Oetzel & Ting-Toomey, 2003).

An important influence on face-saving communication responses is the cultural dimension of individualism–collectivism. At one end of a continuum, individualism describes a social pattern in which individuals prioritize their own personal goals. At the other end, collectivism is a social pattern in which individuals give more priority to the goals of group, such as a family or community, of which they are a member. Although individuals within a culture can differ along this individualism–collectivism dimension, cultures, as a whole, vary in ways that affect how individuals use communication to manage difficult face-negotiation situations (Oetzel & Ting-Toomey, 2003; Shpeer & Howe, 2020).

Pearce and Malhotra (2022) are interested in finding out what face maintenance strategies young people in India use when correcting misinformation shared on social media by older relatives. They conducted in-depth interviews with 26 young adults in Delhi, India.

Their interviews show that the participants express respect, honor, and concern for the person, their mutual relationship, the family, and their social reputation. This concern guides their evaluation of how to use the affordances of CMC to maintain family honor and relationships. When an older family member shares a falsehood on social media, participants rarely respond in an open forum or conversation. Instead, they choose another CMC medium in which to respond. Their choice involves the affordances of synchronicity, nonverbal cues, and publicness.

Synchronicity

Many participants prefer a synchronous medium to correct misinformation in a relationally sensitive manner. They perceive the synchronous medium as facilitating a more sensitive and immediate approach in the discussion and sharing of opinions. Other participants choose an asynchronous medium, such as private messaging. This asynchronous communication allows them to create a well-crafted message that they can edit for politeness to get the point across in a face-saving manner. In each case, whether choosing a synchronous–asynchronous medium, participants perceive the CMC affordance chosen as showing respect, honor, and concern for the person, their mutual relationship, the family, and social reputation while correcting the misinformation.

Nonverbal Cues

Participants also express a concern for the ability to communicate nonverbal cues in their message. They mention the importance of being able to perceive the facial expressions and body language of the individual responding to their correction. As a result, many would choose a phone call or personal videoconference to allow the expression of vocal tone and nonverbal cues that a text-based medium does not. They express the concern that a lack of emotional cues may show a disrespect. Paying attention to the corrected person's reaction also allows adjustment and response.

Publicness

The third affordance that participants consider important is the presence of witnesses. Correcting misinformation or falsehoods is a face-threatening act. Others being present makes the communication more face threatening. In general, participants choose a private medium, such as a personal phone call, text, or email, to reduce the embarrassment of the corrected person.

Sometimes, however, participants perceive publicness as a beneficial affordance. Some participants strategically correct in the presence of one or two others, such as close friends or family members, whom they believe will support their position. Confronting falsehoods with correct information and supportive others who can second that correction can make the position appear more reliable and acceptable. Other participants use a semi-public social media site to correct politely or to educate more broadly. They observe that the semi-publicness affords the opportunity for others to learn and adjust their attitudes, beliefs, and opinions after witnessing someone else's correction.

Participants differ in their perceptions of the appropriate medium to use for face-saving communication with their family member. In each case, however, they are looking for CMC affordances that facilitate their ability to correct the misinformation while respecting and honoring the person, relationship, family, and social reputation.

Perspective in Context

Analysis and Critique

Numerous scholars use the affordances terminology in their research. Differences appear in their use of the concept. This can lead to some confusion in the field (Fox &McEwan, 2017).

Some of the major issues surrounding how affordances have been used in recent research include researchers treating CMC as an entity and ignoring differences in the affordances of each medium, such as email, texting, social media, and videoconferencing. Others ignore the relational communication and social implications of CMC affordances. Some CMC platforms provide relatively safe spaces for the private expression of opinions. Other platforms allow the reposting or broadcasting of a personal comment or short video to a wider audience than originally intended. This can cause embarrassment and either fame or infamy. Other researchers ignore the user perceptions of the medium. Affordances exist in the reciprocity of the perceiver and the medium. Neglecting either the perception or medium ignores the affordance.

Current research efforts continue to develop the conception and implications of CMC affordances. Anders (2016), for example, shows that CMC affordances that allow participant attention allocation and simultaneous communication with numerous people can facilitate a group's ability to share knowledge, integrate diverse information, and collaborate more effectively. Fox and McEwan (2017) provide a scale for measuring the affordances of multiple CMC platforms. Leonardi (2013) shows that groups can use shared affordances to work together more efficiently, compare results of independent efforts, and achieve group consensus more quickly. These researchers continue to develop the influences and effects of CMC affordances.

Affordances in Practice: Social Media Discussion of Police Shootings

Social media provide popular places for discussing controversial issues. Fox and Holt (2018) examined how participant understandings of Facebook affordances affect their communication decision to discuss a politically sensitive and divisive topic, in this case police discrimination. The authors define *police discrimination* as "citizens being treated differently by police because of their race, including racial profiling and the disproportionate number of Black individuals targeted by police brutality and shootings" (p. 534).

Past studies show that chat room participants are more willing to share personal opinions, even on politically divisive topics, because of the affordance of relative anonymity. Facebook, however, affords less personal anonymity than chat rooms. Fox and Holt think this difference in perceived anonymity will affect how people communicate on the platform. People who believe their opinion is in the minority are not as likely to voice that opinion on Facebook for fear of a backlash. Conversely, people who think their opinion matches that of the majority will be more willing to speak out.

They find that people's perceptions do influence whether they were willing to express their opinions about police discrimination on Facebook, but not in the way they expected. People who think that Facebook affords them anonymity are less likely to speak up. They interpret this finding as indicating that people who think they are identifiable, and *not* anonymous are more likely to expect people in their network to support them, if needed. As a result, they are more willing to express their opinion publicly.

Participants who believe Facebook affords them networked associations with people who know them personally are more likely to share their opinions as well. This is probably because they assume that people in their network think like them and are more likely to come to their defense if attacked. Finally, participants who think their posts will have persistence over time are less likely to share their opinions, possibly because they fear that someone in the future, such as a potential employer, might view their expressed opinion, and think differently.

The results of their study indicate that the affordances of CMC influence participant communication. Participant perceptions of Facebook affect the messages they are willing to post, how they engage with others, and their communication on the site. Perceived anonymity, networked association, and message persistence all influence participant communication choices on Facebook. This influence represents more than the constraints of the medium. These affordances identify the influence of the relationship between participant perceptions and medium characteristics on communication.

Illustration of Concepts

Jasmine enjoys her job and wants to develop a career in home product sales. She likes working with Pam and accepted the position after interviewing with several larger home furnishing stores. Cheryl was in town that day, and, as part of the interview process, Pam invited Jasmine to go to lunch with them. Jasmine was impressed by both women and sees them as role models.

Jasmine is able to maintain social presence, accessibility, and network association through CMC. She uses text messages to respond quickly to questions and concerns and adjusts her use of CMC to her customers. Jasmine also uses the editability, persistence, and personalization affordances of CMC to help her achieve this goal. These affordances allow her to write, edit, and carefully redraft her email and text messages before sending to make them clear, precise, and easily understandable to her customers. In addition, she adds furniture dimensions and other technical specifications to her email so that they have more persistence than verbal conversations. Customers can reread the specific information and think about it over time before making a final decision. She personalizes her messages, describing how the placement of specific pieces of furniture will meet the specific customer needs. In doing all of these things, Jasmine is developing a strong professional identity with her customers. Her customers indicate appreciation for her professionalism and expertise and her furniture product sales numbers are up.

Looking Forward to Person

The affordances perspective has moved the discussion of CMC from the constraints of the medium, person, and communication context to the interaction of perception and environment. In the next chapter we analyze the experience of the person in a CMC environment. That environment offers new ways to express personal, social, and virtual identities through CMC. The chapter explores what these identities are, where they come from, and how they are constructed through communication.

COMMUNICATION ETHICS CHALLENGE

Facilitating Group Discussion Through Affordances?

An affordance facilitates communication using a medium. The decision about what type of communication to facilitate can become an ethical choice.

For example, imagine that you facilitate a virtual work group. The group consists of highly competent experts who are geographically dispersed. The group meets once a month by computer audioconferencing. As the group moderator you have individual as well as collective and shared affordances. You can activate and mute the individual speaker's microphones. You can also use metavoicing strategically to recognize certain participants, making it more likely that they will contribute to the discussion, while ignoring others. You also know the group participants well enough to strategically use their individual habits of triggered attending to help shape the flow of the group discussion. You can use these to facilitate the group discussion process.

The group must make a recommendation that is important to your organization. Your supervisor, who does not attend these group meetings, has indicated a strong preference for a particular recommendation. You know how various group members feel about this decision and know that there is strong disagreement among group members.

You think about your communication choices carefully. To what extent do you use your knowledge of individual affordances, metavoicing, and triggered attending to shape and facilitate the flow of discussion toward a group recommendation that supports your supervisor's preference? Consider the ethics of using CMC affordances for (a) personal career advancement by obtaining the recommendation that your supervisor wants, (b) arriving at a decision that everyone in the group can support even if that takes longer than the organization would like, (c) potentially damaging the future prospects for generative role taking within the work group if you assert the authority of your individual affordances to subtlety advance personal goals and centralize authority in control of the group process.

1. What are your options?
2. How do you engage the communication affordances of CMC in an ethical way?

KEYWORDS AND PHRASES

Affordances describes features of the environment that are perceived and used by a participant in that environment to behave in a specific manner.

Anonymity is the degree to which a source is unknown or unspecified.

Collective affordances allow the members of a specialized work team to use the CMC medium in complementary ways.

Communication affordance refers to the interaction between a person's perception of the communication potential of a medium and its desired use.

False perception refers to a potential that an individual perceives but that the medium does not provide.

Generative role taking is a third form of conversation control. Participants can alternately take on leadership roles and engage in behaviors that sustain productive group dialogue.

Hidden potential refers to features of a medium of which an individual user may not be aware.

Individual affordance represents an ability one member may have due to a particular role in the group or technical expertise.

Metavoicing describes engaging in the ongoing conversation by commenting on the presence and participation of others.

Persistence describes the extent to which communication remains accessible after its original presentation.

Shared affordances provide all group members common access to a CMC medium characteristic.

Social affordance describes the relationship between a person and the medium in a way that changes social practice.

Technological affordance refers to an adaptation of the technical characteristics of a medium to a particular communication purpose or goal. It emerges through the interaction of technology and sociocultural uses.

Triggered attending allows a participant to be part of an online conversation but remain relatively uninvolved until alerted to a topic of interest.

Visibility recognizes the relative ease with which information can be located.

QUESTIONS FOR FURTHER DISCUSSION

1. Select a specific social media platform and identify an affordance.

   - Describe whether this affordance aids with message construction, interaction, or group communication.

   - Describe how it can be used to facilitate communication.

   - Can the affordance be used differently for either beneficial or detrimental communication purposes?

   - Are there detrimental or annoying aspects to how some participants use the affordance?

2. Consider some popular methods of CMC (e.g., email, texting, FaceTime). What are some common false or hidden affordances of these methods of communication?

3. People tend to use different CMC platforms for different purposes based on their affordances. Consider the platforms you use the most; what affordances render these platforms attractive to you?

Experience

Goal of this approach: To analyze the experience of the person, presence, and propinquity in CMC. Approach II shifts attention away from the constraints to focus on how individuals experience CMC and the implications of those experiences for human relational communication. The chapters in this approach analyze the CMC experiences of personal identity, presence, and relational propinquity.

Person describes the experience of creating a personal and social identity, the communication of identity, and the expression of a virtual identity in a CMC environment. It examines the influences of CMC characteristics on one's ability to actualize a possible self in the environment that CMC provides.

Presence examines the experience of immersion within a CMC medium and of closeness to others (social presence) that participants can experience in CMC. It then builds on these concepts to discuss how patterns of CMC usage can generate feelings of ambient and connected presence in participant relationships.

Propinquity looks at how the relational closeness that people experience to others when using CMC is affected by their interpretations of the decisions made in that use. The experience of electronic propinquity is integrated into a larger sense of relational closeness that both affects and is affected by those interpretations.

5

Person

Sean just graduated from college. He is a fun-loving person, but he is shy and can feel out of place in social situations. He grew up in a small, rural, town and started working at the Home Products store on weekends while he was in college. He was responsible for restocking supplies, cleaning the show room, and occasionally helping with furniture deliveries. When he graduated, Pam offered him a full-time, entry-level job in the store as a product consultant/salesperson. He is still getting familiar with the product lines, how to deal with customers, and the computer database system.

FIGURE 5.1 Sean.

Identity

Identity represents a person's sense of self. A person constructs that identity through an iterative process of communication, feedback, and cognitive reflection. This process involves interaction with other people and takes place within an environment of social and cultural norms (Koles & Nagy, 2012). Four perspectives describe how this process works.

William James (1918, 1948) provides an early discussion of identity development in his *Principles of Psychology*. He describes identity as the interaction between an internal "I" and a "me." The "I" is the knower, an awareness that underlies the understanding of the self. The "me" is the known self with multiple internal and external levels that a person can actualize in possible identities (James, 1948, p. 176).

Mead (1962) describes the social influences on this identity development process. A person's social identity develops in the symbolic interaction of the individual with a generalized other. This generalized other is an internalized sense of self that developes in response to how individuals think others see them. This internalized sense of self is developed through communication with others, in response to their feedback. Hecht (1993) describes the role of communication in this process of personal-social identity development. Koles and Nagy (2012) extend these concepts to the role of CMC in actualizing people's virtual identities.

Personal Identity

In his description, James captures the complexity of developing a personal identity, describing it as an active, self-conscious process of becoming oneself (Koles & Nagy, 2012). He defines the "I" as the energy of a "passing state of consciousness" that generates an internal sense of "me" (James, 1948, p. 196). The internal "me" represents a person's spirit and sense of being. It is the "very core" of being (p. 181).

The "I" is pure consciousness without any self-awareness. The "me" is the self of which a person is aware. The awareness of this "me" is what allows people to actualize their possible selves in different sociocultural environments. These possible selves represent the multiple potentials a person has for self-expression. Through the process of identity development, a person actualizes some of these possible selves into ways of thinking and being (Comello, 2009; James, 1948).

These actualized selves become the external material identity and social roles that the person enacts in life. The material "me" is the physical embodiment, appearance, and performance of ethnicity, gender, and other demographic characteristics. It includes self-perceptions and presentations of self through the expression of body, clothes, physical ability, health, beauty, and affiliation with family, friends, possessions, and home. An individual develops a set of habitual expressions of self through this material presentation and interaction with others.

In addition, a social "me" develops in the roles, relationships, and social performances that a person enacts in everyday life. These include family, work, and community interactions. They incorporate the feedback of others on the performance of these social roles across multiple relationships within a community and cultural environment. There are "as many different social selves as there are distinct groups of persons ... whose opinion" matter (James, 1948, p. 179).

Table 5.1 describes the main characteristics of a personal identity. "I" is the consciousness of the internal spirit that lies at the foundation of the external material and social expressions of "me." These material and social expressions of "me" actualize the possible selves of a person within the cultural environment of a community.

TABLE 5.1 **Personal Identity**

I	
An active awareness	An active awareness of oneself. The knower of "me."
ME	
Internal spirit	Self-reflection that integrates thoughts, beliefs, and ideas about the self into a coherent conception of self
Material expression	Perceptions of physical appearance, race, ethnicity, gender, socioeconomic, and other demographic characteristics
Social roles	Performances enacted in interpersonal, group, organizational, and social relationships
SELF	
Possible selves	Personal concepts of self with the potential to become actualized
Actualized selves	The identities a person enacts in life

Identity as Perceived Competencies and Expectations of Actualized Selves

Together, the material and social selves form an identity of perceived competencies and expectations in the roles of child, sibling, parent, teacher, colleague, customer, laborer, employer, employee, competitor, companion, acquaintance, friend, and lover. The energy of "I" connects a person's internal spirit of "me" to the external material and social selves. Through this interaction of the external-internal reflection the "me ... changes as it grows [and] ... identity [is] found" (James, 1948, p. 205).

Figure 5.2 illustrates this multilayered construction process of personal identity. It is a process that integrates

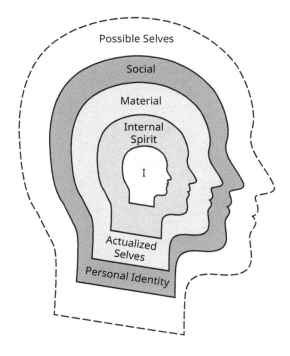

FIGURE 5.2 James Personal Identity.

the internal and external representations of self into a coherent whole. The energy of "I" interacts with the internal "me" to actualize the selves that are possible to express in the external material and social environment.

Social Identity

This personal identity links inextricably to the social world through communication with others. Parents, family, social groups, community, and the broader cultural environment all shape the personal identity. These influences constrain expression and give meaning to identity performances. Mead (1962) develops this aspect of social identity when he conceptualizes these influences as a generalized other that "gives to the individual [a] ... unity of self" (p. 154).

The generalized other communicates the appropriate ways of thinking to an individual through a multitude of mundane, everyday comments and behaviors. The individual internalizes, organizes, and generalizes these comments and behaviors into a pattern of expected social perceptions, attitudes, relationships, and ways of expressing oneself. These patterns constitute the individual's social identity. "So the self reaches its full development by organizing these individual attitudes of others into the organized social or group attitudes and thus becoming an individual reflection of the general systematic pattern of social or group behavior" (Mead, 1962, p. 158).

The influence of this generalized other develops in two phases. First, the conversations, actions, observed behaviors, and attitudes of parents, family members, and friends influence a person's way of thinking. Over time, in a second phase, a person

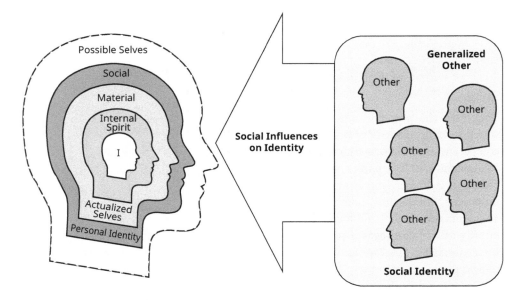

FIGURE 5.3 Mead Social Identity.

becomes aware of a general underlying community system of acceptable actions, behaviors, beliefs, and attitudes. The individual gradually accepts this belief system as an implicit perception and understanding of social reality and one's place in it. This social reality is the taken-for-granted ways of expressing oneself, through language and action, and of relating to others. It represents the influence of the generalized other on one's identity.

Mead (1962) emphasizes the role of communication in this process. The generalized other influences identity development through the symbolic interaction of a person with the larger group. This symbolic interaction involves the verbal and nonverbal communication of an individual "I" responding to the groups and communities that make up the generalized other by providing feedback and instructing the person on the "me" to become the socially acceptable identity within the community.

Figure 5.3 represents the influences of the generalized other on a social identity. The generalized other organizes the community attitudes and beliefs of "me," in negotiation with the internal "I," to create a person's social identity. The process begins in childhood, with family, and generalizes to the attitudes and beliefs of the community.

Communication of Identity

Hecht (1993) describes the role of communication in this identity formation. Identities are constructed and maintained through conversation with others—family, friends, and community. Four levels, or frames of identity, influence this process. These are the personal, enacted, relational, and communal frames (Hecht, 1993; Jung & Hecht, 2004, 2008).

The **personal frame** is the meaning that people attribute to themselves, their motivations, perceptions, and expectations. The **enacted frame** describes how identity comes into being through the dynamic performance of that identity in conversation with others. These conversations allow individuals to express themselves, receive feedback, and internalize the responses in their ongoing presentation of self. The relational frame refers to the individual identity created in relationship with others. The relational frame emerges as an individual defines and refines a self-identity through presentations of the self within these relationships, working with the expectations of others, such as family, friends, employers, colleagues, and community. This frame includes the influence of people's expectations and of the role one takes on in those relationships, such as what it means to be a daughter or son. The communal frame places that identity within the group to which the individual belongs. It contextualizes the personal expressions, perceptions, and expectations within the broader attitudes, values, and expectations of that community (Hecht, 1993).

These identity frames interact to form a person's sense of self in relationship to others. Any inconsistencies among the expectations of the frames create tension in one's identity. Inconsistency between the personal and enacted frames, for example, constrains a person's ability to converse freely with another individual. A personal–relational inconsistency creates tension in the relationship. A personal–communal inconsistency produces a broader social tension in feelings of acceptance within the community. A person can manage a small amount of tension by temporarily suppressing one identity frame or another. However, suppression generates stress, which an individual negotiates through communication (Hecht, 1993; Jung & Hecht, 2004, 2008).

Figure 5.4 positions the communication of identity between the James and Mead conceptions of the personal and social. It is through everyday conversation that an individual enacts a personal and social identity. Hecht frames this process at the multiple personal, enacted, relational, and communal levels of communication.

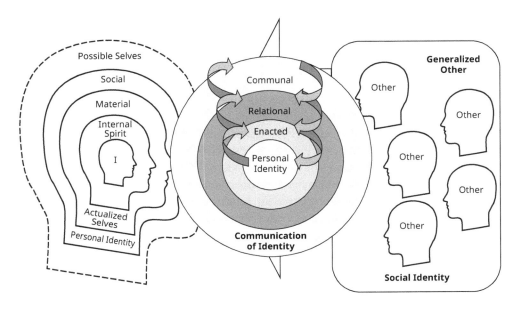

FIGURE 5.4 Hecht Communication of Identity.

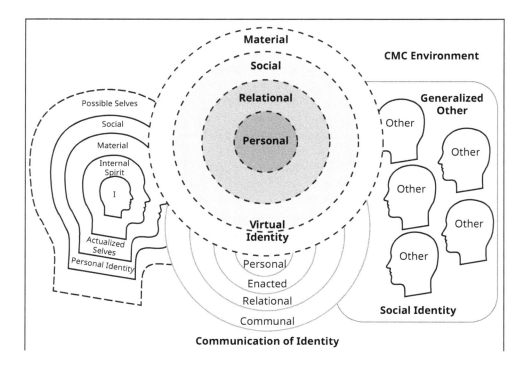

FIGURE 5.5 Virtual Identities in a CMC environment.

Virtual Identity

James (1918) describes personal identity as the expression of an "I" in possible and actualized selves. Mead (1962) develops the generalized other influences on that person's social identity. Hecht (1993) emphasizes the role of communication in framing that identity.

Koles and Nagy (2012) approach their analysis from the perspective that one's virtual identity "integrates certain aspects of an individual's self, incorporating personal, relational, social, and material elements" (p. 4). The personal element contains the relatively stable set of traits, goals, beliefs, and values that an individual holds. The relational element centers on the social roles that an individual embodies. The social element emphasizes a person's group membership, ethnicity, religion, nationality, gender, family norms, and social expectations that influence identity. The material refers to the physical attributes of clothing, property, and places to which a person attributes meaning.

The CMC environment influences the construction and expression of this virtual identity. Figure 5.5 illustrates the personal, relational, social, and material levels of a virtual identity. The figure superimposes these elements on the personal, social, and communication influences identified by James, Mead, and Hecht.

Private and Public Self-Consciousness

How personal, social, communication, and virtual environments influence identity expression depends on a variety of circumstances, including an individual's self-consciousness. Private self-consciousness reflects the inner feelings, emotions, beliefs, and thoughts of a person. It connects a person with the inner aspects of identity. A public self-consciousness pays attention to the social aspects of identity, such as appearance, behaviors, style, and the feedback of others. The private and public self-consciousness of a participant in the virtual environment shapes their identity orientation and expression (Koles & Nagy, 2012).

Koles and Nagy (2012) find that the overall composition of identity orientations is similar in both the physical and virtual presentations of self. When people create avatars, they generally use their physical selves as a starting point, appearing as an avatar of the same gender, for example. Furthermore, private self-consciousness influences the personal and relational orientations to identity expression in both the physical and virtual environments.

However, Koles and Nagy's research also shows that the expression of private feelings, thoughts, and actions affects the personal identity orientation more in the physical presentations of self than in the virtual environment. Public self-consciousness influences the virtual social identities of participants in their self-presentation and the feedback of others in a virtual environment. This social orientation is more important to their virtual expression of identity, while the personal and relational orientations and the extent to which people view themselves as part of a group affect their offline physical identity expressions more.

These results support the role that the virtual social environment plays in shaping identity expression while also demonstrating the influence of private thoughts and emotions in these expressions. Private self-consciousness affects both participant online profiles and their virtual appearances. Participants consider the expression of their inner, personal identities as important as the social impressions they make in the virtual environment.

Virtual Environment and Identity Expression

The experience of immersion, persistence, anonymity, and editability in a CMC medium affect this private–public enactment of a virtual identity. Each of these influences the participants' private–public self-consciousness and the orientation of their identity expression. In addition, the perception of the CMC medium as a third place further influences that identity expression (Koles & Nagy, 2012, Nagy & Koles, 2014a, 2014b).

Immersion
The immersive experience of CMC allows for the development and performance of a strong personal identity. People become emotionally involved in who they are online. They express themselves in creative, and often strategically selected, edited, and easily modifiable ways. The immersive nature of CMC facilitates actualizing a virtual identity that expresses a possible self of personal identity (Nagy & Koles, 2014b).

Persistence
Virtual time is continuous and "cannot be paused" (Nagy & Koles, 2014b, p. 280). This persistence allows ongoing conversations and the development of reputations. Individuals

participate in multiple conversations, across networks of relationships. These relationship networks evolve over time as participants tell stories express values, take positions, share experiences, refer to earlier conversations, and remember past interactions. Participants develop reputations for being gregarious, friendly, generous, dependable, kind, honest, trustworthy, grumpy, or shy. These reputations develop as much through what others say about a person as from an individual's self-disclosures, expressing a relational identity.

Editability and Anonymity

Many CMC environments allow varying levels of editability and anonymity. The ability to edit one's presentation of self to others provides an opportunity for personal reflection on thoughts, feelings, emotions, and beliefs. Being able to maintain a level of anonymity facilitates both experimentation and self-reflection, as participants explore possible selves, allowing a greater variety of possible social identities (Green-Hamman & Sherblom, 2016).

A Third Place for Identity Enactment

Identity develops through conversations in multiple environments. For most people, the first place for identity development is in the home with family. It offers a degree of privacy and place to relax. A person can explore inner thoughts and feelings and evaluate personal attitudes, emotions, beliefs, values, ambitions, and goals. Work provides a second place, one that is more public. At work, acquaintances, strangers, supervisors, and rivals can judge appearance, mannerisms, verbal style, and performance adequacy and provide feedback. A person develops a social identity in anticipation of these reactions to the material expression of self and expectation of fitting into the expected social relationship status of others. Both family and work, for most of us, present relational hierarchies in which to express identities (Oldenburg, 1991).

A third place for identity development occurs in informal social gatherings at neighborhood pubs, cafés, or community centers. These third places provide a neutral ground where people interact with others and "conversation is the primary activity and the major vehicle for the display and appreciation of human personality and individuality" (Oldenburg, 1991, p. 42).

Many of the virtual environments of CMC provide this type of third place. People gather in these virtual environments without the implicit hierarchies embedded in families and work relationships. They serve "as neutral grounds for socializing and experiencing realities" (Nagy & Koles, 2014b, p. 280).

Actualizing Possible Selves

Individuals can use these communication characteristics of a medium to develop multiple, unique presentations of self within their independent networks of social relationships. They can experiment with public expressions of a private identity, reflect on it, and modify that presentation of self. They can creatively experiment with actualizing possible selves and fit identities to their different CMC relationships, networks, and communities.

Even though CMC affords individuals with the opportunity to alter their virtual identities, participants typically preserve a congruence between their physical and virtual identity. They actualize virtual identities that express possible selves rather create false presentations of self. These virtual identities may accentuate different character-istics of the participants, but they generally present a psychologically consistent aspect of the person. They may express the inner thoughts, feelings, and emotions of a private self-consciousness or present an ideal material or social self to which the person aspires. The feedback that others provide and the impression that CMC participants believe they are making also affect their virtual identities, but these virtual identities incorporate the personal, relational, social, and material into a congruent self-presentation (Koles & Nagy, 2012; Nagy & Koles, 2014a, 2014b; Papacharissi, 2011).

Applying Identity: CMC Incivility

Jaidka et al. (2021) explored how personal and social identity affect people's (in)civility. They designed a community-based social media site for research participants to engage in synchronous discussions on gun control in the United States. They randomly assigned participants to groups. In some groups, both participant personal and social identity were absent and participants remain anonymous. In other groups, personal identity, including a picture, was visible. Still other groups revealed the social identity of a political affiliation, but without personal identity information. Finally, in the fourth type of group, personal identity, picture, and political affiliation appeared for other group members to see.

The groups engaged in 25-minute discussions of gun control. A pro-gun rights bot began the discussion session with a set of scripted comments excerpted from arguments made in internet forums on gun control. Another bot, scripted with comments opposing gun rights, attended each group session as well. The bots remained passive observers to the discussion, except for the initial comments, unless there was a lag in the discussion.

Researchers measured the participant argument construction, use of justification, and incivility in the comments of the 940 contributors. Results show that when participants can see each other's political identities, they are more likely to compose rational conversa-tional messages. Revealing personal identity information does not affect the rationality of discussion, but, when coupled with the political social identity, it does decrease incivility and facilitates more rational discussion.

The results of the study suggest that identity influences group discussion. Revealing or concealing personal and social identity in CMC affects participant conversational style. Participants shape their communication style in discussing a controversial topic to their perceptions of personal and social anonymity.

Perspective in Context

Analysis and Critique

Identity is an ongoing process of expression, feedback, and modification. This means that personal, social, and virtual identity can appear to be vague concepts. The work of James, Mead, Hecht, and Koles and Nagy help describe some of the complexities of identity and the implications for self-expression in a virtual environment.

Virtual identities change due to many influences, such as physical life circumstances, the amount of time spent using CMC, on particular social media sites, and the relationships that people engage in through CMC. Over time, individuals may shift their social media use or their reasons for using specific social media sites, or they may communicate with different groups. They may change jobs, develop different relationships, and have children. All of these changes can affect their virtual identities.

In addition, participation in a virtual environment may facilitate thinking about potential aspects of self that have remained hidden and unexplored in physical life. Exploration of these can lead to self-discovery. A virtual identity, in general, both expresses and reflects on a person's physical self and the cognitive, relational, and physical changes in their life.

This analysis of personal, social, and virtual identities, however, does not explore how people sometimes will manipulate their presentations of self to deceive others. This is a shortcoming of describing identity only as an authentic personal, social, communication expression of self. This does not invalidate the authenticity of most people's virtual identities but does recognize their relational and communicated nature.

Personal identities and social reputations change as roles and relationships change. Virtual identities change as online relationships change. Most people are authentic in their presentations of self. Some, however, may use the anonymity and editability of CMC to deceive and take advantage of others.

Virtual Identity in Practice: Learning the Irish Language Through CMC

Collins et al. (2019) examined the role played by personal, relational, social, and material identities in the use of a virtual environment to teach the Irish language. Language learning is a process that involves more than just memorizing words and syntax. It includes adjusting one's personal, relational, and social identity in becoming a speaker of another language and a member of that language community.

They designed an immersive virtual experience in which participants learned to speak Irish. Each participant wore a wireless headset and underwent a training session. After training, participants entered the virtual environment of an Irish shop, where they had to interact with characters in Irish to collect the items they needed to purchase. Participants only heard and spoke Irish in the shop. They reported feeling immersed in the virtual environment and motivated to learn Irish after using it in the shop.

This experience demonstrates the importance of engaging people's personal and social identities in learning a new language. While purchasing the items in the shop, they received feedback and recognition as a member of an Irish speaking community. They participated in a meaningful activity and system of cultural practices within a language-speaking community. This interaction involves the personal, relational, social, and material dimensions of self in a way that stimulates the language-learning processes.

Illustration of Concepts

Sean strives to create a professional identity both on and offline. He makes sure that his professional abilities are documented online. Additionally, he scans social media platforms for pictures in which he has been tagged and removes himself from embarrassing baby pictures posted by family members and less-than-professional party pictures posted by friends. His website accentuates his identity and abilities as a graphic designer and showcases his talent in using furniture layout software to show how pieces will fit together in a room.

When he interacts with customers through CMC, Sean spends time editing and revising his messages before sending. He recognizes that he needs to build a professional reputation with customers and attempts to do this with clear, enthusiastic, and informed professional responses to customer questions. He often asks Pam to review his messages for informational accuracy, completeness, and professional tone before sending them. This allows him to orient each message and email to a specific customer need and informational desire. Sean uses CMC to develop his relationships with customers. CMC facilitates his ability to later talk with them face-to-face.

Looking Forward to Presence

In order to develop a virtual identity, a person must experience an immersive presence within a CMC medium. In addition to a personal presence, participants need to develop a social presence in relationships to others in order to communicate. In the next chapter, we discuss these experiences of CMC presence and social presence.

COMMUNICATION ETHICS CHALLENGE

Expressing My Virtual Self or Catfishing?

Most people create a virtual identity that expresses some aspect of themselves. A few, however, create a virtual identity to engage in what is popularly known as catfishing: creating a false online virtual identity for nefarious purposes, such as a romantic or financial scam. Catfishing is a trend in cyberbullying as well. Some teens have committed suicide after being catfished by someone in their school or community. Many more have been deceived, abused, or teased after falling for a deceptive catfish scheme (Lohmann, 2013).

1. Do you know someone who has been catfished? How were they tricked, and how did they find out? (If you can't think of any, Google provides some interesting catfishing examples.)

2. What are the communication ethics of creating a genuine virtual identity? Is it ethical to creatively portray oneself as how you would like to be seen by others, including as a different gender, race, ethnicity, or age than you are in physical appearance? How far can one change one's presentation of virtual self before engaging in unethical communication behavior?

3. When does portraying a virtual self that differs creatively from a physical identity become unethical?

4. Is it the intent to do harm to another person, or the interpersonal deception in presentation of self, that makes this communication unethical?

KEYWORDS AND PHRASES

Actualized selves are the external material identity and social roles that the person enacts in life.

Communal frame places the individual identity within the group to which the individual belongs.

Enacted frame describes how identity comes into being through the dynamic performance of that identity in conversation with others.

Generalized other describes the influences that parents, family, social groups, community, and the broader cultural environment have on personal identity.

Identity represents a person's sense of self. A person constructs that identity through an iterative process of communication, feedback, and cognitive reflection.

Material element of identity refers to physical attributes such as clothes, property, and places to which a person attributes meaning and that contribute to their sense of self.

Personal element of identity references the mostly unchanging collection of traits, goals, beliefs, and values that an individual holds.

Personal frame is the meaning that people attribute to themselves, their motivations, perceptions, and expectations.

Private self-consciousness reflects the inner feelings, emotions, beliefs, and thoughts of an individual. It connects a person with the inner aspects of identity.

Public self-consciousness pays attention to the social aspects of identity, such as appearance, behaviors, and style.

Relational frame refers to the individual identity created in relationship with others.

Social element of identity emphasizes group membership, ethnicity, religion, nationality, gender, and family norms and expectations, all of which might influence a person's identity.

Third place references public spaces where identity development can occur without the social hierarchies implicit in family gatherings or at work. These include informal social gatherings at neighborhood pubs, cafés, or community centers and groups meeting through CMC.

QUESTIONS FOR FURTHER DISCUSSION

In this chapter, we describe identity as a relational process of communication. This perspective describes the self as an "I" and a "me," shaped in response to a "generalized other." "I" is my internal, subjective, spontaneous, unpredictable, driving force of self. "I" is who I am inside, but most of the time I am aware of "me." "Me" is defined by the roles, relationships, and self-concepts negotiated with and defined by the generalized other, including significant others, family members, community, and society at large.

1. Do you think this provides a good description of the processes of identity? If not, how would you describe identity? Do you think identity is a process or a personal attribute?

2. Given this way of viewing identity, do you agree with the statement made earlier in the chapter that people's online identities are often a fairly authentic representation of themselves? Why (not)? Do you think that a virtual identity might be a more authentic expression of one's inner self, the "I," than a physical identity? Why(not)?

3. If this is the case, do you think this freedom of expression of a personal identity might have positive, negative, or potentially both types of consequences for a person? Explain what you think about this and why.

Image Credits

6

Presence

P am bought the Home Products Store about 15 years ago. The store specializes in high-quality commercial furniture products for condo associations, retirement communities, large residential rental units, and professional buildings. Pam works long hours, spending most of her time in the office doing the bookkeeping, staying up-to-date on product lines, tracking customer accounts, and providing sales support to Sean and Jasmine. She focuses her attention on her customers, employees, the store, and her career.

FIGURE 6.1 Pam.

Personal Presence

Presence means being in the moment, focused, and not distracted by other things. It describes the experience of immersion in a conversation, relationship, narrative, or mediated experience. It means "being fully conscious and aware in the present moment … deep listening, being open beyond one's pre-conceptions and … consciously participating" (Senge et al., 2004, p. 13).

In a face-to-face conversation, we experience a sense of presence when actively listening to a conversation partner discuss a topic of mutual interest. We become involved in the conversation and often lose track of the time and place. In mediated communication, presence can mean having consciousness transported away from an awareness of one's physical surroundings into the flow of a good movie or the interaction of a video game. In CMC, presence means being aware of and, perhaps at least momentarily captivated by, what is happening on a social media site or in a virtual reality, becoming involved, and losing awareness of one's immediate physical surroundings (Oh et al., 2018).

CMC Presence

Presence is the experience of being there, becoming involved, engaging with, and immersed within the communication flow of a medium. It has an effect on the participant experience of CMC and the relationships developed within a medium. There are multiple terms used to describe various forms of presence. First among them is *telepresence*.

Telepresence

Telepresence is a general term that describes a person's psychological state and subjective perception of reality as filtered by a technology. It is an immediate, personal, immersive experience in a medium, one in which people are no longer aware that their experience is mediated by technology. The presence of a physical reality is suspended, and the action of the mediated experience captures one's attention (Lee, 2004; Lombard & Ditton, 1997; Slater & Wilbur, 1997).

Telepresence does not require interaction with another person, just involvement in the medium. Bourdon (2020) challenges the use of the word *presence* as a substitute for telepresence, but increasingly the literature uses *presence* as the term to describe the multiple aspects of a mediated telepresence experience. That experience involves the "high quality sensory feedback [for] ... achieving that sense of being there" (Minsky, 1980, pp. 45–46).

Social Presence

Social presence is a feeling of psychological proximity, closeness, connectedness, and intimacy with another person (Short et al., 1976). It describes a dynamic and ongoing process of connection, interaction, relationship, and involvement with others in a CMC environment. Presence describes the experience of being immersed in a medium that becomes the background environment within which participants communicate. Social presence describes the relationships experienced with others within that environment (Biocca, 1997; Houtman et al., 2014; Short et al., 1976).

Social presence refers to the degree to which participants feel connected, accepted, and close to each other in their personal-social-virtual identity expressions. It facilitates the communication interactions and is the experience of relationships with other people in a CMC medium. Social presence is the sense of a "socially salient other" present in the same online space that creates the opportunity for social engagement (Öztok & Kehrwald, 2017, p. 262).

Self, Personal, and Copresence

Three additional concepts further define the experience of presence and social presence. These are self, personal, and copresence. They recognize the importance of an awareness of one's self, others, and the relationship within a CMC environment. They are important to a person's expression of a virtual identity in CMC, whether participating in an online game, network, work team, or community.

Self-presence refers to an individual's awareness of, and personal-emotional involvement in, a virtual identity and self-presentation. It is a person's awareness and embodiment of a sense of self within the virtual environment. It describes how people perceive their bodies, emotions, ideas, beliefs, and character traits, as expressed in that virtual environment (Biocca, 1997; Lee, 2004; Ratan & Hasler, 2009).

TABLE 6.1 **Terms Defining Social Presence in Relationship to Others Within a Medium**

Self and Other Awareness: Experience of oneself and others in a virtual environment

Personal presence	Extent to which you feel you are in a virtual world
Self-presence	Awareness of and emotional response to a virtual self-representation
Copresence	Feeling the presence of other people in an online virtual environment

Social Presence With Others: Relational immediacy and "being there" with others

Social presence	Interpersonal immediacy, psychological proximity, relational intimacy communicating with others in a virtual environment

Personal presence is the degree to which an individual is involved in a virtual environment. It is the extent to which the individual feels a part of, and participates in, the virtual environment. The closeness or distance of the virtual environment to physical reality can affect this feeling, such as in the ability to create an avatar that looks like the individual, or to see virtual objects move in response to physical hand movements (Heeter, 1992; Lee, 2004).

Copresence refers to CMC participants being aware of each other. It has a bidirectional meaning and is not about a single participant's awareness of another person's presence but about both people being aware of each other. It describes a psychological connection made within a virtual space in which participants feel that they share the same feelings and ideas (Fägersten, 2010; Leonard et al., 2015).

Summary: Presence

Presence is the psychological state of an immersive experience in a virtual environment. This experience of presence is necessary but not sufficient for communication. Communication requires an awareness both of oneself and of others within the space in order to connect on an informational, emotional, and relational level. Social presence describes the experience of relational communication, built on that awareness of others in the virtual environment. It is the experience of forming relationships within a CMC medium. Table 6.1 lists the terms defining the multiple aspects of social presence.

Conceptualizing the Relationship Between Presence and Social Presence

Figure 6.2 organizes the terms and concepts that describe presence and social presence into a cube. As the cube illustrates, presence in the medium is the necessary foundational experience. Without this presence, social presence is not possible. An inner wall of self-presence represents one's sense of personal identity and awareness of self within the medium. The outer wall depicts the experience of copresence with others. Personal presence exists in the relationship between this self-awareness and experience of copresence with others, in the expression of personal and social identities. Social presence is the overall experience of relationships with others within the medium.

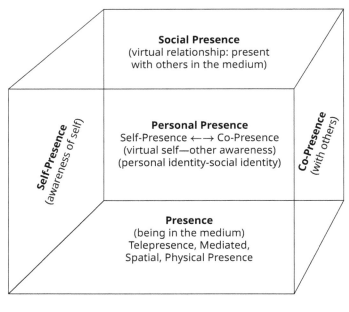

FIGURE 6.2 The Social Presence Cube.

Social Presence in CMC

Each type of CMC medium affects the development of social presence differently. Some forms of CMC feature synchronous, visual communication, which facilitate a social presence. Others provide visual anonymity, asynchronous communication, and text-based messaging. Each of these constraints can reduce the sense of social presence. Table 6.2 lists these constraints.

Visual Anonymity

Visual anonymity means that participants cannot see each other while they interact and may not know what each other looks like. Many CMC platforms, such as online forums, are visually anonymous. The visual anonymity reduces the nonverbal communication cues exchanged and can make it harder to create social presence (Rogers & Lea, 2005).

TABLE 6.2 **CMC Constraints on Social Presence**

1. Visual anonymity

2. Asynchronous communication

3. Text-based messaging

The communication behavior of participants in these online spaces, however, can increase the sense of social presence. Users of text-based social media platforms, for example, often share personal details that alleviate the social distance created by the lack of visual information. They can share pictures and other details about their personal lives that facilitate the development of personal relationships. Text-based messaging users often use visual cues such as emojis and gifs. In other online environments people create avatars, which while not direct visual representations, often stand-in for others' perceptions of them (Jin, 2011; Kang & Watt, 2013; Kear et al., 2014).

Asynchronous Communication

The degree to which a CMC medium reduces synchronous communication among participants can also adversely affect social presence. Synchronous communication allows participants to speak and listen simultaneously and to provide interactive feedback. Asynchronous communication denotes a lack of interactivity and often involves conversational delays that can reduce the experience of social presence.

Synchronicity of the communication varies with the medium. Videoconferencing is synchronous, but watching a recorded livestream is not. How communicators use a medium further influences the synchronicity and experience of social presence. Texting, for example, can provide a nearly synchronous form of written communication. How synchronous it is, however, depends on how quickly participants respond. Email is asynchronous, but when people respond immediately, it can feel almost synchronous. In each case, the responsiveness with which participants engage the communication, as well as the medium itself, affects the synchronicity and sense of social presence. The more immediate a communication partner responds, the more connected and together people feel (Park & Sundar, 2015).

Despite the asynchronous nature of most CMC, such as texting, email, and social media, the rate at which people respond to messages affects the experience of synchronicity. Most text conservations are immediate and instantaneous, with messages moving rapidly back and forth, creating a sense of synchronicity and social presence. Often, when a person does not respond immediately, it is perceived as an indication of a momentary distraction, not a relational absence. It may disrupt the immediate synchronicity but does not necessarily reduce the sense of overall social presence (Licoppe & Smoreda, 2005; Park & Sundar, 2015).

Text-Based Messaging

Facilitating social presence in a videoconference, when participants can see each other's facial expressions and hand movements and hear people's voices, is easier than in a text-based medium. The text-based nature of CMC can reduce the clarity of meaning in a message and the experience of social presence. Text-based environments lack many of the nonverbal cues, facial expressions, gestures, and vocal subtleties that express human emotion. This lack of emotional connection means that creating social presence is more difficult and may take longer (Liu et al., 2018).

In response, people use textual paralinguistic cues to communicate facial expressions, gestures, and other nonverbal cues. These cues include misspelling words, the use of specific symbols, punctuation, emojis, emoticons, and gifs. These textual paralinguistic cues add emotional depth to the communication expression. They facilitate emotional expression, project an active, warm feeling of connection, and increase the sense of social presence in the message (Hayes et al., 2020; Liu et al., 2018; Luangrath et al., 2017).

Summary: Social Presence in CMC

Although visually anonymous, asynchronous, and text-based CMC can reduce the experience; social presence is a relational perception, not an attribute of the medium. Participants create social presence through their communication behaviors. Responding quickly to a message creates more synchronicity. Sharing personal information and explicitly recognizing the contributions of another participant reduces anonymity and builds relational connection. Editing one's posts and comments to be clear and easily understood, and including nonverbal paralinguistic textual cues, facilitates social presence with others, regardless of the medium.

Social Presence With an Audience Across CMC Platforms

Turner and Foss (2018) expand the concept of social presence by acknowledging that CMC is no longer something that takes place within a single medium. They recognize CMC as the multiple, inter-related forms of communication that occur across a variety of media platforms and contexts. Social presence occurs across this broad range of CMC platforms, environments, information resources, and media. This broader CMC environment provides a competitive communication context within which participants must construct and manage their identities and relationships. To be effective, participants must develop a social presence that is salient to others across the CMC environment.

This competitive multiplatform environment of CMC requires that communicators first secure the attention of an audience and establish a social presence in their relationship to it. They must draw that attention away from other distractions in competing CMC sources. Then they must maintain that attention, regardless of those distractions. Turner and Foss (2018) suggest four strategies to achieve this. Each takes a different approach to establishing a social presence with an audience.

First, communicators often focus on an audience who has a budgeted social presence. This approach assumes an audience that allocates and manages its social presence across a number of interactions and platforms. Participants are likely to be simultaneously engaged in multiple text, email, other social media interactions, and face-to-face conversations at the same time. To create social presence, the key strategy for communicators is to first activate the audience's attention to a message, and then communicate that message efficiently. The focus on efficiency recognizes that an audience's social presence for any communicator is budgeted across these multiple interactions. In addition, a focus on return on investment for the communicator is essential. In other words, how much availability does a communicator have, and how much attention does an individual need or deserve at that time? This approach can mean that relationships become more superficial, with people only communicating in short bursts or through brief messages.

Second, in some contexts, communicators may attempt to promote social presence by limiting the number and variety of CMC sources available to the audience. This represents a communicator sense of entitled social presence. This strategy is sometimes successful in organizational videoconferences when a supervisor requests that participants stop reading emails, or in an educational classroom setting with the collection of cell phones or prohibition on use.

For the strategy to be successful, the audience must accept the communicator's entitlement to enforce this rule. Otherwise, participants may continue reading emails and using their phones. This approach, although sometimes effective, does create an asymmetrical relationship, with the communicator seen as superior.

Third, communicators may use a competitive social presence strategy to focus audience attention on a message. To stand out from a background of CMC noise, communicators must make their message more interesting, stimulating, exciting, or provocative. Communicators using this strategy develop motivating messages by changing the words, adjusting the message, and providing evidence to appeal to a particular audience. Although this approach also renders the relationship asymmetrical, in this case, it is the audience that holds the power of communication.

Fourth, communicators can create an invitational social presence that focuses on a specific audience and their needs, by listening to participants with respect and understanding the value of their perspectives. Recognizing that participants are the authorities of their life experiences, allowing them to describe those experiences in their own words, and explicitly acknowledging the worth of their contributions creates a feeling of conversational safety, value, and freedom of expression. This facilitates social presence through the recognition and value of audience members as participants in a CMC relationship. In practice, this may involve asking a specific friend out for lunch or a teacher inviting several students to help come up with an in-class activity.

These four approaches move the concept of social presence beyond CMC relationships in any one medium. They describe approaches to developing communication relationships with audiences across multiple, and often competitive, CMC environments (Turner & Foss, 2018). Table 6.3 lists these four approaches to developing social presence with an audience.

TABLE 6.3 Four Approaches to Social Presence With an Audience Across CMC Platforms

BUDGETED SOCIAL PRESENCE	Assumes audience allocates and manages attention across a large number of CMC interactions. Focus on communication efficiency.
ENTITLED SOCIAL PRESENCE	Attempts to promote social presence by limiting the number and variety of other CMC sources available to an audience.
COMPETITIVE SOCIAL PRESENCE	Assumes lack of audience attention due to competing CMC sources. Creates more interesting, exciting, stimulating, or provocative messages.
INVITATIONAL SOCIAL PRESENCE	Invites audience to interact, understand their perspectives by listening, considering alternatives, and creating feelings of safety, value, and freedom of expression among participants.

Ambient and Connected Presence in Relationships

Other researchers further expand the concept of social presence to mean a relationship influenced by broader patterns of CMC use. They describe how people use CMC to maintain the quality of social presence in their relationships with acquaintances, friends, business associates, family members, or intimate partners. Two terms recognize this patterned use of CMC, often carried out through phone calls, texting, or social media use, to maintain the social presence of important relationships. Ambient presence describes the sense of presence that is the result of two people in geographically different locations using CMC. Connected presence describes the regular use of CMC across time that maintains expected patterns of relational communication (Licoppe, 2004; Madianou, 2016; Rao, 2008; Wadley et al., 2013).

Ambient Presence

When we live in close proximity to others in the physical world, we often hear their footsteps, rustling noises, doors opening or closing, muted conversations, or other background noises. This provides a sense of the presence of those others who are nearby. When someone is not physically close to us, these sounds are missing. Ambient presence describes how CMC can stimulate that closeness by creating a perpetual awareness of what people who live across geographical distances are doing (Madianou, 2016).

In the past, couples often overcame this physical separation by writing long, descriptive letters about the mundane events and activities in their lives, sending pictures to one another, or placing international phone calls. The recipient could reread the letter multiple times, maintaining a relational connection and ambient presence with the other at each reading. Today, couples often maintain this type of relational connection by texting, Skyping, or using WhatsApp to communicate with each other multiple times a day.

Social media can provide an ambient presence as well. People use Facebook, Twitter, Snapchat, Instagram, and other social media to post about the everyday events, special memories, and important occasions of their lives. They also maintain an ambient presence by sharing mundane, even random, pictures of a room or an outdoor landscape, emojis, quotes, short videos, or messages. These maintain an ambient presence by providing others with constant updates about their personal lives.

The popularity of the cell phone renders the creation of an ambient presence even easier. People use their cell phones to maintain a relatively unobtrusive relational connection by sending messages or to check social media sites to see what their connections are doing. Participants in intimate relationships often use this type of ambient copresence to maintain their emotional connection and sense of belonging throughout the day, even when separated by physical distance (Madianou, 2016).

Connected Presence

Connected presence describes the extent to which the sense of being together in a relationship is mediated by CMC. It describes how people use multiple platforms and devices to maintain their sense of closeness to others. It represents the "patterns of mediated interactions that combine into connected relationships" (Licoppe, 2004, p. 136; see also Schroeder, 2005).

Connected presence creates a sense of shared time and space; geographical boundaries disappear, and CMC creates a "mediated intimacy" that feels as tangible as a physical presence (Wilding, 2006, p. 133). It reduces the perception of geographic separation, and the distinction between absence and presence becomes blurred. The act of communication affects this sense of connected presence as much as the content. Through frequent communication, people get a sense of being copresent through CMC, even when the messages they exchange are short and mundane (Licoppe, 2004; Wilding, 2006).

The medium of connection, however, matters. Letters, for example, often create highly detailed, idealized, perceptions of a communicator's world and relationships. Frequent exchanges of email can provide a more mundane and timely insight into those lives and realities. Texting can provide even more immediacy and connection to the moment (Wilding, 2006).

The nature of the CMC technologies and the social expectations associated with them affect the practice of connected presence. Participant preference in the use of medium, available technology, and communication habits interact to create relationship expectations. A cell phone, or a medium such as Skype or Facetime, support personal conversations. These conversations may occur at preplanned times and involve shared personal information that shows a relational trust, commitment, and engagement. In addition, cell phones facilitate texting and the maintenance of a connected presence through short, frequent messages and quick responses. These demonstrate relational engagement through accessibility and continuous connection.

Connected presence can develop through the use of any type of medium. It may involve short, frequent interactions, or long conversations, whether spoken or texted. The conversational content may be secondary to the relational communication, and the multiple, short points of contact can form a perceptual continuous conversation across time, creating the sense of connected presence (Licoppe & Smoreda, 2005)

Applying Connected Presence: Building Relationships

Connected presence, in either synchronous or asynchronous communication, builds on participant interactivity and openness that help sustain relational trust and satisfaction. Developing or maintaining these relationship qualities with another person in any medium can be difficult. The anonymous, asynchronous, text-based characteristics of many forms of CMC can hinder their development as well. Participants can work on building interactivity, openness, trust, and satisfaction in their relationships by developing communication habits that respond to the social presence of others online (Sherblom et al., 2018).

Interactivity identifies the turn taking, immediacy of feedback, and rate of conversational exchange. Face-to-face discussion is synchronously interactive. In a text-based CMC interaction, the rate tends to be slower. People type and read slower than they speak and listen. Turn taking is less rapid. Feedback is slower. Nonverbal cues are subdued, and the conversation can become less of a dialogue and more of a series of monologues expressing

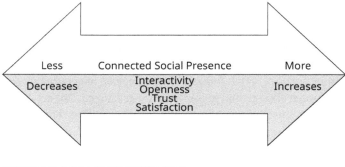

FIGURE 6.3 Connected Social Presence.

opinions. Explicitly encouraging interactivity is important to building conversational openness in a CMC relationship.

Openness describes a person's willingness to self-disclose. It reflects a participant's level of comfort in expressing personal thoughts, ideas, opinions, and emotions. This disclosure occurs reciprocally in a relationship. Reciprocal disclosure improves relationship trust and satisfaction.

Trust is the relational expectation that another person will treat you with respect, cooperation, and benevolence. Participants build trust through their patterns of communication. Consistent, personalized, frequent responses build trust and stimulate interactivity.

Satisfaction is a feeling that a conversation and relationship are enjoyable and worth pursuing. Conversational and relational satisfaction require developing a social presence with another person in a CMC medium. Participants must be able to use the medium effectively to experience social presence, trust, interactivity, openness, and satisfaction (Sherblom et al., 2018).

Figure 6.3 shows how these relational characteristics increase and decrease with the connected social presence created through communication. Frequent, short, or longer, more thoughtful communication can maintain that connection. The key is the interactivity and openness of the communication that builds trust and satisfaction in the relationship.

Perspective in Context

Analysis and Critique

Presence and social presence are important concepts in CMC. Achieving participant interactivity, conversational openness, interpersonal trust, and communication satisfaction are dependent on them. Developing presence and social presence, however, can be a challenge.

In a face-to-face relationship, you can look a person in the eye; read nonverbal cues of interest, distraction, or boredom; and ask direct questions. In a CMC environment, some participants may be reticent to interact, preferring to lurk or engage in social loafing. It is more difficult to know if a person is paying attention, multitasking, or away from their computer or phone. A person cannot be socially present in a conversation if not present in the medium.

Social presence is a relatively abstract relational concept. I may think that I am socially present in an asynchronous, text-based, CMC conversation, even while I multitask, read my email, or do other mundane chores. After all, I am good at multitasking, and am simply using the time delays in the asynchronous communication to accomplish other important things. If you are my conversational partner, however, you may notice my lack of involvement and social presence.

Measuring social presence, interactivity, openness, trust, and satisfaction can be a challenge. Do we ask the communicator, question the communication partner, or examine the text of the conversation to estimate it? What if one communication partner disagrees with another about the level of social presence experienced?

Face-to-face relationships facilitate the greatest opportunity for social presence, but they do not guarantee it. A leaner medium, such as a text-based conferencing system, may provide more of a challenge. With time and experience, however, participants in text-only CMC groups can develop social presence and share rich personal, social, emotional, and relational communication. Online social support groups provide an example.

People participate in these online social support groups for many reasons. They can participate in them from home. They often receive numerous, quick responses to important personal questions and issues from relatively knowledgeable sources. The anonymity of the medium enhances a sense of personal control over the information (Campbell & Wright, 2002).

More importantly, these CMC social support groups develop a social presence among participants by doing four things. First, participants offer explicit statements of emotional support, affection, encouragement, sympathy, and understanding. Second, they provide information in the form of instruction, advice, situational appraisals, expertise, and suggestions for reducing uncertainty in challenging situations. Third, they express esteem with compliments, personal validation, positive statements, and relief from blame. Fourth, they support each other in the expression of similar feelings, interests, concerns, and willingness to help. Through these four communication practices, CMC support groups build social presence, interactivity, openness, trust, and satisfaction among participants (Green-Hamann et al., 2011).

Social Presence in Practice: Holograms and Videoconference Presentations

In *Star Wars: A New Hope*, Princess Leia sends R2-D2 to project a hologram of her imploring Obi-Wan Kenobi for help. She must have thought this would be the most persuasive way of producing a sense of social presence, connection, and urgency in her need for assistance. Of course, that was a long, long time ago, in a galaxy far, far away. Does a three-dimensional holographic image produce a greater sense of social presence and copresence than a two-dimensional video? Mazgaj et al. (2021) explore this question.

They compared the social presence and copresence responses of real human participants to video and hologram projections in a high-tech laboratory setting. They create two kinds of messages. For the first, they used a digital holography process to create, store, and project a three-dimensional holographic image. For the other, they communicated the same message through a two-dimensional videorecording. They showed the message to 98 student participants, half of whom saw the three-dimensional holographic projection. The other half viewed the two-dimensional video message.

After showing the message, they asked participants to respond to a questionnaire about their experience of social presence and copresence with the person communicating the message. They measured social presence in participant responses to psychological proximity, closeness, connectedness, and intimacy with that person. They measured copresence in the participant perceptions that their feelings of emotional closeness were mutual. Mazgaj et al. (2021) report differences in the responses they obtained from the two conditions.

Their results show that the experience of social presence overall differs only a little between the two conditions. The three-dimensional hologram condition produces a slightly higher level of perceptual awareness. This does not significantly change the participants' experience of social presence but does produce a difference in copresence. The perception of a copresence is significantly stronger in the holographic projection than in the video presentation. These results suggest that Princess Leia was right to choose a holographic presentation in the hopes of building a sense of copresence and emotional connection with Obi-Wan Kenobi.

Illustration of Concepts

Pam works hard to develop a sense of social presence with Jasmine, Sean, and with her customers. She responds quickly to text messages and emails and personalizes her messages, asking how previous projects are serving current customer needs. When needed, she suggests using a less visually anonymous, asynchronous, text-based medium to develop a social presence to work through informational details and more complex information. But Pam always allows the customers to choose a medium, according their preferences. She also makes sure to set aside time to meet with Sean and Jasmine in the store each week. Using a variety of CMC media and face-to-face meetings, and focusing on generating social presence in each, Pam maintains her relationship connections.

Looking Forward to Propinquity

In the next chapter, we look at electronic propinquity and the implications of communication choices on relationships. The electronic propinquity perspective predicts that our selection of a communication medium affects our experience of relational closeness. Sometimes texting is the most efficient method of communicating, while other times leaving a phone message is the most logical thing to do. Our choice of medium, however, can affect the perception of our relational closeness or propinquity.

The Ethics of Social Presence

Being socially present means being with another person. It takes time, energy, and attention. I must stop what I am doing, think about, and focus my attention on them and what they are thinking and feeling. I have to become aware of their emotions, anxieties, fears, uncertainties, joy, excitement, exhilaration, or exhaustion. Being socially present can be a challenge even in a face-to-face situation. In a CMC medium it is often easier to maintain an interpersonal distance, multitask, or delay a response until it is convenient for me to reply. I may offer to be there for a friend but then be slow or non-responsive to a phone call, text message, or email. It can be more difficult to interrupt my life to make an effort for a friend right now. What are the communication ethics of relationship? Do the ethics of responsiveness to a friend change when a communication medium is asynchronous rather than synchronous?

1. Is there an appropriate time period within which to write a response to an asynchronous text message or email from a friend who writes about a serious emotional concern?

2. Does my response time depend on the nature of the friendship? (Sometimes I just can't handle the drama.)

3. Does an appropriate response time depend on what else I have going on in my life? (A true friend will understand that I have my own concerns and issues to deal with.)

4. What are the communication ethics of social presence with a friend in CMC?

KEYWORDS AND PHRASES

Ambient presence describes the sense of presence that is the result of two people in geographically different locations using CMC.

Budgeted social presence assumes an audience that allocates and manages its social presence across a number of interactions and platforms.

Competitive social presence is a strategy used to describe when communicators make their message more interesting, stimulating, exciting, or provocative to stand out from a background of CMC noise.

Connected presence describes the extent to which the sense of being together in a relationship is mediated by CMC. It describes how people use multiple platforms and devices to maintain their sense of closeness to others and maintain patterns of relational communication.

Copresence refers to CMC participants being aware of each other. It has a bidirectional meaning and is not about a single participant's awareness of another person's presence but about both people being aware of each other.

Entitled social presence describes when communicators attempt to promote social presence by limiting the number and variety of CMC sources available to the audience.

Interactivity identifies the turn taking, immediacy of feedback, and rate of conversational exchange.

Invitational social presence means that communicators focus on one specific audience and work to relate to them.

Personal presence is the degree to which an individual is involved in a virtual environment.

Presence means being in the moment, focused, and not distracted. It describes the experience of immersion in a conversation, relationship, narrative, or mediated experience.

Self-presence refers to an individual's awareness of, and personal-emotional involvement in, a virtual identity and self-presentation.

Social presence is a feeling of psychological proximity, closeness, connectedness, and intimacy with another person.

Synchronous communication allows participants to speak and listen simultaneously and to provide interactive feedback.

Telepresence is a general term that describes a person's psychological state and subjective perception of reality as filtered by a technology.

Textual paralinguistic cues are cues that people use to communicate facial expressions, gestures, and other nonverbal cues. These cues include misspelling words, the use of specific symbols, punctuation, emojis, emoticons, and gifs.

Visual anonymity means that participants cannot see each other while they interact and may not know what each other looks like.

QUESTIONS FOR FURTHER DISCUSSION

1. Do you use CMC to maintain one or more of your relationships with family and friends? Are those relationships as close and intimate as your face-to-face relationships?

2. Often people maintain close, personal relationships through a combination of face-to-face and CMC. These are sometimes called hybrid forms of communication, with relationships developed and maintained through the use of face-to-face conversations, phone calls, texting, and social media platforms. Do you think this is an effective way of developing social presence and relational trust? Why (why not)?

3. Many of us multitask while using CMC; we chat with others during a videoconference meeting, or we scroll through our social media while watching a livestream. Do you think this hurts your presence? Why (not)?

7

Propinquity

C heryl likes her job as regional vice president of commercial and residential furniture product sales. She works hard to maintain good business relationships with her employees and customers. Cheryl thinks about the relationship implications of her CMC choices as she tries to build closer working relationships with both customers and colleagues.

FIGURE 7.1 Cheryl.

A Perspective on Electronic Propinquity

Electronic Propinquity

Electronic propinquity is a systems perspective that seeks to understand the influences of CMC use on the closeness people feel in their relationships with others. Propinquity means physical closeness in time and space. The dimensions of time and space define our physical world. They structure our perceptions of reality and make it accessible to us through our sensory awareness and cognitive interpretations. Time and space spent together define the dimensions of our human relationships as well. This physical closeness to others constitutes a fundamental condition of relationships in a face-to-face context. Although CMC lacks the physical closeness of face-to-face conversation, people often feel a connection to others online. Electronic propinquity is the experience of a psychological closeness and feeling of connectedness to another person through CMC (Korzenny, 1978; Walther & Bazarova, 2008).

Korzenny (1978) originally developed electronic propinquity as "a general theory of mediated communication" (p. 3). Walther and Bazarova (2008) extend the perspective to include the more recent forms of interactive CMC. Electronic propinquity uses psychological closeness as a substitute for the embodied, physical closeness of face-to-face conversation. In this sense, electronic propinquity is similar to the experience of online social presence. Social presence, however, refers to a sense of proximity to another person in a CMC environment; electronic propinquity is the experience of a relational closeness (Short et al., 1976; Westerman, et al., 2015).

TABLE 7.1 Influences on Electronic Propinquity

1. The existing closeness in a relationship

2. Mutual directionality of communication

3. Bandwidth of the medium

4. Complexity of the information

5. Communication rules

6. Communicator skill with medium

7. Amount of choice in selection of communication medium

Electronic Propinquity and Relational Closeness

Electronic propinquity is a sense of online relational closeness but places that feeling within the larger context of interpersonal relationships. The perspective moves beyond the experience of online social presence to describe the implications of people's CMC choices on that feeling of psychological closeness in their interpersonal relationships, or their sense of propinquity. In other words, the electronic propinquity perspective captures the feeling of emotional intimacy with another person, whether an acquaintance, client, colleague, friend, or family member, and examines the influences and consequences of people's CMC choices on this feeling of relational closeness (Korzenny & Bauer, 1981; Walther & Bazarova, 2008).

Influences on Electronic Propinquity

There are seven factors that **influence electronic propinquity**. These influences are the existing relational closeness, the ability to provide and receive feedback (i.e., the mutual directionality of communication), bandwidth, information complexity, communication rules, communicator skill, and amount of choice available in the selection of a medium through which to communicate (Korzenny, 1978; Korzenny & Bauer, 1981). Table 7.1 lists these influences.

Seven Propositions of Electronic Propinquity

Seven propositions describe the implications of each of these influences on the interpersonal closeness of a CMC-based relationship. First, propinquity is a perception of relationship closeness rather than a characteristic of the medium. Second, if the CMC message exchange includes more nearly synchronous, direct, and immediate feedback, people will perceive more relational closeness. Third, the greater the bandwidth of the medium used to communicate, the more relational closeness people will experience. Fourth, the greater the complexity of the information, the less relational closeness people will perceive as a result of the message. Fifth, the more the communication is governed by social and technological rules, the less perceived relational

TABLE 7.2 **Seven Propositions of Electronic Propinquity**

1. Propinquity is a perception of relationship closeness.

2. The more synchronous feedback, the more relational closeness perceived in a message.

3. The wider the medium bandwidth, the more relational closeness perceived in a message.

4. More complex information, the less relational closeness perceived in a message.

5. More formal communication rules, the less perceived relational closeness in a message.

6. More communicator skill with medium, the more perceived relational closeness in a message.

7. Fewer choices in available medium, the more perceived relational closeness in a message.

closeness. Sixth, the more a communicator is skilled in using a medium, the more relational closeness they will experience. Seventh, if there are fewer media to choose from, people will perceive higher levels of relational closeness through whatever medium they end up using (Korzenny, 1978; Korzenny & Bauer, 1981). Table 7.2 lists these propositions.

Examining Propinquity: Three Levels of Analysis

These electronic propinquity propositions enable three levels of analysis for examining electronic propinquity in more detail. The first, most immediate, level of analysis involves examining the experience of electronic propinquity within a CMC medium. The second compares the experience of electronic propinquity across different CMC media. The third focuses on the implications of electronic propinquity for relational closeness.

First Level of Analysis: Propinquity Within a Medium

The first level of analysis examines electronic propinquity as the experience of psychological closeness or proximity to someone in a particular CMC medium. Studies focused on this level of analysis often treat propinquity as similar to the experience of social presence in a medium. Westerman et al. (2015), for example, treat "both social presence and electronic propinquity [as] ... the experience of feeling connected/being with another entity [and as] similar, or even the same" concepts (p. 95). They use the concept at this level of analysis to examine the expression of connection between participants and the people presented in a set of CMC news stories. Wombacher et al. (2017) also note the similarity between the concepts of social presence and propinquity when they assess how online learning affects the electronic propinquity of students who experience CMC anxiety.

Second Level of Analysis: Comparison of CMC Media

A second level of analysis examines electronic propinquity across media. It uses electronic propinquity to compare the experience of different CMC media. Similar to the media richness perspective, the electronic propinquity perspective places CMC media along a continuum that recognizes face-to-face conversation as the most facilitative of relational communication. Unlike media richness, which compares the ability of media to convey content information efficiently and effectively, the electronic propinquity perspective compares their ability to facilitate relational closeness.

Five of the electronic propinquity propositions suggest comparisons that can be made among different types of CMC. These are the implied differences in media characteristics of immediate or synchronous feedback, bandwidth, communication rules, and the communicator skill needed. The implications of these comparisons rank CMC media in an order similar to the media richness perspective.

Face-to-face conversations produce the highest levels of relational closeness; we are freer to express ourselves because we can express our thoughts in incomplete sentences and ignore formal rules of grammar. This personal expression facilitates mutual understanding and increases the relational closeness. It is more difficult to reproduce this experience through electronic propinquity in a CMC medium. Videoconferencing maintains the relational closeness of time and space, with conversational interaction and nonverbal expression, but it generally requires more formal rules for speaking order and turn taking, and more communicator skill. A phone call maintains a mutual directionality in synchronous conversation but reduces the amount of nonverbal feedback in physical cues. Texting further reduces the shared space of vocal cues and expression. Email both reduces time and space synchronicity and generally requires adherence to more formal rules.

Walther and Bazarova (2008) compare the experiences of electronic propinquity in groups whose members use a single medium to communicate to those in which some members are able to use a higher bandwidth media than the others. They find no differences in the experience of electronic propinquity among the participants of groups whose members use a single medium to communicate. However, when some group members can communicate using a higher bandwidth, those who can use only the lower bandwidth medium report experiencing less propinquity in their group relationships. The effect holds regardless of the medium, whether chat, voice, video, or face-to-face conversation, used to communicate.

In their study of CMC anxiety and electronic propinquity, Wombacher et al. (2017) note that participants viewing self-advancing slides without narration report lower electronic propinquity that those viewing self-advancing slides with narration. The experience of CMC anxiety also reduces the electronic propinquity. Electronic propinquity, however, does not affect student learning, as measured in quiz scores.

Third Level of Analysis: Implications for Relationships

More recent research often examines the implications of electronic propinquity for participant relationships. These analyses provide more than a description of an online experience or comparison of the effects of different media characteristics. These analyses use the sixth and/or seventh propositions of electronic propinquity to explore effects of communicator skill and choice of a medium on relationship closeness.

Social Presence and Propinquity in Online Gaming

Banks and Carr (2019) analyzed the social presence of players in an online multiplayer video game and the experience of electronic propinquity that participants develop in their relationships with each other while playing. Player interactions through their avatars elicit perceptions of an immediate social presence within the game. At the same time, the players engage in informal conversations, sharing memories and experiences, developing a relational closeness over time.

Using an online experiment carried out among *World of Warcraft* players, Banks and Carr (2019) find that players perceive both the avatars and the human behind them as social actors and develop relationships with both, experiencing propinquity with other players as well as their avatars. This increases the complexity of cognitive-social demands of playing the game and impacts the communication the gameplay. Players must interpret and respond to not only the expressive cues embodied by the actions of the avatar, but also the strategic goals held by the players.

Sexual Assault Nurse Examiners' Use of Electronic Propinquity

Downing et al. (2022) used the electronic propinquity perspective to examine whether a CMC medium can be used to connect with people who have been sexually assaulted. These victims face multiple adverse physical and emotional health risks. Sexual assault nurse examiners (SANEs) provide initial examinations and follow-up appointments for counseling, pregnancy testing, and immunizations against sexually transmitted infections. Patients, however, often do not complete this course of follow-up care; less than three quarters of sexual assault victims answer their phones when called.

Downing et al. (2021) describe designing a program based on the principles of electronic propinquity to help sexual assault survivors be more informed, comfortable, and engaged in their follow-up care. The program uses texting rather than phone calls and allows the patient to decide the type of message and time of day they want to receive them.

Their results show that participation in the texting program is higher than other forms of follow-up care. Downing et al. find that giving patients control and allowing them to incorporate the messaging into their daily lives promotes a sense of psychological closeness, affiliation, trust, and relational propinquity with the nurses and increases the willingness to participate in the program. Participants prefer texting as a convenient, supportive, and noninvasive form of CMC for maintaining their privacy about the potential health issues surrounding sexual assault. The messages are relatively silent, can be reviewed when and where the recipient wishes, and are easily deleted. They give recipients a sense of control over the information, which can be tailored to their specific requests. The texting program creates relational propinquity without adding stress.

Summary: Electronic Propinquity

Figure 7.2 illustrates the three levels of analysis. First, the experience of electronic propinquity within a medium is similar to social presence. Second, electronic propinquity, like the media richness perspective, provides a method to compare CMC media, but one that focuses on relational closeness rather than informational efficiency and effectiveness.

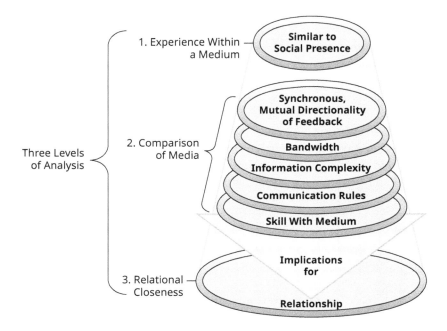

FIGURE 7.2 Three Levels of Analysis.

Third, electronic propinquity has implications for developing feelings of closeness in a relationship.

The Implications of Electronic Propinquity for Relational Closeness

The implications of electronic propinquity for relationship closeness are of particular interest, as demonstrated in the works of Banks and Carr (2019) and Downing et al. (2021). These analyses focus on the communication choices a participant makes when using a CMC medium and the implications these choices have for their relationships. In addition to the experience of electronic propinquity within a medium and comparison between media, this level of analysis focuses on participant perceptions and expectations of the relationship and their CMC choices.

First, the perception of relationship closeness depends on preexisting conditions in the relationship communication habits and expectations of participants. For Banks and Carr (2019), these conditions exist in the medium and objectives of the game, as well as the gamer experience, expertise, and playing strategies. For Downing et al. (2021), these conditions exist in patient perceptions of their health care needs, relationship to the clinic, and habits of cell phone use.

Second, these preexisting conditions form the context of perceptions about the relationship and the choice of medium used to communicate. Banks and Carr (2019) describe the perception of social agency experienced by gamers as "a result of [their] shared experiences and memories, which is used to guide subsequent interactions" (p. 288). Downing et al. (2021) discuss the purposeful choice of a medium to facilitate an ongoing relationship with patients. The perceived interactive feedback and bandwidth capabilities of the medium inform this choice.

The choice of medium, made from among the available options, affects the ongoing closeness of the future relationship. Banks and Carr (2019) describe the use of the medium for not just immersive play in the game, but for the development of relationships with both the avatars and the humans behind them. A relational closeness develops in understanding the human players as social actors with strategic goals, expertise, and experience. Downing et al. (2021) demonstrate the importance of medium choice in facilitating an ongoing relational closeness. The selection of a medium that allows patients control over the interaction and feedback facilitates the potential for an ongoing relationship better than one with more synchronous communication and bandwidth, such as a phone call.

Summary: Implications for Relational Closeness

Electronic propinquity is a psychological perception that exists in the experience of relational closeness. It can change over time. Communication habits and expectations affect these perceptions of propinquity. For example, if we are professional colleagues who typically use email to exchange important business messages with each other, regardless of whether we are accessible by phone or occupy offices near each other, then my sharing important information with you by email will not reduce our relational closeness. If, however, we have a history of exchanging important information verbally, either by talking on the phone or in face-to-face conversation, then sending that information by email threatens our relational closeness. Other characteristics of our relationship can affect the interpretation of propinquity as well. Interpersonal uncertainty, conflict, or the experience of difficulties in the relationship can reduce the perception of propinquity intended by a message. On the other hand, a desire to overcome relationship turbulence or hope for a future relationship can increase the perception of propinquity in the message.

The choice of a communication medium from among the available alternatives affects a receiver's sense of propinquity as well. Participants evaluate the propinquity of a message through their perceptions of the features of a medium. An interactive medium that facilitates more feedback and has more bandwidth generally facilitates a greater sense of electronic propinquity. For example, a person commonly perceives more relational closeness from a phone call when a medium with greater bandwidth, such as a face-to-face conversation, is not readily available. That same person generally feels less propinquity when that phone call replaces an expected face-to-face conversation. Likewise, a recipient likely feels more propinquity from a personal phone call than a short text message containing the same information. This, however, is not always true. As illustrated by Downing et al. (2021), a recipient sometimes perceives a text message as more convenient, confidential, and time efficient than a phone call. In either case, it is the recipient perception of the electronic propinquity implied by a message that affects the ongoing relationship.

In conclusion, the choice of a medium, within the available alternatives, affects the ongoing relational closeness. The interpretation of this choice maintains, enhances, or

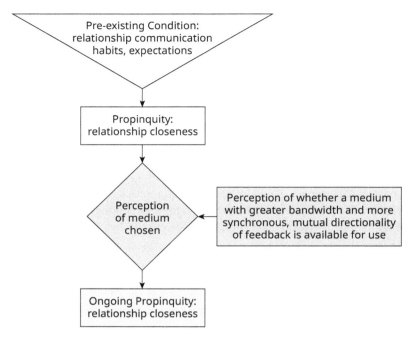

FIGURE 7.3 Influences on Relationship Closeness.

diminishes that relational closeness (Downing et al., 2021; Korzenny, 1978; Ramirez et al., 2008). Figure 7.3 summarizes the connections of electronic propinquity to relational closeness.

Cycles of Perceptual Influences

The choice of a medium through which to communicate, within the available alternatives, affects the ongoing relationship closeness. It also influences perceptions of the medium chosen for that communication. Perceptions of the chosen medium, within the perceived alternatives, influences the receiver impressions of the synchronicity of feedback, bandwidth, information complexity, communication rules, and communicator skill displayed in the message. These perceptions form a cycle of influences that affect both the experience of the medium and the ongoing relational closeness (Korzenny, 1978).

The receiver of a CMC message perceives the sender as making a choice among possible media through which to communicate. When a richer medium is available for use, but a leaner one is chosen, the receiver's perception of that choice reduces the experience of mutual directionality in the feedback available in that medium. That is, a receiver may not believe a response is desirable or needed, or they may not know how to respond to information sent through a text or email when a richer medium allowing for a fuller discussion is available. The perceptions of communicator choice and reduced directionality in feedback work together to reduce the receiver's experience of the chosen medium's bandwidth. This perception of a smaller bandwidth increases the apparent complexity of the information conveyed and formality of the communication rules employed. These perceived characteristics of the message, in turn, reduce the impression of communicator skill, and the overall cycle reduces the sense of electronic propinquity in the message and the resulting relational closeness.

When the receiver believes that a richer medium is not available for use, the experience of mutual directionality in the feedback available in a medium increases. The medium choice and experience of increased feedback directionality increase the perception of bandwidth. This perception of greater bandwidth decreases the apparent complexity of the information and formality of communication rules. These, in turn, increase the impression of communicator skill in using the medium for that message. This cycle of perceptions increases the sense of electronic propinquity in the message and the relational closeness produced by it.

For example, if I am out of town and text you an important piece of information, you are likely to respond quickly, providing a mutual directionality in feedback. The texting medium is adequate to our communication, the information straightforward, and the rules informal, and I appear to be a skilled communicator in using CMC in that way. My choice to send the message through that medium at that time is likely seen as the result of my having limited options and will likely strengthen the feeling of closeness in our relationship.

If, however, I text you that same information instead of walking a few steps down the hall from my office to yours, you are likely to perceive my choice of texting as an indication of less relationship closeness and as requiring less immediate response from you. The bandwidth of the text message, in comparison to a face-to-face conversation, appears small. The information conveyed without discussion, appears more complex, conveyed with more formal rules, and by a less skilled communicator. Figure 7.4 depicts these two cycles of influence that affect perceptions of the medium, the message, and the ongoing relationship closeness.

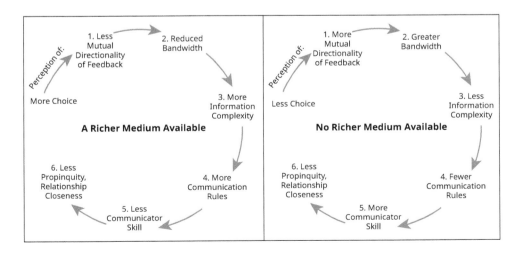

FIGURE 7.4 Cycles of Influences on Medium Perceptions and Relationship Closeness.

Perspective in Context

Analysis and Critique

Walther and Bazarova (2008) suggest that the propositions of electronic propinquity lack clarity and that empirical tests do not always support its predictions. Korzenny and Baurer (1981), for example, predict that electronic propinquity will increase with bandwidth, feedback, and communicator skills and decrease with information complexity and communication rules. They report inconclusive results, however, with feedback accounting for 55% of their differences. Bandwidth, complexity, rules, and skills contribute little. They conclude a need for further specification of the electronic propinquity propositions.

Walther and Bazarova (2008) provide a more carefully detailed specification and comparison, finding that bandwidth and medium choice affect electronic propinquity. Furthermore, their research demonstrates that it is not the actual features of the medium that determine the propinquity, but the perceptions of these features. This finding supports a major proposition of electronic propinquity, which states that these perceptions are interpretations based on the choices made among those available for CMC.

The electronic propinquity perspective indicates that these communication choices have relational consequences, which is the most interesting, useful, and comprehensive proposition of the perspective. The person to whom I am communicating interprets my choice of medium as an indication of my perception of our relational closeness. In turn, that person's interpretation of my CMC choice affects their perception and, subsequently, the ongoing closeness of our relationship. When other CMC options are available, choosing a lean medium may create distance in our relationship. Choosing the richest available medium enhances that relational closeness.

Propinquity in Practice: Medical Practitioners in Malaysia

Rahman (2017) examined the relational implications of media choices made by hospital medical officers and physicians in Malaysia. He uses electronic propinquity to analyze these choices and their relationship implications. The Malaysian government provides computer applications, and hospital management requires the use of them.

Rahman (2017) reports high proficiency among the medical professionals in the use of word processing, spreadsheets, and CMC applications, with somewhat less skill with graphics and databases. In addition, most physicians carry cell phones while treating patients and use them to stay in touch with colleagues, to get the latest information on new diseases, and to keep up-to-date on any new outbreaks in the country. Respondents report using the CMC applications to resolve medical issues quickly, speed up their work cycle, increase their individual productivity, and ensure an efficient working environment. The medical officers in this study also reported participating in online meetings to engage in annual and strategic organizational planning, especially when they need the input of specialists.

Furthermore, the medical officers in this study rely on CMC to overcome the physical distance from colleagues, especially specialists, who work at other hospitals. Medical officers at different locations, therefore, must create their own communication networks with colleagues, using their personal cell phones. They especially use their cell phones to seek the views of other medical professionals on proposed treatments, send information on a patient's progress, or share photos of a patient's condition. This helps reduce patient treatment cost by eliminating the need for transportation. In addition, medical professionals use CMC to share experiences or findings related to a particular health care issue. Others participate in ongoing CMC groups to discuss specific medical concerns, increase knowledge of diseases, access the most recent information on new diseases from domestic or foreign websites, and improve the accuracy, timeliness, and completeness of information to make better medical decisions. Rahman reports that these medical professionals experience electronic propinquity with others. The technology helps them overcome barriers of time and space to create a relational closeness with other medical professionals.

Illustration of Concepts

Cheryl uses her cell phone to maintain closeness with her employees, regardless of where they might be working at the time. When Alex and Darius are on the road or at a customer job site she often uses text or email to stay in touch. However, if she has not talked with them recently, she usually calls. This gives them the opportunity to talk through multiple smaller issues as well as sharing the information of immediate interest, which helps them maintain their working relationship.

Cheryl often calls new customers to tell them about information she will be sending them by email. This takes time and energy but helps build the relationship; the use of a medium that allows for synchronous and direct communication increases their propinquity. Cheryl thinks these communication habits are important to building closer working relationships with her employees and customers.

Looking Forward to Social Information Processing

Person, presence, and propinquity describe the experiences of individuals with CMC. Propinquity, in particular, extends the implications of these experiences into the interpersonal relationships of participants, both online and off. In the next section of the book, we discuss perspectives on how participants use CMC to present themselves and interpret others. In the next chapter, we begin with a discussion of social information processing and how people use CMC to reduce their interpersonal uncertainty and develop relationships based on the social cues embedded in language.

Selecting a Medium as an Ethical Communication Choice

Imagine that we have been working on a major project for weeks. This project is very important for your career, as it will help you showcase your talents as our newest employee. This morning I found out that we won't be able to carry out a major portion of the project due to budget cuts. I could walk down to your office to give you the bad news, but I am exhausted and disappointed by the news myself, so I send you an email late in the afternoon, saying we can talk about it on Monday. My real reason for choosing email is that I want to limit your opportunity to express your disappointment. I do not want to hear your emotional response.

So, I postpone the opportunity to talk about it face-to-face, and I make it your responsibility to approach me about it. I make no further effort. I limit the relational closeness of our communication through my selection of a medium.

1. To what extent do I have a responsibility of making a communication effort to talk with you openly about bad news rather than selecting a medium to avoid that discussion?

2. Does the type of bad news make a difference? How?

3. Does the closeness and type of relationship we have make a difference? How?

4. What are the ethics of relational communication in the workplace? Are they different from the ethics of relational communication with a friend or family member?

KEYWORDS AND PHRASES

Electronic propinquity is the experience of a psychological closeness and feeling of connectedness to another person through CMC.

Influences on electronic propinquity refer to (a) existing relational closeness, (b) the ability to provide and receive feedback (or the mutual directionality of communication), (c) bandwidth, (d) information complexity, (e) communication rules, (f) communicator skill, and (g) amount of choice in the selection of a medium through which to communicate.

Propinquity means physical proximity or closeness in time and space.

Time and space structure our perceptions of reality and make it accessible to us through our sensory awareness and cognitive interpretations. Time and space spent together define the basic dimensions of human relationships.

QUESTIONS FOR FURTHER DISCUSSION

1. Have you ever been in a situation where you were planning on using one medium with a lot of bandwidth (e.g., a videoconferencing app such as FaceTime or Zoom) but then had to resort to using a medium with less bandwidth (audio only or texting)? What did that do to the conversation? How did it make you feel? How did that experience compare to when you were planning on using the lower bandwidth medium in the first place? How does this relate to the importance of choice in creating relational closeness?

2. When you have to send a professional email that is tied to more communication rules than a text message to a friend, what do you do to still create a sense of closeness? Are there cues one can give that adhere to the rules but still increase propinquity?

3. The electronic propinquity perspective argues that people with higher communication skills in a particular medium will be better at creating relational closeness using that medium. Explain why this is. Have you ever seen this play out in how other people use certain media?

Relationships

Goal of this approach: To compare and contrast the perspectives of social information processing, hyperpersonal relationships, and social identity model of deindividuation effects on human communication relationships. Approach III describes how people build relationships through CMC. The chapters examine how people reduce their uncertainty to create CMC relationships, how these relationships gain depth and intimacy, and the potential influences of CMC on the development of group identities.

Social Information Processing and Hyperpersonal Relationships first examines how people strategically engage in social information processing to reduce their interpersonal uncertainty and develop personal relationships through CMC. Next it analyzes the processes of hyperpersonal relationship development with a sense of relational intimacy that can exceed the experience of participants in face-to-face contexts.

Social Identity Model of Deindividuation Effects describes the influences of text-based language cues and visual anonymity on relationships within and between different CMC groups. The model analyzes how these influences can accentuate the norms of an immediate group context and emphasize in-group–out-group boundaries, membership status, biases, and stereotypes.

8

Social Information Processing and Hyperpersonal Relationships

Pam and Alex maintain a close business relationship through CMC. They have never met in person, but Pam knows that she can text Alex with a technical question about lighting at 6 in the evening and he will respond. His responses are always polite, informational, and contain the technical details that Pam needs. Those responses help Pam develop her customer job quotes for the next day. They also form Pam's impressions of Alex as a person, even though the nonverbal cues of eye contact and facial expression are missing from their CMC interactions. Pam wonders whether her impressions of Alex might change if they met in person.

FIGURE 8.1 You. Me. Text Is All I See.

Forming Relationships Through CMC

When we communicate with people, whether at work or in our personal lives, we form social impressions and interpretations of who they are, and we use the available social cues to make decisions about what type of relationship we want to have with them, if any. As we develop the relationship, we work to reduce our interpersonal uncertainty and increase the predictability of what we can expect from the relationship. These processes of uncertainty reduction in our relationship formation rely on the ability to interpret both the verbal information and nonverbal cues contained within the communication (Altman & Taylor, 1973).

Many methods of CMC provide only text-based information, which filters out some of these nonverbal social cues. Even videoconferencing, especially when it takes place on a small screen, mutes the facial expressions and other social cues readily available in a face-to-face conversation. Yet humans are motivated to communicate and process the available social information in much the same way, regardless of the medium and nature of the social cues (Walther, 1996).

The social information processing perspective describes how we form relationships through CMC. It applies the concepts of social penetration and interpersonal uncertainty reduction to the CMC context. Social penetration describes the phases and types of information assessed during relationship formation. Uncertainty reduction describes the communication strategies used to obtain that information.

Social Penetration

The social penetration perspective presents a social psychological perspective on relationship development (Altman & Taylor, 1973). It describes relationship formation as a process of peeling back layers to get to know increasing levels of personal information about someone. Some call this social penetration perspective the onion approach to interpersonal relationships because both onions and relationships have layers, and both can make you cry.

Through social penetration, we generally gain increasing amounts of information about a person in a specific order. At first, we perceive only a person's general demographic information, then social preferences, goals, aspirations, hopes, anxieties, beliefs, and finally personal self-concepts. That is, when we first meet someone face-to-face, we often perceive only general physical characteristics such as height, weight, and appearance. Then, through conversation, we gradually learn about a person's social preferences, orientations, likes, dislikes, frustrations, and attitudes toward life. As we get to know a person better, we discover their goals and aspirations, and then their hopes, anxieties, and belief systems. Finally, when we become friends, we learn their personal joys, fears, issues, and concerns.

For example, when we first meet, you might notice my height, weight, approximate age, clothes, body posture, and general physical appearance. In our first conversation, I might tell you where I grew up. Later on, I might mention my frustrations with school, job, roommate, or life in general. Next, I might tell you my aspirations and that I am studying to become a nurse, lawyer, or auto mechanic. Only when I get to know you better, and trust you will I tell you my deeper aspirations in life, personal concerns, anxieties, and

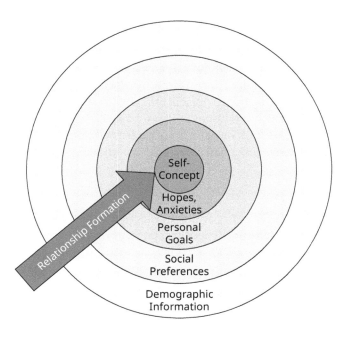

FIGURE 8.2 Relationship Formation Through Social Penetration.

self-doubts. Revealing them too early in the relationship would make me vulnerable to your judgment and possible ridicule and derision. I need to trust you before I share my deepest aspirations, beliefs, feelings, and self-concepts. Figure 8.2 illustrates this multi-layered process of relationship formation.

Interpersonal Uncertainty Reduction

Interpersonal uncertainty reduction builds on this social penetration concept of relationship formation. When we first meet, we have a relatively high level of interpersonal uncertainty about each other. We know little about each other, except what we can see. We engage in information-seeking communication to reduce that uncertainty. **Uncertainty reduction** describes the interpersonal motives and strategies for seeking information about another person with whom we plan to develop a relationship (Berger & Calabrese, 1975; Douglas, 1994).

Motivations to Reduce Interpersonal Uncertainty

There are some people we may not care to get to know, in which case we likely will not be motivated to reduce interpersonal uncertainty. However, if we plan to develop a relationship, for either work or personal reasons, we generally pursue a social penetration process of getting to know that person, at least a little, to reduce our interpersonal uncertainty. Novelty and surprises can be exciting in a relationship, but too much uncertainty about what someone will do or say can have a negative effect on the relationship. This is particularly true when two people have just met and are attempting to gain a better understanding of who they are and their relationship to each other. This uncertainty reduction is also important at times when an event makes participants less certain about each other and their relationship (Baxter & Wilmot, 1984; Emmers & Canary, 1996).

In short, we seek uncertainty-reducing information if we (a) anticipate a future relationship, (b) want something from a person, or (c) find that person either interesting or threatening. If none of these conditions exists, we may have little motivation to reduce our interpersonal uncertainty. If one or more of these conditions exists, we are motivated to gather the information (Kellerman & Reynolds, 1990).

Uncertainty Reduction Strategies

We generally use four types of uncertainty reduction strategies to gain the interpersonal information about someone. These are active, passive, interactive, and extractive information gathering strategies. Passive information gathering strategies include quietly watching how someone interacts with others in a social setting or on social media, observing the person's responses to particular situations and drawing comparisons to the behaviors of friends or people we know. Active information gathering strategies involve finding out information about a person without interacting with them. This can include asking a shared network of friends about the person. Interactive information gathering strategies include engaging a person in conversation,

TABLE 8.1 **Interpersonal Uncertainty Reduction Strategies**

PASSIVE	Casually observe the person in social settings:
	Observe people unobtrusively as they interact and react to others.
	Observe person interacting with people you know. Draw comparisons of similarities to friends (social comparison)
	Watch person when less inhibited, less affected by social norms. Identify candid behaviors (disinhibition-deviation testing).
ACTIVE	Seek relevant information about the person:
	Ask others about the person.
	Select or change the environment to observe a person in different or unfamiliar surroundings.
INTERACTIVE	Interact with the person to seek personal information:
	Engage in a conversation with the person.
	Ask direct questions (verbal interrogation).
	Listen for self-disclosure of information that is new and not known publicly (new self-disclosure).
	Watch for hedges, enhancements, distortions, evasive responses, omissions, falsifications (deception detection).
EXTRACTIVE	Do some research on the person:
	Read newspaper accounts or look up information about a person.
	Search public records, newspaper, library, the internet, or other sources for information about the person.

asking questions, listening to statements of self-disclosure, and paying attention to any apparent enhancements, evasive responses, omissions, distortions, falsifications, or contradictory statements. Extractive information gathering strategies include looking up information about the person in the newspaper, library, or searching the internet (Ramirez et al., 2002; Sherblom et al., 2009).

Social Information Processing in CMC

Active, passive, and interactive uncertainty reduction strategies rely on the observation of nonverbal social cues, such as eye contact, facial expressions, and body language as well as the verbal content of communication. Many CMC platforms filter out the expression and interpretation of one or more of these nonverbal social cues. A cues filtered-out perspective suggests that this lack of nonverbal cues may reduce a communicator's interpersonal awareness and affect their ability to form an accurate impression of the other person. This inability to create accurate impressions can hinder the social penetration and interpersonal uncertainty reduction processes of relational communication, creating a social context in which participants are more self-centered and less mindful of others (Walther, 1992, 1996; Walther & Parks, 2002).

Human communicators, however, are motivated information seekers. Social information processing argues that people will strategically use whatever social cues are available as a substitution for the missing nonverbal information. CMC users will adapt their communication style and information-gathering strategies to the characteristics of the medium. As a result, the verbal content and the other types of social cues that are available in a medium replace the relationship information of any filtered-out nonverbal cues (Walther, 1996).

People may employ different interpersonal strategies, but they are motivated and obtain the relational information that is available through CMC. They adapt their uncertainty reduction strategies to the CMC platform, but engage in the same cognitive processes as in face-to-face contexts to gather the interpersonal information that is needed to develop their relationships (Tidwell & Walther, 2002; Walther et al., 2005).

Time and Impressions

Accessing social information in a CMC medium can take more time. The lack of physical and vocal cues can slow down the communication process, but the relationship formation processes are the same. Given sufficient time participants can and do gather the necessary information to develop their interpersonal relationships.

In a face-to-face conversation, participants can speak, listen, and interact. Participants can quickly develop initial impressions of each other. They can observe physical and vocal nonverbal cues simultaneously. In CMC, participants typically exchange fewer messages in the same amount of time; typing and reading simply take longer than talking and listening. In addition, much CMC is asynchronous. This means that participants are often not online at the same time, adding further delays to their relational communication processes (McEwan, 2021; Walther, 1996; Walther & Parks, 2002).

The social information processing perspective acknowledges this difference in time for information exchange. It recognizes that initial impressions may develop more quickly in face-to-face conversations as participants share demographic information and personal preferences. Using different information-gathering strategies, CMC communicators can express and acquire that same information and develop their personal relationships. With the accumulation of this relational information, CMC participants can, over time, get to know each other relatively well, just as well as when they converse face-to-face (Walther, 1992, 2009; Walther & Parks, 2002).

The Nature of Cues

When CMC is mostly text based, such as in email, texting, and online forums, participants can substitute verbal expressions, such as OMG and LOL, to replace absent nonverbal cues. They can use interactive questioning and compare it to information and impressions they develop through other means to obtain reliable personal impressions. In addition, CMC provides participants access to text-based language cues that are not available in face-to-face conversations (Tidwell & Walther, 2002; Walther & Parks, 2002).

These language cues differ from the physical and vocal ones, but participants can use them in similar ways to form social impressions. Observing how someone uses language, such as their word choices and spelling, for instance, can provide impressions of personal competence, levels of psychological anxiety, and perceptions of gender, ethnicity, socioeconomic background, and social attitudes. Verbal immediacy, language intensity, and vocabulary use all create impressions that can increase or diminish feelings of relational intimacy (Baron, 2004; Herring & Martinson, 2004; O'Sullivan et al., 2004; Walther et al., 2005).

CMC also provides cues not available in face-to-face conversation, such as the use of emoticons, emojis, and gifs. These provide stylized substitutes for the missing nonverbal cues that augment the verbal communication of face-to-face conversation. They can enhance the communication and play a role in relationship formation in CMC. Emoticons, such as ;-), :-(, and :-) can provide a substitute for a communicator's facial expression to more clearly show an attitude toward a topic and to distinguish statements intended as humor or sarcasm from an assertion of fact or opinion. Emojis can set the tone of a conversation, expressing a communicator's personality, playful attitude, emotional state, or approach to informational succinctness. Gifs help participants share complex emotions and show their engagement in the relationship (Cramer et al., 2016; Jiang et al., 2018; Konrad et al., 2020; Utz, 2000; Walther & D'Addario, 2001).

Audio, video, and streaming platforms include a wider variety of interactive and synchronous social cues than text-based CMC. They typically, however, do not provide all the nonverbal cues readily available in a face-to-face conversation. Because of this difference in available nonverbal cues, CMC relationships tend to develop more slowly (McEwan, 2021). Figure 8.3 depicts the trajectories of CMC and face-to-face social information processing paths. Social information gathering typically starts more slowly in CMC but over time accumulates the necessary information to form relationships.

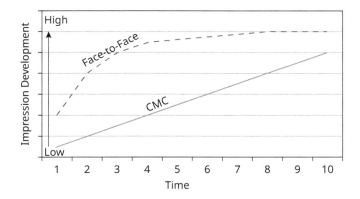

FIGURE 8.3 Projected Paths of Relational Impression Development, Face-to-Face and in CMC.

Summary: Social Information Processing

Communicators use the same processes to develop their interpersonal relationships in CMC as in face-to-face communication. Motivated communicators strategically gather the interpersonal information needed to reduce their uncertainty and develop relationships through CMC in similar ways as in face-to-face communication. It may take longer to observe and interpret an adequate amount of relational information, but the social penetration and interpersonal uncertainty reduction processes are the same.

The Hyperpersonal Perspective

In some cases, relationships can take less time and form more quickly and intensely through CMC than face-to-face. The **hyperpersonal** perspective (pronounced "hyper-personal") describes how these feelings of intimacy can develop in less time and with more intensity in a CMC medium. The experience of relational intimacy in these CMC relationships sometimes exceeds that of participants in similar face-to-face contexts. The hyperpersonal perspective describes this phenomenon by building on the same social penetration and interpersonal uncertainty reduction processes as social information processing. It, however, "stresses the role of strategic message design, attributional processes, and feedback in [this] relationship formation" (Ramirez & Burgoon, 2004, p. 424).

People seek being liked and approved of by others. To obtain this approval, some participants use CMC strategically to present themselves in a favorable light. Those who see these presentations often interpret them in highly positive ways that can create feelings of relational closeness to the presenter. The strategic messaging, available social cues, and idealized interpretations work together to facilitate reciprocal feelings of interpersonal connection, liking, closeness, and intimacy. When this occurs, a hyperpersonal relationship forms "more quickly and intimately than in face-to-face interactions (Walther, 1996; Walther & Parks, 2002).

Expedited Intimacy in CMC

CMC allows participants to optimize the impressions they present to others through careful message composition and editing. Participants commonly self-censor, edit, and engage in a creative online presentation that represents them in a positive light. They are selective and edit the personal information they want to share, and they avoid potentially embarrassing or controversial topics (Walther, 2010; Walther & Parks, 2002).

People try to create good impressions in face-to-face contexts as well, but CMC facilitates this process. When presenting oneself in a face-to-face conversation, a person must simultaneously interpret the other person's nonverbal cues. This requires cognitive resources, which, in an asynchronous CMC medium, people can use to plan, compose, edit, and review their own self-expression. In a CMC medium, participants can reallocate the cognitive resources used to create an immediate positive first impression in face-to-face interactions to create a more long-term, positive self-image (Hancock & Dunham, 2001; Walther, 1996).

In addition, CMC-based conversational partners have fewer nonverbal cues that might contradict the personal information provided and fewer opportunities to ask questions or interrogate the honesty of a self-presentation. Participants can ignore inconvenient questions and inquires more easily than in a face-to-face conversation, and they can take advantage of the visually anonymous, text-based, asynchronous characteristics of the CMC medium to enhance their relational goals and self-presentations. This creates the opportunity for a presentation in which a participant creates a very likeable online self (Walther & Parks, 2002; Walther & Whitty, 2021).

In addition, the reduced nonverbal social cues in CMC and subsequent efforts at uncertainty reduction often leads participants to fill in the missing social information using the highly edited and positively skewed relational cues that are available. This creates a positive interpretation that is likely to exaggerate the already embellished presentation. It uses only the available subset of social cues, such as an apparent sense of humor, to infer the whole of a person's identity, and then confirms that impression using the communicator's positive informational presentation of self. The combination of this presentation and interpretation can lead to a hyperpersonal relationship (Hancock & Dunham, 2001; Parks, 2017; Ramirez et al., 2002; Walther, 1996; Walther & Whitty, 2021).

Figure 8.4 illustrates the reciprocal process of a hyperpersonal relationship. Participants progress through the same process of sharing demographic, personal preferences, goals, aspirations, beliefs, and self-concept information. The participant desire to present a positive self-image and the lack of any contradictory nonverbal information, however, expedites the process.

CMC Influences on Hyperpersonal Relationship Development

In a face-to-face conversation, a nonverbal expression can reveal unintended emotional responses or negative personal information. Text-based forms of CMC allow participants more control over producing a coherent, positive presentation of self without interference from these unintended nonverbal leaks. Participants can use CMC strategically to edit posts, comments, and pictures before and after they have shared them. They can also

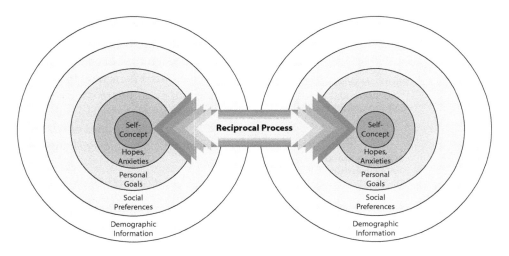

FIGURE 8.4 Relationship Development Through Social Penetration Is a Reciprocal Process.

decide who will see which parts of their profiles. In addition, the asynchronous nature of much CMC further allows participants to consider their responses to comments from others and to carefully design a positive and acceptable response (Walther, 1996; Walther & Parks, 2002).

Furthermore, the visual anonymity of CMC can reduce interpersonal inhibitions, facilitate greater self-disclosure, and encourage more interactive communication. Platforms centered on the sharing of visual information, such as TikTok, allow confession-style videos, which people often perceive as authentic presentations of a person's identity. This can increase the sense of interpersonal trust, feelings of intimacy, affection, and positive emotions toward the person. These feelings often surpass those of face-to-face interactions (Barta & Andalibi, 2021; Joinson, 2001; Tidwell & Walther, 2002).

Hyperpersonal Relationships

Communication is a reciprocal process between at least two people. The nature of feedback available through CMC adds to the potential of a hyperpersonal relationship process. When two participants feel a mutual attraction, both are likely to engage in personally enhancing messages. This means that when a person receives an idealized message they generally reciprocate with a positive and affirming message. This encourages the other person to respond in a positive way that continues their self-presentation. This response may be a reply, a comment, thumbs-up, or an emoji. All of these reinforce the participant's behavior, creating a spiral of positively skewed relationship messages that are favorably interpreted by both participants in ways that enhance the relationship development (Walther, 1996; Walther & Whitty, 2021).

When both participants engage in this hyperpersonal impression management, the reciprocal hyperpersonal relationship process emerges. The positive feedback loop between the participants intensifies the interaction and encourages a mutual disclosure

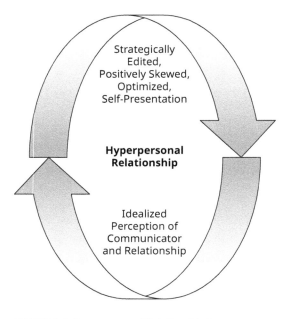

FIGURE 8.5 Hyperpersonal Relationship Loop.

of more positively skewed intimate relational expressions at earlier in the relationship than one might see in a face-to-face interaction. In addition, participants inflate the relational importance of these disclosures, generating greater feelings of relational intimacy more quickly (Jiang et al., 2011).

This hyperpersonal sequence explains how dating apps and websites that show no more than a picture, a name, an age, and a few key words are so successful. In this case, it isn't the feedback loop resulting from interacting with someone's profile that explains the hyperpersonal communication; it is the lack of nonverbal cues. Users of these sites and apps use the simple, nonverbal cues that make up a profile to draw general conclusions about someone's personality. The "magnifying effects" of these small cues are in line with the foundations of the hyperpersonal perspective (Dai & Robbins, 2021, p. 6).

Not all CMC relationships become hyperpersonal. It depends on people's motivation, ability, and desires. The lack of synchronous communication, discrepant feedback, or dissonant nonverbal cues, and the ability to reallocate cognitive resources to produce a carefully edited, text-based message, facilitates this rapid relationship growth. This type of CMC can foster rapid relationship growth that outpaces face-to-face interactions. When hyperpersonal relationships do develop in CMC, they do so quickly. The intimacy experienced in these relationships at times surpasses the intensity of face-to-face interactions (Tidwell & Walther, 2002; Walther & Parks, 2002). Figure 8.5 illustrates this cyclical relationship process.

Constructing Authentic CMC Relationships

The self-selection process through which people present themselves online has led to concerns about deception and misrepresentation (Gibbs et al., 2006). How people present themselves through CMC, however, often is connected to real-life environments (e.g., connecting with friends and family on social media) or goals (e.g., finding work or a partner through a dating app). This means that CMC participants need to be thoughtful about the extent to which they edit and curate self-presentations, as the connections made in a CMC environment may persist and affect face-to-face relationships (Toma & Hanock, 2010).

Some CMC users do not feel that an honest online self-presentation will be as successful as a carefully crafted, edited, overtly positive presentation. Participants often consider what others may think of them and selectively curate their personal characteristics, especially on dating apps. They sometimes choose to embellish their looks with flattering pictures or less-than-truthful statements about their physical size while remaining honest about attributes unrelated to their physical appearance, such as income and occupation. As a result, individuals rate their odds of finding a date through an online dating app as higher than through a real-life event. This creates an interesting predicament when an online connection leads to a face-to-face interaction with the possibly of a long-term relationship (Fullwood & Atrill-Smith, 2018; Gibbs et al., 2006; Toma & Hancock, 2010).

Relationship goals matter in determining whether a CMC relationship becomes hyperpersonal. Participants seeking long-term relationships with others are less likely to engage in hyperpersonal communication strategies. They are more likely to be more honest in what they say and share about themselves. They probably realize that if they meet their online acquaintance face-to-face, any dishonesty will become obvious (Gibbs et al., 2006).

Applying Social Information Processing and Hyperpersonal Perspectives

Developing Customer Relationships on a Company Website

Pang et al. (2018) propose that organizations can use the social information processing and hyperpersonal perspectives to improve how they communicate with their customers. They suggest that the best way to build interpersonal relationships with customers is by engaging in a dialogue. This dialogue should rely on a variety of social cues adapted to the CMC environment and include positive affect and feedback.

They recommend that the dialogue move through three stages of relationship development. The initiating stage aims to build credibility, trust, and liking with the customer. This can be achieved by creating a favorable impression through personal disclosures and asking questions that facilitate conversation and build familiarity.

In the second stage, the company should aim to intensify the relationship by showing immediacy in the conversation through language use. This involves the use of first- or second-person pronouns, colloquial language, providing contact information, and demonstrating an expertise in the topic of interest. It also includes politeness in greetings and signoffs, using affective punctuation such as exclamation marks and ellipses, and personalized language to indicate involvement, understanding, and responsiveness to a customer's needs. These language immediacy tactics reduce uncertainty and lead to greater perceived caring, credibility, competence, and trustworthiness.

The third and final stage involves creating a bond with the customer. This can be achieved by creating an expectation of future interactions. When people think they will engage with another person or organization in the future, they are more likely to disclose information and be more honest in their interactions. Companies that employ these dialogic communication strategies on their websites and social media pages can create a sense of belonging among their customers that can produce beneficial results for the company in both the short- and long-term.

Meeting an Online Romantic Partner Face-to-Face

Reints and Wickelgren (2019) interviewed 16 individuals about their experiences of finding a potential romantic partner online and then meeting face-to-face. Participants ranged in age from 21 to 27 and included people who self-identify as queer, gay, or heterosexual. The researchers asked the participants how they presented themselves online, what impressions they formed of online their partners, and what happened when they meet an online partner face-to-face.

All participants readily admitted to producing optimized self-presentations online. They indicated that they considered the design of their profiles, photo selections, and bio statements to create positive images of themselves while explicitly censoring aspects they considered undesirable. Participants made an effort to be witty, but not quirky, and to match their tone and language to that of their conversation partner. They also indicated an awareness of a potential partner's judgment of their misspellings, punctuation, tone, and language use.

Interestingly, participants were apparently not fully aware of the idealized perspectives they created for their partners, even while admitting to modifying their own profiles, photos, and language. They articulated even less awareness to having positively inflated perceptions of their partner's optimized self-presentations. Participants reported both positive experiences that fulfilled their expectations and negative ones that violated them when eventually meeting people face-to-face. They reported having their expectations fulfilled only two of six times meeting someone face-to-face after developing a short-term online relationship. In both cases, these meetings led to positive relationship outcomes. Four participants had their expectations violated. Three of these led to negative relationship outcomes, but surprisingly one produced a positive result. The length of time spent communicating online before meeting did not affect the relational outcomes or participant evaluations.

Catfishing

Catfishing is the deliberate misrepresentation of oneself through a CMC medium with the purpose of deceiving others. It is commonly associated with online dating but also applies to situations in which an individual assumes an online persona with the intention of financially defrauding others (Mosley et al., 2020; Simmons & Lee, 2020). The idealized perceptual processes of the hyperpersonal relationship formation help explain how catfishing can be successful. Perpetrators rely on an individual's willingness to extrapolate from the limited social cues and minimal personal information that the catfish provides to construct an idealized perception of them.

The catfish provides fake information, romanticized profiles, and regular responses to their victims over time, building the relationship. By responding positively to the feedback of their victims, they gain information and create an apparently reciprocal hyperpersonal relationship. The relationship can become so intense that upon discovering the lie, victims often refuse to believe it is fake (Mosley et al., 2020; Walther & Whitty, 2021).

Perspective in Context

Analysis and Critique

The social information processing and hyperpersonal perspectives provide useful insights into how people self-present and develop relationships through CMC. Walther (2009), himself, however, provides a critique of each. First, he recognizes that the social information processing of increasing amounts of relational communication does not necessarily lead to a closer relationship. Communication is important to the interpersonal uncertainty reduction process, but it does not guarantee that an intimate relationship will develop. Reducing that interpersonal uncertainty may mean discovering that you really do not like that person. You may have similar demographic backgrounds and personal preferences but not share the same goals, beliefs, or aspirations in life. Gathering social information and reducing interpersonal uncertainty may mean drifting apart rather than getting closer together. Second, while the hyperpersonal perspective provides a descriptive account of how certain CMC relationships may develop rapidly, it fails to explain how personal attributions, message design, and feedback work together to affect this relationship formation. It does not prioritize which of these is most influential or how they might interact to affect the intensity of that relationship development.

Despite these critiques, the social information processing and hyperpersonal perspectives each provide useful insights into relationship formation processes of CMC. They provide insight into different ways in which the availability of social cues affect relationship development. The social information processing perspective describes how asynchronous, text-based communication can slow relationship formation in business, professional, and social relationships. The hyperpersonal model shows how the same lack of corroborating nonverbal cues can focus attention on the positive and quicken the intensity of relationships when participants wish to optimize relationship development through the available social information. Each perspective describes important influences on the interpersonal uncertainty reduction and relationship development processes as they occur through CMC.

Hyperpersonal Communication in Practice: Dating Apps

Considering the popularity of dating apps and platforms in finding a romantic partner, Antheunis et al. (2020) investigated participant perceptions of potential romantic partner attractiveness on an online dating site. They compared the use of available audiovisual versus text-only cues on a dating platform. They also explored whether meeting through a videoconferencing call might reduce any subsequent disappointment a person experiences when meeting face-to-face for the first time.

The limited social cues available in a text-based CMC medium, such as a dating app and website, allow people to create positive self-presentations and idealized perceptions of the other person. A text-based CMC medium also invites more self-disclosure. Video-conferencing does not allow the same amount of time for editing and modifying one's self-presentation. Participants can observe each other's facial expressions and physical nonverbal cues during the synchronous conversation. Therefore, the researchers predicted that potential romantic partners using the text-based medium will develop more social and romantic attraction to each other than those communicating through videoconferencing.

People who meet potential romantic partners online, however, are often disappointed when they meet face-to-face. Switching from text-based to face-to-face communication can weaken the hyperpersonal relationship that people have developed. Therefore, Antheunis et al. predict that when people meet face-to-face after communicating through text-based CMC, their attraction to each other will drop more than if they meet after videoconferencing.

Using an actual speed-dating event, where participants interacted with potential partners either through text-based CMC or videoconferencing and then met face-to-face, Antheunis et al. found that participants using the text-based CMC experience more social attraction than those who use videoconferencing. Those who communicated first through the text-based CMC also showed greater persistence in this attraction to the other person when they meet face-to-face. These results suggest the formation of a hyperpersonal relationship. The results, however, also show that meeting face-to-face reduces the romantic attraction among participants, regardless of the CMC medium used for their first conversation. This suggests that both the text-based CMC and videoconferencing allow participants to create favorable impressions and idealized perceptions, which meeting face-to-face then challenges.

Illustration of Concepts

Pam enjoys her late afternoon, text-based interactions with Alex through CMC. At first, she was tentative with her questions about lighting, and, as predicted by social information processing, their professional relationship started slowly. Gradually, as Alex responded positively to her inquires, she relaxed and began to feel more comfortable asking questions and occasionally sharing some personal information about her weekend plans or vacation trips. She thinks he is kind, competent, funny, and a big help with lighting issues when she is working with a difficult customer. She likes him and, as predicted by the hyperpersonal model, thinks highly of him. Pam hopes to meet Alex in person someday and, as shown in Figure 8.6, expects that he will be well dressed and confident.

Looking Forward to the Social Identity Model of Deindividuation Effects

In the next chapter, we discuss the social identity of deindividuation effects (SIDE) model. This SIDE model describes other some other influences of text-based communication on relationships. It highlights important considerations for group relationships in a CMC medium.

FIGURE 8.6 Pam imagines Alex to Be well dressed and confident. In reality, Alex is socially awkward, even shy at times, but uses his words to project a more confident impression.

Is an Edited Self-Presentation Ethical?

We all want to make a positive impression. Text-based CMC allows us to do that through editing, rewording, selectively presenting, and shading our presentation of self in a way that is difficult to do face-to-face. Where is the line between an ethical, authentic presentation of self and a deceptive presentation?

When we first meet face-to-face we share social demographic and other visible characteristics of ourselves. As we engage in conversation, we gradually open up to each other sharing our deeper, true feelings, beliefs, and thinking. Through text-based CMC we engage in the same process, but with the ability to engage in more editing of our self-presentation.

It is easier for me to stretch the truth about myself—my accomplishments, looks, strength, and abilities—through CMC. It is more difficult for you to verify that what I am telling you is true. I can lie to you face-to-face, as well, but our communication is more interactive, and you are more likely to notice. You can watch my nonverbal affect, and I don't get the chance to reread, edit, and polish my message before you see it. You can ask questions, and it is more difficult for me to avoid answering them. In CMC I can more easily ignore your questions, skirt sensitive issues, and present myself in more positive ways.

1. Is it ethical for me to embellish my self-presentation?

2. How authentic a presentation of myself must I make to develop an ethical inter-personal relationship?

3. Is the authenticity of my self-presentation only an issue in CMC if we are likely to meet in person when you are likely to see the deception?

4. Does the ethical nature of embellishing one's self-presentation depend on the context of the presentation? Is editing one's self-presentation through CMC more or less ethical when making friends, applying for jobs, or looking for a romantic partner?

KEYWORDS AND PHRASES

Active information gathering strategies involve finding out information about a person without interacting with them. This can include asking a shared network of friends about the person.

The **cues filtered-out** perspective suggests that the lack of nonverbal cues common to CMC may reduce a communicator's interpersonal awareness and affect their ability to form an accurate impression of the other person.

Extractive information gathering strategies include looking up information about the person in the newspaper, library, or searching the internet.

Hyperpersonal perspective describes how these feelings of intimacy can develop in less time and with more intensity in a CMC medium.

Interactive information gathering strategies include engaging a person in conversation, asking questions, listening to statements of self-disclosure, and paying attention to any apparent enhancements, evasive responses, omissions, distortions, falsifications, or contradictory statements.

Passive information gathering strategies include quietly watching how someone interacts with others in a social setting or on social media, observing the person's responses to particular situations, and drawing comparisons to the behaviors of friends or people we know.

Social information processing argues that people will strategically use whatever social cues are available as a substitution for the missing nonverbal information.

Social penetration provides a social psychological perspective on relationship development. It describes relationship formation as a process of peeling back layers to get to know increasing levels of personal information about someone.

Uncertainty reduction describes the interpersonal motives and strategies for seeking that information about another person with whom we plan to develop a relationship.

QUESTIONS FOR FURTHER DISCUSSION

1. How would you compare the relationships (romantic, friendship, professional relationships) you have created through face-to-face interactions with the relationships you have created through CMC? How fast did the relationships progress? How (if at all) did you find your impression of the other person change over time? Do you see the principles of the social information processing and hyperpersonal perspectives reflected in your experiences?

2. It has been said that the social information processing perspective may be more characteristic of professional and social affiliations and hyperpersonal developments more common in romantic relationships. What do you think? Do you think the social information processing perspective and hyperpersonal effects are contextually influenced?

3. When you meet someone online, how do you go about reducing your uncertainty about that person? Do you have specific cues you look for? What kinds of cues do you use to create a favorable impression? How much do you embellish your online impression? Do you think other people embellish their presentations of self? Does this embellishment differ by the social media context? If you have ever met someone in person after meeting them online, how did that experience go? Did your experience reflect the research findings presented in this chapter?

4. Can you think of a way of combining the social information processing perspective and hyperpersonal perspectives into a single theory for making predictions? For example, (a) describe contexts, such as professional versus personal, when each is likely to occur; or (b) describe sequences, such as that the social information processing perspective predicts early relationship development for reducing uncertainty about demographic information and personal preferences, but the hyperpersonal perspective becomes more relevant when people begin exploring aspirations, goals, beliefs, and self-concepts in their relationships.

Image Credit

9

Social Identity Model of Deindividuation Effects

Sean was the first person in his family to graduate from college. He is from a small, rural town and started working for the Home Products store while he was in college. Jasmine is from the city. Since graduating from the college that her parents and grandparents attended she has gained 3 years of professional experience working in the furniture sales business.

The Cognitive Salience of Identity

Identities are not fixed, and neither is our awareness of them. Different aspects of one's identity are salient at different moments in time. Awareness shifts along a continuum from a personal to a social identity, depending on the immediate context. At one

Sean   Jasmine

FIGURE 9.1 Sean and Jasmine develop social identities as coworkers at the Home Products store.

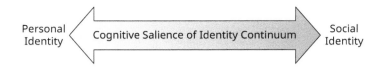

FIGURE 9.2 Cognitive Salience Continuum From Personal to Social Identity.

moment in time, an individual may be thinking about a personal issue, concern, or per-spective. At another time, that same individual may be involved in a group activity and thinking more about social roles and expectations (James, 1918; Martindale, 1981).

This shift in awareness is largely automatic. It occurs without much thought and is affected by the immediate social context. Personal identity becomes salient during quiet times, in thoughts about personal ambitions, motivations, accomplishments, satis-factions, desires, regrets, relationships, and meaning. Social identity becomes salient in the awareness of social roles, activities, responsibilities, and obligations to others, such as family, friends, colleagues, professional and social groups, or communities to which someone belongs. Along with these shifts in awareness from personal to social identity come changes in cognitive schema and the language and behaviors perceived as accept-able and appropriate to the roles as a member of a family, group, or community (Lea & Spears, 1991; Sassenberg & Boos, 2003; Spears et al., 2002). Figure 9.2 illustrates this shift in cognitive awareness along a continuum from personal to social identity.

Communication Accommodation

People express the shift from the personal to various social identities through their language and communication style. Communication accommodation describes how changes in language use expresses both a conscious and unconscious affiliation with or difference from a group. This accommodation includes such language characteristics as speaking rate, average word length, sentence structure, and the use of nouns, verbs, and qualifiers. Communicators show affiliation with a group through convergence in their language use and distance through divergence (Giles, 1973; Giles et al., 1987; Giles & Ogay, 2007; Street & Giles, 1982).

Convergence means using a communication style similar to a person or group with whom a person identifies. A convergent style stimulates both a verbal and a cognitive reciprocity with the other person or group, and it facilitates mutual understanding among participants. Divergence in language style distances participants from people and groups with whom they do not identify. People adjust their communication style to be less similar to, or more divergent from, a person or group they see as different from them, and with whom they do not wish to be associated. Divergent language patterns mark differences between groups and distinguish group boundaries. In addition, divergent styles may be used to acknowledge the social status differences between group members. In this case, divergence is not an indication of a desire to distance oneself but an indication of complementarity. A style that is complementary appears divergent but represents a reciprocal pattern of communication behaviors that recognize and reinforce these social status differences in group member relationships, such as the differences between managers and employees or doctors and patients (Gasiorek & Giles, 2015; Giles & Ogay, 2007; Muir et al., 2017).

Thus, social identity is recognizable in a person's communication style and language use. People use language and communication style as social cues to identify their social identity and economic, ethnic, gender, race, or social group membership. This becomes particularly important in the expression and interpretation of social identities in text-based forms of CMC where it can raise concerns for the potential of deindividuation effects (Adams et al., 2018; Giles & Ogay, 2007).

Social Identity Model of Deindividuation Effects

The **social identity of deindividuation effects (SIDE)** perspective describes people's tendency to identify with a group when engaged in CMC. This renders the group identity salient, even when other members of the group are not visible. When CMC users believe they have some knowledge of the social groups to which other users belong, such as through profile pictures, descriptions, or the use of specific language or other expressions, they often assume that these individuals hold the characteristics commonly attributed to the group (Lea & Spears, 1991; Postmes et al., 1998; Tanis & Postmes, 2003).

SIDE describes two processes that can occur in the interpretation of social identities: deindividuation and depersonalization. Both of these processes affect the interpretation of oneself and of others as individuals. They also have implications for the development of group relationships and communication behaviors. The SIDE model describes the influences on these processes and their implications for CMC.

Deindividuation

Deindividuation is a state of decreased cognitive salience of oneself as a person and increased awareness of a social identity within a specific group context. This shift in cognitive awareness affects the social behavior of the individual in several ways. Participants become more attentive, sensitive, and responsive to the social rules and situational norms of the group, and as a result, in-group and out-group membership distinctions become more important. At the same time, participants pay less attention to either personal ethics or the general norms of society. They conform more to their role within the group, focusing on the expectations that come with that role and the relevant situational norms defining it. When they experience deindividuation, participants are more likely to look to the group for guidance for their behaviors (Postmes et al., 1998; Spears et al., 2002).

Participants who experience deindividuation are thus more likely to conform to the expectations of the group and adhere to the immediate situational norms in their attitudes, language, and behavior. A physical mob in which participants become unruly and engage in acts of vandalism and destruction provides an example of deindividuation. The flaming that occurs on some social media sites offers a CMC-based example. The immediate situational norms of the physical mob or social media group replaces both personal ethics of behavior and general social standards of civility and politeness. Participants accept the immediate group norm, even when that norm indicates that physical violence or verbal rudeness to others is acceptable and even expected (Giles & Ogay, 2007; Kim et al., 2016; Lea & Spears, 1991; Postmes et al., 1998).

Depersonalization

This deindividuation can foster a depersonalization process. Depersonalization is the tendency to perceive oneself and others not as unique individuals with multiple idiosyncratic characteristics, talents, behaviors, and ways of communicating, but as defined only by membership in a group, community, or social category. The awareness of any individual differences becomes less salient and the perception of group stereotypes more prominent.

Depersonalization affects perceptions of and attitudes toward both the group and the individual. Stereotypes associated with age, education, ethnicity, gender, race, political affiliation, or socio-economic class become the defining characteristic of the group, as well as the single, salient, defining marker of the individual. This affects perceptions of both in-group and out-group identities. It heightens the favorableness of impressions and attraction to in-group members and increases the negative perceptual biases that accentuate differences, justify rejection, and foster hostility toward out-group members.

Depersonalization occurs when the deindividuation processes of social identity become salient and participants perceive both themselves and others no longer as individuals but as representatives of a demographic category with stereotyped group characteristics, values, attitudes, and behaviors. In-group–out-group membership boundaries become accentuated, and the stereotypes associated with group membership, whether age, ethnicity, gender, race, or socio-economic class, become the defining characteristics. The individual becomes a token representative of that stereotype (Postmes et al., 1998; Spears et al., 2014).

Social Identity Deindividuation Effects (SIDE) in CMC

Certain characteristics of a CMC medium can affect these processes of deindividuation and depersonalization. The social cues that are readily available to participants in a text-based, visually anonymous CMC medium are less diverse than in a face-to-face context. In a text-based medium, participants often gain their knowledge of other CMC participants through their profile pictures, self-descriptions, and language use. Participants often assume that these other CMC participants hold the same or similar attitudes, beliefs, and characteristics that they attribute to the group to which they belong. The SIDE model describes how this can facilitate in-group stereotyping and expectation of adherence to a set of group norms (Lea & Spears, 1991; Postmes et al., 1998; Tanis & Postmes, 2003).

Sometimes CMC can facilitate participant freedom in communication. At other times, it can have the opposite effect, reinforcing social group boundaries. A CMC medium does not produce equality and democratization or discrimination and hostility, but it can enhance the social constraints and normative demands within a particular social context. The SIDE model focuses attention on the influences of the increased focus on text-based language use and visual anonymity on these deindividuation and depersonalization processes (Postmes et al., 1998; Spears et al., 2014).

Text-Based Language Influence

The text-based nature of some CMC media focuses attention on language use. However, it diminishes access to the more personalized cues such as people's body language and facial expressions; and it removes the unique individual nonverbal cues of vocal pitch, tone, pause, hesitation, urgency, excitement, and anxiety, emphasizing instead the more social features of language such as word choice, grammar, and spelling. This hinders the process of individuation and the potential for viewing another person as a unique individual. Instead, the media highlights information about social identities, such as the socio-economic, political, or racial groups to which a person belongs.

This increased awareness of the language used can perpetuate the deindividuation of participants by increasing the social identity while simultaneously reducing the salience of personal identity. As people use language to indicate membership to some groups and to distance themselves from others, participants who use language in similar ways may perceive a common social identity. This creates a positive social bias toward in-group membership and an accompanying bias, potential for stereotyping, and discrimination against those outside of the group (Giles & Ogay, 2007; Postmes et al., 1998).

Visual Anonymity

Many types of CMC offer relative visual anonymity, meaning that participants cannot see each other while communicating. With this visual anonymity, participants often become less self-aware and more depersonalized in their CMC. Individual differences among group members become less salient, and the social identity of the group and of being a group member, become accentuated.

When social identity in a group is salient, this visual anonymity can contribute to depersonalization and stereotyping. It reduces the individual personal cues conveyed by facial expression, body stance, physical closeness, and social presence. This minimizes individual personal differences within the group and emphasizes a common social identity. Visual anonymity does not produce depersonalization, but it can contribute to the group communication conditions that facilitate it (Spears et al., 1990, 2014).

Summary: Social Identity Deindividuation Effects

In a CMC medium that relies on text-based communication coupled with visual anonymity, differences among individuals become less salient and the social identity of being a group member becomes more salient. The text-based reliance on language cues and visual anonymity interact with the salient social identity and norms of an immediate group context to facilitate processes of deindividuation and depersonalization. These can

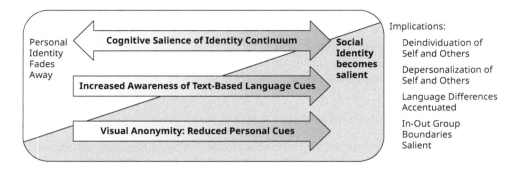

FIGURE 9.3 Deindividuation: Unique Individuals Perceived as Stereotypical Group Members.

accentuate the importance of group boundaries, in-group–out-group membership status, and perceptions of individuals based on group stereotypes. The SIDE model examines the implications of this on group communication (Lea & Spears, 1991; Tanis & Postmes, 2003). Figure 9.3 illustrates this multilayered, interacting perceptual process.

Strategic Use of SIDE

Much like communication accommodation, the cognitive processes that produce social identity deindividuation effects often function automatically, influenced by the immediate group context, reduced social cues, focus on nonverbal cues, and visual anonymity of CMC. However, people will sometimes use these processes strategically to express or enhance their group social identity. Participants may highlight certain aspects of their social identity, use the word *we* in statements to the group, express opinions, and act in ways that they perceive as acceptable, typical, and approved of by the group. They often use this behavior for multiple purposes, such as protecting their social identity, supporting others within the group, or seeking approval from in-group members. In addition, participants sometimes use expressions of social identity to articulate ideas that those outside of the group would perceive as extreme and unacceptable (Guegan et al., 2015; Klein et al., 2007; Li & Zhang, 2021; Rains et al., 2017).

The desire to strategically promote a social identity that distinguishes the in-group, to which one belongs, from a perceived out-group can lead to an increase in uncivil communication and behavior toward others, such as insulting them. This occurs most often in a CMC medium when a group is relatively small and members perceive a need to defend themselves. When the CMC group is larger in numbers there appears less of a desire to insult outsiders and less inter-group bias (Korostelina, 2014; Rains et al., 2017).

The lack of social cues on CMC platforms can facilitate resistance to a dominant out-group as well. Seeing participants as unique individuals becomes more difficult, and seeing them as a member of the group becomes easier, which can lead to deindividuation. This can increase a sense of group solidarity and mutual feelings of support among in-group members. This sense of support and solidarity can encourage people to adhere to in-group norms and values and resist the pressures of a dominant out-group. This tight adherence to the social norms of the group, however, can also lead to depersonalization, increasing an in-group preference and out-group negative bias, accentuating group boundaries, and increasing stereotyping and discrimination (Lea & Spears, 1991; Spears et al., 2002, 2014; Tanis & Postmes, 2003).

SIDE and Visual CMC

In the past, scholars and activists predicted that the text-based anonymity of CMC would equalize status differences among people. They assumed that visual anonymity would remove the power differentials present in conversations between people with different gender identities. Subsequent research, however, shows that when CMC users are anonymous, and become depersonalized, they often act in line with gender stereotypes. Depersonalization, as represented in the SIDE model, often leads to higher acceptance of social identity norms rather than more egalitarian communication (Postmes & Spears, 2002).

Recent forms of CMC include more visual platforms, such as Zoom and FaceTime videoconferencing. On these platforms, CMC users are able to see each other, reducing visual anonymity as well as the reliance on text-based communication. However, SIDE model analyses of these forms of CMC suggest that, even on these platforms, a group identity associated with visual cues, such as age, ethnicity, or gender, can enhance the salience of social identity. Some CMC participants on these platforms who identify as female, when given the choice to select a visual representation of themselves that is less gender defining (e.g., an avatar) often do so to avoid gender stereotyping in these contexts (Spears et al., 2014).

Applying Accommodation in CMC

Accommodation occurs at many levels of language use and communication styles, across CMC platforms. Boghrati et al. (2018) look at accommodation in the syntax of comments posted on Reddit. Adams et al. (2018) explore accommodation in participant use of emojis, emoticons, and lexical surrogates in their cell phone messages, and Muir et al. (2017) examine the accommodation of chat room messages between people placed in positions of high and low social power.

Accommodating Syntax on Reddit

Boghrati et al. (2018) analyzed the communication accommodation in Reddit conversations to understand how participants accommodate their linguistic styles to those of their conversation partners. They found that when participants comment on a post, they tend to use a syntax similar to the one used in the original post. The syntax of the comment was more similar to the original post than to any previous posts made by the commenter, indicating an accommodative syntax shift. The first sentence of the comment was also the most similar to the syntactic structure of the first sentence in the post. Additional sentences showed syntactic similarity as well. These results indicate that Reddit users display a cognitive tendency toward accommodation and point to a social group dynamic among Reddit users that encourages syntax accommodation.

Accommodating Emojis and Emoticons in Cell Phone Messages

Similarly, Adams et al. (2018) explored the extent to which people use accommodation in their use of textisms in cell phone messages. They defined textisms as digital cues that convey nonverbal meaning and emotion in a text message. These included emojis, emoticons, lexical surrogates that stand in for nonverbal sounds (haha), purposeful use of extra or missing punctuation, intentional word expansions (wooonderful!), and word substitutions using a number as part of a word (4tunate). Study participants produced text message interactions with five different people on their smartphones, generating a collection of 889 text messages.

Their results show that conversational participants generally converge in the use of textisms across the course of a conversation. A conversational partner's initial use of textisms affects the number that a responding conversational partner uses. These respondents use more textisms in their return messages after viewing a message that uses textisms.

In addition, participants converge more in their use of textisms when they like their conversational partner. These results demonstrate the intentional use of nonverbal displays in text-based CMC. Conversational partners generally converge, adapting their message behaviors to convey the nonverbal meaning and emotion of their text-based digital communication.

Accommodating Power in a Chat Room

Muir et al. (2017) examined the effects of social power differences on linguistic style accommodation in a chat room messaging system. They asked pairs of participants to converse by typing messages in a private chat room. Participants role-played as either someone in a high (judge) or a low (worker) position of power. They conversed with someone in the opposite position, representing a social power differential in the relationship. Participants created their own usernames within the system, and no other personal information was available to their conversational partner, providing anonymity in a text-based communication.

The study's results show that conversational partners diverge in their language use and that their linguistic style similarity decreases with each successive turn across the conversation. Both the judges and the workers show divergence in their messages. The divergence, however, functions to recognize and to reinforce the assigned social power differentials of judge and worker, creating complementarity between the two roles. These results indicate a cognitively automatic communication accommodation of these CMC participants who are simply role-playing positions with different amounts of social power.

Applying SIDE to CMC: Implications

Social identity deindividuation can have either negative or positive effects for participants in a CMC group. Li and Zhang (2021) analyze the negative influences of SIDE on the responses to out-group participant requests for support on a social media site. Conversely, Dai and Shi (2022) demonstrate the potential of using SIDE as a positive influence for stimulating young people who lurk in CMC mental health support communities to participate.

SIDE Bias in Social Media

Li and Zhang (2021) analyzed the social identity deindividuation effects of in-group and out-group membership of participants seeking support on an interactive social media site. They looked at responses to text-based, visually anonymous requests for support from participants identified only by either an in-group and out-group social identity status. The study relied on participants who attended the same university. The researchers manipulated messages so that support-seeking posts from apparent in-group members appeared with a symbol of the university, such as a flag or cake with the university logo. Out-group member posts contained similar images, but with the symbols of a rival university.

Results indicate that the salient group member identities and scarcity of other personal, individuating cues affect the supportiveness of participant responses to the posts. Participants replied to the support-seeking messages posted by an in-group member more often than they did to one posted by an out-group contributor. Participants also provided more action-focused supportiveness in their responses to requests that receive positive comments from other in-group members. They did not do the same for posts supported by out-group members. In addition, participants provided lower levels of person-centered support to a post after reading unsupportive comments written by an in-group member. As predicted by the SIDE model, these results suggest a positive in-group and negative out-group bias to requests seeking support on this social media site.

Positive SIDE for Lurkers

Dai and Shi (2022) investigated whether the social identity deindividuation effects of visual anonymity can provide a positive influence on the mental health and well-being of young people who lurk in online mental health support communities. People drawn to these online support communities often suffer from, or have friends or family members with, mental health concerns. Participating in one of these communities can decrease stigmatization, enable social support, and encourage seeking help. The active involvement of young adults communicating with their peers in these online communities reduces feelings of anxiety and depression. Yet a large number of young people lurk instead of actively participating or engaging in communication with others in these virtual support communities.

Dai and Shi (2022) presented 326 participants (ranging in age from 18 to 29) with screenshots of fictitious online mental health support community conversations between two people. In each conversation, a support seeker posted a message about experiencing a mental health issue and expresses worries about seeing a mental health professional. The provider responded with a comforting message and supportive comments.

Both male and female study participants identified more with a support seeker who was visually anonymous than with one who was identifiable in a photo. This suggests that visual anonymity and depersonalization have a positive effect on perceptions of greater similarity and identification with the support seeker. In addition, the conversations identified both the support seeker and provider with gender-specific names and personal pronouns in the messages. When the conversation portrayed the support seeker as a woman, female participants find the support provider messages more convincing, although there was a nonsignificant difference found for the males.

These findings suggest that online support communities can facilitate the effectiveness of their mental health support messages by prioritizing social identity markers on their sites. Using text-based, visually anonymous messages that reduce personal cues and bolster social identity characteristics can stimulate the SIDE perceptual processes of online support seekers who tend to lurk but do not participate in these communities. Viewing virtual conversations in which participants are visually anonymous but appear similar in social identity may stimulate further health-seeking behaviors among lurkers in these communities. In addition to gender, other salient categories of social identification, such as age, race, ethnicity, and occupation, may facilitate meaningful in-group identification.

Perspective in Context

Analysis and Critique

The SIDE model offers some insight into the processes of identity development and expression. It indicates how a salient social identity can shape group relationships in a CMC medium. At the same time, the model is limited in scope. The model describes communication between individuals and groups within a social space at a particular point in time. It ignores the potential for relational development or change over time. The model analyzes the effects of a shift in salience from personal to social identity, increasing deindividuation and depersonalization, and the implications of that for individual communication within a group and for in-group–out-group relationships, but only at that single point in time.

In addition, the SIDE model does not examine the influence of human agency on the personal or social expression of identity, even when recognizing the potential for strategic use. Communication accommodation explores both the conscious and subconscious uses of language as an expression of individual affiliation with or distinction from a group of people; SIDE, however, does not. Instead, the SIDE model assumes a relatively passive acceptance of a social identity and portrays that as rendered salient mostly through an automatic process. Even when modeling the strategic expression of identity, it offers little insight into how people can consciously construct and manage their personal and social identities as responsible social agents within groups (Giles & Ogay, 2007; Spears et al., 2002).

Negotiating a social identity is a complex process that has many influences. Language is one way that people construct, as well as express, their social identity. Personal motivation, past experience, and cultural orientation also play roles in the salience of tha social identity. These influences remain under investigated in the SIDE model (Laurin 2008; Spears et al., 2014).

The SIDE model, however, does provide insight into some of the important influenc of a text-based, visually anonymous medium on CMC. To the extent that individuals all these influences to remain unconscious and to guide their perceptions of other peo based on language use, they run the risk of accepting negative stereotypes, mindless prejudice, bias, in-group favoritism, and out-group exclusion. Only by being mindful of these potential influences can individuals and groups exercise personal agency in their communication. The SIDE model calls on competent communicators to (a) be aware of the potential negative influences, (b) interrogate their assumptions when interpreting language use, and (c) make a conscious effort to understand the communication intent and meaning of others, even when they use language differently (e.g., Giles et al., 2012).

SIDE in Practice: Social Media Communication During a Pandemic

Social media, and the support people can experience when using a CMC platform such as Facebook, can play an important role during times of crises. This became especially apparent during the early days of the COVID-19 pandemic, when people were physically isolated from one another but connected through social media. However, social media can encourage aggressive and uncivil behavior, as well. Seiter and Brophy (2021) used the SIDE model to investigate how visual anonymity and prosocial orientations of social media influenced how CMC users engaged in supportive or aggressive communication during the first few weeks of the COVID-19 pandemic.

Seiter and Brophy (2021) examined the use of three platforms at the beginning of the COVID-19 pandemic. They focused on Reddit, YouTube, and Facebook because of their varying reliance on text-based communication, levels of visual anonymity, and degrees of expectations for prosocial behaviors. Reddit is one of the most anonymous platforms. It does not allow profile pictures and does not ask for personal information. YouTube allows the use of pictures and names. Facebook actively encourages the use of real names and pictures.

Seiter and Brophy (2021) asked what kinds of communication, aggressive or supportive, appear most often on each of these platforms in the first week after the World Health Organization declared COVID-19 a global pandemic. They selected the top posts on each platform that included the words *coronavirus* or *COVID-19* and then selected the top five conversations from the comment section. They analyzed 100 conversations on each platform for evidence of emotional support, esteem support, informational support, and aggression.

Results show that Reddit users are more likely to offer emotional support than are the Facebook or YouTube participants. The Facebook and YouTube users are more likely to engage in aggressive communication than are the Reddit users. These findings suggest the influence of salient group identities within each platform.

Seiter and Brophy (2021) interpreted these results using the SIDE model. The visual anonymity of these platforms increases the salience of social identity, which means that people are more likely to behave in accordance with what they perceive to be the group norm. Reddit tries to enforce pro-social group behaviors through a set of community rules. Because Reddit users perceive this as the dominant group norm, they are more likely to communicate in a supportive, prosocial way. Aggressive communication sometimes occurs on Reddit, but the platform asks users to adhere to their code of civility. In doing so, Reddit tries to enforce pro-social group behaviors. Because Reddit users perceive these as the dominant group norm, they are more likely to communicate in a supportive, prosocial way. Facebook and YouTube both have codes of conduct posted, as well, but these are not a defining element of the platforms' identities. These results suggest the possibility of promoting supportive behaviors on a social media platform through the promotion of clear-cut pro-social norms and values. This, coupled with the anonymity of participants on these platforms, could lead to more pro-social communication among users.

Illustration of Concepts

Sean and Jasmine share a mutual respect and have a good working relationship. Jasmine is quick to respond to Sean's questions and happy to share her knowledge about the business with him. Sean, however, is intimidated by Jasmine's knowledge, experience, ability, and background. She sometimes uses words, expressions, and technical terms that Sean does not understand. This makes Sean feel inexperienced and like he doesn't know what he's doing.

Sean likes Jasmine as a person and respects her work and success with customers. He makes an effort to communicate with her face-to-face to clear up any misunderstandings. Jasmine recognizes this as well and is happy to explain the meaning of the various terms and any important concepts behind them. When it is not possible to meet face-to-face, they Facetime, rather than email, to discuss the issue. This reduces their reliance on text-based and visually anonymous CMC and increases their awareness of each other's personal identities. They frequently end up laughing about the misunderstanding, and it has become a running joke between them, which makes Sean feel less insecure about his abilities and knowledge.

Looking Forward to Identities

In the next chapter, we discuss individuals and their CMC interactions. The SIDE model introduces some of the basic concepts useful in describing the implications of those interactions. In the chapters that follow individuals, we discuss the interactions of CMC groups and communities.

COMMUNICATION ETHICS CHALLENGE

What Are the Ethics of Personal Identity Expression and Social Role Conformity?

SIDE develops a contrast between a personal presentation of self and a social role identity. It describes the CMC influences that increase the likelihood of identifying strongly with a social group and focuses on the negative aspects of deindividuation and depersonalization. Yet, we each have a responsibility to perform some social roles to the best of our ability. We have family, work, and community obligations. Always expressing a personal identity, and never identifying with the interests and perspectives of the group, would be self-centered and selfish.

Finding a balance in the cognitive salience of personal expression and social role is important to ethical communication. How do I find this balance? Is it ethical to place my own family or local group interests ahead of those of groups of other people? What are the communication ethics of strongly advocating for myself, my family, or my community? What are the ethics of using the visual anonymity and text-based communication of CMC for that advocacy?

A local high school drama instructor discovered that parents had formed a group on social media that was critical of the drama program. He tried to join the group but was excluded. So, he applied for membership in the group using an anonymous alternative identity and was accepted. He used his text-based communication through this visually anonymous identity to present the facts about the drama program, showing the benefits, citing student accomplishments, and announcing upcoming events. When his participation in the group through his alternative identity was discovered, the parents were outraged and he was fired from his job. What are the communication ethics of this case?

1. Most people will say that the instructor's deception in creating the alternative identity was unethical. What do you think? Is it ever ethically justifiable to communicate deceptively?

2. Aside from the initial identity deception, did the drama instructor act unethically?

3. The most interesting SIDE questions revolve around the communication ethics of the parents group. Were the participants of the parents group unethical in their communication? They are not subject to public open meeting laws, but when is it ethically appropriate to have ongoing, closed meetings that exclude members of the larger community, especially when the main purpose of those meetings is to criticize the work of those excluded people? Should those people not be allowed to hear the criticism and speak in their own defense?

4. What are the personal and social communication ethics of participating in a visually anonymous, text-based CMC group?

KEYWORDS AND PHRASES

Communication accommodation describes how changes in language use expresses both a conscious and unconscious affiliation with or difference from a group.

Complementarity refers to a style of communication that appears divergent but represents a reciprocal pattern of communication behaviors that recognize and reinforce social status differences in group member relationships.

Convergence (in communication accommodation) means using a communication style that is similar to a person or group with whom someone identifies.

Deindividuation is a state of decreased cognitive salience of oneself as a person and increased awareness of a social identity within a specific group context. The deindividuation process shifts identity salience from the personal to the social, increasing sensitivity to the environmental cues and social influences while decreasing an awareness of oneself as a unique individual.

Depersonalization is the tendency to perceive oneself and others not as unique individuals with multiple idiosyncratic characteristics, talents, behaviors, and ways of communicating but as defined only by membership in a group, community, or social category.

Divergence in language style distances participants from people and groups with whom they do not identify.

Personal identity means viewing oneself as a unique individual. This identity becomes salient in thoughts about personal ambitions, motivations, accomplishments, satisfactions, desires, regrets, relationships, and meaning.

Social identity means seeing oneself within a social role, as a member of a group or community, and behaving in accordance with the social norms appropriate to that role. It becomes salient in the awareness of social roles, activities, responsibilities, and obligations to others, such as family, friends, colleagues, professional and social groups, or communities to which someone belongs.

The **social identity of deindividuation effects (SIDE)** perspective describes the tendency of people to identify with a group when engaged in CMC.

QUESTIONS FOR FURTHER DISCUSSION

1. How much influence does our perception of race, gender, age, or ethnicity have on our perceived ease of communicating with someone?

2. Communication accommodation is a common element of how people communicate. Do you think this is a contextual process? In other words, do you think people are more likely to engage in accommodation when they see people face-to-face or when they communicate with them through CMC? Why (not)?

3. How do processes of deindividuation and depersonalization influence people's tendency to engage in communication accommodation?

4. Online spaces often lack civility; discussions through CMC often become aggressive and hostile. This has been attributed, in part, to the effect that deindividuation has on how we behave. How could online spaces utilize our tendency to look for and adhere to group norms to reduce such incivility?

Interactions

Goal of this approach: To analyze the multiple implications of CMC interactions for individuals, groups, and communities. Approach IV examines the communication interactions of CMC participants. The chapters look at the implications of these interactions for how people make sense of themselves and relate to others as individuals, groups, and communities.

Individuals describes the presentation of self through CMC, focusing specifically on how interactions are shaped by impression management, imagined audiences, context collapse, authenticity, identity shift, warranting, social comparison, and privacy management concerns.

Groups discusses how CMC groups form, and the competency requirements and benefits of participating in CMC groups. It analyzes the group network influences on the activation and mobilization of informational and emotional social capital among participants and suggests six rules for effective group CMC.

Communities examines how interactions shape virtual communities. The chapter describes the differences of networked individualism, virtual settlements, and permeable communities. Then it discusses the implications of accessibility, boundaries, community practice, leadership, and lurking for the experience of virtual community.

10

Individuals

S ean, Pam, and Jasmine strive to present professional images of themselves in multiple online spaces. They create and maintain online identities across a number of social media platforms and through numerous professional CMC interactions each day. These identities link to their employment at the Home Products store but also include personal relationships with family and friends. They monitor and edit both the appearance and style of their CMC self-presentations to maintain a professional image for their colleagues and customers.

Presentation of Self

When people communicate information about themselves, in-person or through CMC, they are engaging in a form of self-presentation. Self-presentation is a communication activity

FIGURE 10.1 Presentation of Self in CMC.

that conveys who someone is, but it also helps a person construct a sense of self. Sometimes a person adjusts how they present themselves to meet audience expectations. When and how people do this has implications for their self-identity (Baumeister & Hutton, 1987).

Goffman (1959) likens this self-presentation to a live theater performance. The action of this presentation takes place simultaneously in front- and backstage areas. The frontstage is accessible to a wide audience. The backstage is more personal and private.

A frontstage presentation of self includes both the appearance and manner of performance. Appearance involves an audience's perception of the social status and appropriateness of the activity performed. Manner describes the competence, integrity, and coherence of the performance within those social expectations. The audience to a performance expects the presentation to be consistent in appearance and manner and to fall within social norms.

In the frontstage area, the actor presents a version of self that consciously conceals any perceived personal flaws and accentuates a fit with social role expectations. The physical setting (including appropriate clothing, furniture, scenery, and accessories), personal characteristics (demographic markers indicating age, gender, race, social status, physical size, appearance, and posture), and expressive use of language, speech, facial expressions, and bodily gestures collectively constitute an idealized, and as socially acceptable as possible, presentation of self.

The backstage region is a more personal, private space where an actor "can relax ... step out of character", and review any aspect that might offend the audience in the ongoing frontstage presentation (Goffman, 1959, p. 112). The backstage helps the actor achieve the perception of consistency in the frontstage performance. Backstage, actors can adjust their costumes, reflect on the performance, and choose from a repertoire of actions, styles, characters, and phrasings to create the desired impressions for the front stage presentation.

An actor moves the presentation of self from that private backstage area into the view of a select audience for the frontstage performance. The dynamic action of that frontstage performance manages the audience impressions, using the backstage preparation of costumes, sets, and lighting to support the acting. In a good production, the front- and backstage work together to present a character that the audience judges authentic within the confines of the theater walls.

There is also an area outside of the theater. The theater walls separate the actor, audience, and performance from the view of those in this outside region. The performance is not intended for them. The performer creates the presentation of self as a dramatic interaction with a specific audience in mind, away from the view of the outsiders who might not be used to seeing the performer in this role. Figure 10.2 illustrates the concepts of a front- and backstage in the presentation of self.

Presentation of Self to a CMC Audience

There are notable differences between a live face-to-face performance and a CMC presentation of self. In CMC, unlike in a face-to-face setting, performers can edit their presentations before and after people have seen them. In addition, CMC participants often are not sure who their audience is. They often receive only delayed feedback, and

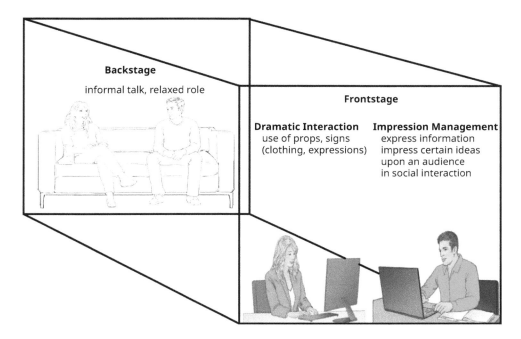

FIGURE 10.2 Backstage and Frontstage.

frequently must create a performance for multiple audiences at once. These differences between a CMC-based self-presentation and a face-to-face self-presentation raise concerns about participant impression management, imagined audiences, and context collapse. Numerous scholars have applied, adapted, and modified Goffman's theater metaphor to account for these differences in CMC self-presentation (Darr & Doss, 2022; Hogan, 2010; Marwick & boyd, 2011a, 2011b; Treem et al., 2020).

Impression Management

Self-presentation in frontstage spaces means deciding which parts of oneself to share with others, and how to best share them so as to create the most favorable impression. This selective self-presentation, or **impression management** is more common when people become aware of an audience and concerned about how they appear to other people (Hogan, 2010; Marwick & boyd, 2011a).

This impression management becomes more complicated in CMC where the distinction between front and backstage can become blurred. Friend and follower lists create an audience with imagined preferences. These preferences can affect the expression of one's presentation. In addition, text-based CMC allows reviewing and editing messages before sending. Yet, the lack of visual cues makes it difficult to assess what members of the audience think until after the message is sent and asynchronous CMC provides delayed feedback, which creates a time lapse before an audience response. As a result, it can become unclear what part of the performance exists in the composition, presentation, and response to the feedback (Marwick & boyd, 2011a; Treem et al., 2020).

Imagined Audiences

In most face-to-face interactions, we know the audience. We can see and hear them. This allows us to predict what kind of self-presentation is appropriate. Without a physical audience present, we must imagine one. This is what authors and screenplay writers do. They imagine who might be reading or watching their work. In many forms of CMC it is unusual to have a live audience, with some exceptions, such as a videoconference or the "live" option of Instagram. Instead, CMC participants usually perform for an imagined audience. When deciding how to behave and present themselves, participants must consider who might see them and base their self-presentation on those imagined audience member preferences (boyd, 2008, 2010; Marwick & boyd, 2011a).

Sometimes these assumptions about an imagined CMC audience are straightforward. When sending an email to colleagues, for example, the sender knows the general audience, even if the list of recipients goes beyond the people a sender knows personally. Other forms of CMC, such as social media sites, allow users to make their audience tangible through the creation of friends or follower lists. These social media sites push users to define their audiences. This can make self-presentations less complicated since the communicator knows something about who the audience is. Friend or follower lists effectively "write their audience into being" (Marwick & boyd, 2011a, p. 116).

Context Collapse

In face-to-face contexts, our presentation of self often differs with each particular audience. We communicate differently with family members than we do with colleagues or with classmates. Face-to-face, we can separate our audiences and adapt our communication accordingly.

An in-class (frontstage) presentation of a topic is likely to contain different content, detail, and verbal style than talking about that same topic with colleagues later in the day (another frontstage) or reviewing it with a few close friend that evening (backstage). We are more likely to tell the friend about how we felt presenting the topic, our nervousness, inarticulateness, and feelings of inadequacy in knowledge or preparation.

In CMC, however, particularly on social media sites, we are much more likely to have a variety of audiences in the same space. This creates a context collapse. Having multiple groups of people on the same platform affects how we present ourselves (Marwick & boyd, 2011a). Figure 10.3 illustrates this context collapse.

Managing CMC Audiences

Social media platforms such as Facebook, TikTok, Instagram, and Twitter allow people to friend and follow folks from all areas of their life. People often add family members, high school or college classmates, neighbors, and colleagues to their friends list. The absence of any kind of physical boundaries, such as time and place, to associating with people on social media allows people to connect with a broad range of others outside of a current context (boyd, 2010).

This means that instead of engaging only with one's peers, colleagues, or family members in separate presentations of self, social media participants must engage all of

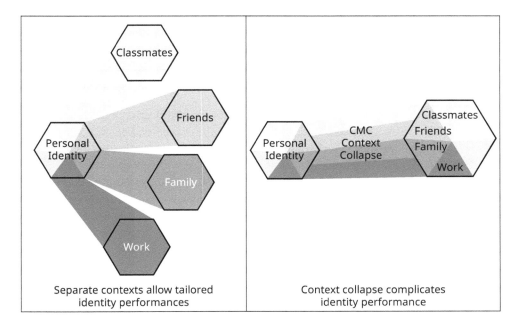

Separate contexts allow tailored
identity performances

Context collapse complicates
identity performance

FIGURE 10.3 Context Collapse

them on a single platform. They must simultaneously be aware of these multiple groups in their self-presentation. Social media users often develop a variety of strategies to navigate this context collapse.

Some Instagram users, for example, create multiple accounts for separate audiences. They post idealized public identities in their "real" Instagram accounts, known as Rinstas. These identities are accessible to multiple audiences, including parents, teachers, friends, acquaintances, and strangers. These frontstage Rinsta accounts provide users with social attention. Users also create additional "fake" Finsta accounts to express themselves to a few close friends they consider trustworthy. These backstage Finsta accounts serve as safe places for participants to engage in humor, have fun, share private feelings, vent raw emotions, and bond with a small group of friends. Through their Finsta accounts, friends share, validate, and affirm each other's presentation of self (Darr & Doss, 2022).

Other CMC user strategies include creating circles of friends with whom participants share certain posts. Some participants use certain platforms only with certain groups of people. Others work with multiple audiences by carefully considering what they share and keep private and balance authenticity and honesty with the need to remain of interest to a variety of audiences (Marwick & boyd, 2011a).

Participant Interactions and CMC Self-Presentations

Self-presentation using CMC is considerably different from self-presentations carried out in face-to-face settings. This can be attributed to how participant interactions are impacted by the nature of the CMC platforms. These interactions determine how self-presentation takes place. The role that participant interactions in CMC play in people's self-presentations is discussed by looking at authenticity, identity shift, warranting, and social comparison.

Authenticity

Authenticity defines the perception of an action or communication as real, sincere, or reflecting a person's inner self. It describes whether an observed behavior is reflective of someone's real feelings and thoughts. Authenticity is not an "inherent quality" that resides within a person, however, but a social construct, which means that it depends on the situation and the interaction (Reade, 2020, p. 3). It is not something that one *has* but a performance. It is an ongoing process through which we figure out who we are and convey that to the world in a "coherent ... narrative of the self" (Duguay, 2017, p. 353). In CMC people choose what personal information to disclose, hoping that an audience will view their performance as authentic (Abidin, 2018; Darr & Doss, 2022; Lee, 2020; Lindholm, 2013; Marwick & boyd, 2011a, 2011b).

Assessing authenticity in CMC, however, can be difficult. The presence of bots, fake social media accounts, and the increase in deep-fake videos complicate the issues surrounding the authenticity of a CMC presentation. Seemingly personalized messages from politicians tweeting out their new political agendas or an apparently personal blog post by a celebrity further confounds the authenticity issue. Yet, considering the authenticity of these types of messages is a particularly important issue, given the ease and speed with which misinformation can spread across the internet (Lee, 2020).

Most social media users strive to create an authentic identity presentation. In addition, many social media platforms promote themselves as authentic, and as even more authentic than their competition. A variety of "markers," including consistency, spontaneity, amateurism, and disclosure of personal information, influence perceptions of authenticity in social media (Salisbury & Pooley, 2017).

Meeting authenticity expectations within the cultural norms and values of a CMC audience, however, is complicated by the context collapse. Most social media users manage multiple audiences who have different ideas about what makes someone authentic. One way individuals manage is through a careful consideration of what they disclose and what they keep private. They balance the kinds of topics they share with which audiences, hoping to please them all (Darr & Doss, 2022; Haimson & Hoffmann, 2016; Marwick & boyd, 2011a, 2011b).

CMC users often balance sharing highly personal, unedited, and "realistic" appearing information, with being positive, creative, and engaging with an audience on a regular basis. Sharing personal struggles, "a day in the life," or pictures featuring skin and body imperfections, create a sense of authenticity among their followers. These kinds of posts, however, are often as carefully edited and as much a performance as more curated presentations (Abidin, 2017; Duguay, 2017; Haimson & Hoffmann, 2016; Marwick & boyd, 2011a, 2011b; Reade, 2020).

In addition, the ability to be authentic is constrained and enabled by the platform. On Twitter (now known as X), for example, the highly public nature of most user profiles means that people must work harder at balancing the expectations of the various audiences who might see their tweets (Marwick & boyd, 2011a). Facebook, for a while, had a "real name" policy that forced users who did not live under their birth name to use that name for their profile, restricting their ability to be authentic (Haimson & Hoffmann, 2016). TikTok's highly visual focus, as well as its reliance on made-up usernames and its association of similar content through the "for you" page, promotes high levels of personal disclosure, considered authentic by many (Barta & Andalibi, 2021).

Identity Shift

The act of presenting ourselves to others is more than self-expression. It is a social process. Interacting with others, and reflecting on those interactions, affects our personal sense of self, as well. Thus, how we behave in front of others affects how we see ourselves.

People assume a consistency between their internal values, beliefs, and attitudes, how they view themselves, and how they behave. This perception of consistency helps avoid cognitive dissonance, or internal discomfort over holding two opposing ideas or beliefs. People strive to make their external behaviors align with how they see themselves. Viewing a behavior that is discrepant with how one sees oneself can result in an internalization process that changes one's self-concept. Observing a public behavior can induce a person to reflect on that behavior, reexamine the aspect of their personal identity reflected in that public behavior, and, if necessary, adjust it to align with that behavior (Bem, 1967; Tice, 1992).

Behaviors that people carry out in public settings are the most influential in this effect. If a behavior is not public and no one else is there to see it, a person may ignore it, and it may not lead to an adjustment in self-concept. If other people are around, the behavior is likely to influence personal identity (Schlenker et al., 1994).

This internalization process of a public behavior that affects a self-concept occurs in CMC as well. Online behaviors are especially likely to engender this type of change because of the amount of work that goes into constructing an online presentation and the persistence of that online communication. Identity shift describes a change in a person's self-concept after observing their online behavior (Carr et al., 2021; Gonzales & Hancock, 2008).

Not all CMC behavior leads to an identity shift. Behavior that takes place in a private setting, such as an email sent to a single recipient, is less likely to lead to a change in a person's self-concept than a behavior that takes place in more public settings, such as an Instagram post to hundreds of followers. The publicness of the behavior makes an individual feel more committed and is more likely to change an internal self-concept (Gonzales & Hancock, 2008). Interestingly, an individual's perception of the behavior being public influences identity shift more than the actual publicness of that behavior (Carr, 2021). Even creating and thinking about sharing a post with others can produce this identity shift (Johnson & Rosenbaum, 2023).

Feedback also influences the changes in self-concept induced by public online behaviors. Positive feedback to a post or other online behavior, by confirming the poster's idea or behavior, is more likely to lead to identity shift than negative feedback. Public feedback, such as a comment on a post, intensifies identity shift more than privately received feedback, such as a private message about a post (Carr & Foreman, 2016; Carr & Hayes, 2019; Walther et al., 2011).

Perception of the audience influences the likelihood of identity shift as well. What a social media user thinks about their audience affects whether an online behavior leads to identity shift. Whom people envision to be in their imagined audience influences, for example, whether posting something to them on a social media site will affect a change in self-concept (Johnson & Rosenbaum, 2023). When people create a post that reflects a trait or value they think their audience cares about, that post is more likely to lead to a change in self-concept as well (French & Hancock, 2016, as cited in Carr et al., 2021). In addition, when people tailor a CMC message to a specific audience, rather than a broad group of people, that message is more likely to lead to identity shift (Carr, 2021).

Another factor that plays a role in whether an online behavior leads to a change in self-concept is identifiability. When a social media post directly connects to a person, because they are using a real name rather than a pseudonym, an actual profile picture, or another identifier such as their hometown, that connection of the person to the post facilitates the potential for a change in self-concept. Others have to be able to link the expression back to the individual to affect a person's self-concept. People who can remain anonymous while posting are less likely to experience a dissonance in self-awareness about what they posted or need to adjust their self-concept (Carr et al., 2021).

In addition, online posts must be relevant to a person's self-identity for them to engender a change in self-concept. The online performance must be salient to the poster's identity, that is, a performance online must be meaningful to the person for it impact their self-identity. Furthermore, some parts of people's identities do not change through identity shift. Some aspects of the self, such as altruism, are too deeply rooted in a person's identity for an online post to affect. On the other hand, most personal characteristics, like brand or art preferences, are more malleable or ephemeral and can change through an identity shift process (Carr et al., 2021; Carr & Hayes, 2019; Johnson & Rosenbaum, 2023; Johnson & Van der Heide, 2015).

In sum, identity shift takes place when CMC participants feel that there is an audience observing their online communication and that the audience cares about the behaviors they display. An attitude that is salient to a person's self-concept and a self-presentation directed to a specific audience are more likely to lead to identity shift. Feedback can intensify the identity shift as well. Figure 10.4 illustrates this identity shift process.

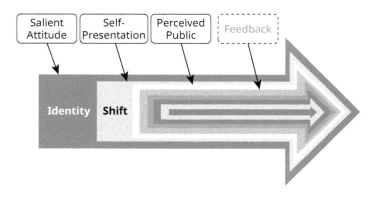

FIGURE 10.4 Identity Shift.

Warranting

It can be challenging to determine what information to rely on when deciding how believable a person's self-presentation is in a CMC environment. Many of the cues used for assessing a person's credibility in a face-to-face situation, such as facial expressions and body language, are absent in CMC. Yet, CMC participants still must evaluate information to determine whether an online behavior is credible and reflective of an offline characteristic.

When evaluating online communication and behaviors, establishing credibility is central. Warrants are online cues, such as a comment, like, or a post, that provide evidence that the online communication is connected to an offline self and thus could be credible. When CMC participants perceive an online communication, such as a comment or post, not to be credible, they are less likely to use it when they create an impression of the individual or organization (Walther & Parks, 2002).

Participants perceive cues that are difficult to alter as more credible. Cues perceived to be immune to manipulation thus have greater warranting value. This includes the number of followers a person has, the number of likes or upvotes a post receives, or the number of posts shared by other people about an individual. These third-party claims are especially relevant to credibility. Information shared by others about a person provide third-party claims that have high warranting value. Interactive social media sites, therefore, render people's self-presentations more credible than static websites because the presence of others who can verify a person's claims provide high warranting value (DeAndrea, 2014; Hayes & Carr, 2015; Rui, 2018; Walther & Parks, 2002).

One caveat here is the extent to which the dissemination of third-party claims can be influenced by the person the claims are about. This influence can reduce the warranting value of the information in three ways. First, when participants believe that the information that someone posted about a third person could have been influenced by this third person, the warranting value of that information decreases and the opinion of those individuals becomes less positive. Second, when there is a perceived relationship between the subject of the post and the person making the claim in the post, the warranting value of the information also decreases. Third, when participants have reason to believe that the third party making the claim might benefit from providing positive information, that information becomes less credible as well (DeAndrea, 2014; DeAndrea & Carpenter, 2018; Rui, 2018).

The warranting value of these cues plays an important role in determining the credibility and authenticity of a source, a message, or an interaction. When participants deem a source credible, they are more likely to judge it authentic. When participants see other users verifying a claim, or see the claim as immune to manipulation, the claim will be deemed to be more credible and thus authentic (Hayes & Carr, 2015; Metzger et al., 2010).

Social Comparison

Social comparison is a common human activity. People constantly assess themselves, evaluating their behaviors, abilities, and ideas in comparison to others, especially when there are no objective means by which to assess oneself. The targets of these comparisons are generally not random. People tend to compare themselves to others who are somewhat like them rather than those who are significantly different or better at something (Festinger, 1954).

People compare themselves to others for the purposes of evaluating the self, making decisions, managing their emotions, and overall well-being. They compare themselves to people they know, people they have only heard about, fictional characters, and people they have made up themselves. Although everyone engages in these social comparisons, people who are naturally oriented toward others and those who report lower self-esteem are more likely to compare themselves to others (Buunk & Gibbons, 2007; Vogel et al., 2014; Wood, 1996).

These social comparisons frequently create skew or biased perceptions of others in ways that can affect people's self-esteem and overall happiness with themselves. Downward social comparisons to someone less well off or worse at something can make people feel better about themselves as they consider the contrast or difference between themselves and the target. Upward social comparisons to another person who is doing better at something can lead to a desire for self-improvement. This is especially the case for people with a higher self-esteem or those who see themselves as similar to the comparison target. Upward social comparison, however, also can be harmful to a person's self-esteem. Subsequently, people will sometimes engage in defensive mechanisms to differentiate themselves from that person so that any comparison becomes meaningless (Buunk & Gibbons, 2007; Collins, 1996).

CMC provides many opportunities for these types of social comparisons. Social media platforms are especially interesting spaces to examine the processes and implications of social comparison as most users of these sites present highly curated, mostly positive, and generally idealized images of themselves (Schreurs et al., 2022). This can produce a **positivity bias** in that social media interactions feel like upward comparisons, which can have negative effects on self-esteem and self-evaluation (de Vries et al., 2018; Vogel et al., 2014). Some research links the negative effects of social comparison to the amount of time social media users spend looking at body image–related content and photographs on social media (Meier & Gray, 2014; Tiggeman & Zaccardo, 2015). Facebook users, for example, may experience negative moods, envy, and depression after extensive exposure to viewing attractive, popular, or healthy profiles (Appel et al., 2016).

This connection between social media upward comparisons and one's ideas about oneself is not entirely straightforward; in some cases, upward comparisons can have positive effects (Meier & Johnson, 2022). This outcome has been attributed to assimilation; when social media users perceive themselves to be similar to high-performing others, they will experience positive consequences of the upward comparison. Instagram users who saw positive posts about nature and travel and who experienced upward comparison did not experience any negative effects. Instead, they reported benign envy and a desire to improve themselves to be more like the target. This benign envy leads to inspiration rather than anything negative (Meier et al., 2020).

Finally, not all social media users engage in social comparison. Social comparison is most likely to occur among users who are younger, have more friends, and spend more time using the media. The effects may also influence members of collectivist societies more than individualistic ones (Burke et al., 2020).

TABLE 10.1 Relational Concerns for the Presentation of Self in CMC

AUTHENTICITY	Social construct based on relationships. Difficult to assess, constrained and enabled by CMC platform
IDENTITY SHIFT	Internalization of public behavior influences self-concept
WARRANTING	Credibility assessment difficult due to reduced or absent nonverbal cues, facial expressions, body language
SOCIAL COMPARISON	Downward, upward, positivity biases influence on self-esteem

Summary: Authenticity, Identity Shift, Warranting, and Social Comparison

Many of these perspectives on the processes of how individuals present themselves find practical and interesting applications in CMC research. Abidin (2017), for example, develops the concept of **calibrated amateurism** to show how family influencers purposely add an amateurish look to their videos to create a spontaneous, relatable, yet entirely staged authenticity. The success of these influencers suggests that their audiences find this appealing. Johnson and Rosenbaum (2023) use identity shift theory to examine how brands can effectively use social media like Facebook and Twitter to improve potential consumer attitudes toward them. They find that sharing and liking on different platforms have different effects on people's brand attitudes. Couture Bue (2020) uses the social comparison perspective to study how social media use affects body image satisfaction among young women. She finds that an increase in appearance comparison to people in Instagram posts leads to an increase in body dissatisfaction and focus of attention on those areas of the body that an Instagram user dislikes. Table 10.1 summarizes these concerns for the presentation of self in CMC.

Privacy Management in CMC

Managing the privacy of one's personal information can be challenging. Privacy management is more than just enforcing personalized rules about who has access to what information; it is an ongoing process of negotiation about the boundaries between private and public. **Privacy management** is about regulating personal informational boundaries. It describes how individuals consider and reconsider who should have access to what information about them under what circumstances (Palen & Dourish, 2003; Trepte, 2021). This regulation of privacy boundaries occurs within a broader context of social and cultural norms and values. These social and cultural norms and values influence what privacy means to each of the individuals in a relationship. Privacy is a social-relational concept, and an important element in CMC usage (Marwick & boyd, 2014).

Communication Privacy Management

Communication privacy management describes the negotiating process of sharing personal information with close friends, acquaintances, and a broader public. To connect with friends and build relationships, people need to reveal private and personal information. But to protect themselves, they also need and desire to keep certain information private. This creates a conflict, and people must choose how much and what information to disclose about themselves, what to keep to private, and how to manage their personal privacy in general. Once someone shares private information with a friend in order to build a stronger personal connection and relationship, that friend becomes a co-owner of the information. Now the two individuals need to negotiate or arrive at a common understanding about when and how to protect or reveal that information. The result is that privacy management is a relational communication negotiation process rather than an individual decision. If this negotiation process breaks down and the owner and co-owner cannot agree on such shared rules, it results in a privacy disruption or turbulence, with private information shared outside the boundaries the original owner had in mind (Child & Petronio, 2011; Petronio, 2010; Trepte, 2021).

CMC complicates this privacy negotiation process. Digital media blurs the boundaries between the public and private sphere. The anonymity provided by some online platforms and ability to edit one's online profile and behaviors provides people with some control over their personal information. Yet, many other features of CMC erode that sense of control over private information.

Participation in social media, for example, requires people to disclose information about themselves when they create a profile. In addition, to use these platforms to their fullest potential, people must share personal information to build their online social relationships. This means that people end up sharing personal information with a large and diverse group of people. They can, to some degree, control who can see what information, but they cannot control what other people do with that personal information. In addition, CMC users cannot control changes in platform policies that affect the visibility of posts and, due to the persistence of online communication, cannot control who might see their online information in the future. (Child & Petronio, 2011; Marwick & boyd, 2014; Palen & Dourish, 2003; Trepte, 2021).

Networked Privacy Management

A networked privacy management perspective involves understanding the technological influences of a CMC network on privacy management. An individual's networked privacy in CMC differs from the assumptions made about personal confidences shared face-to-face. People do have some technological features at their disposal to control who sees what information, but the privacy of their personal information is no longer held within the bounds of family or close friendship relationships.

To ensure their privacy, CMC users must be familiar with and know how to manage the social context in which they operate. They must be aware of the online social relationships, norms, and values that guide these relationships. Social media users can, for example, share posts about having a hard day with certain, restricted, audiences.

If they want to truly safeguard the privacy of that information, however, it is better to use subtle cues that only their intended audience will understand (Marwick & boyd, 2014; Trepte, 2021).

Although people consistently report high levels of concern about privacy violations in online spaces, these concerns do not appear to translate to stricter privacy management practices. In other words, people experience a privacy paradox: They might feel more concerned about privacy but don't act on it. Their evaluation of the risks versus the benefits of sharing personal information, or privacy calculus, contains a level of unawareness about the potential of all present and future risks associated with oversharing. This can lead to privacy cynicism, or the feeling they have no control over how their information is handled. So while they might be concerned about the risk associated with sharing in online environment, they feel that nothing they can do will change that risk, which leads to inaction (Hoffman et al., 2016; Trepte, 2021).

Perspective in Context

Analysis and Critique

Self-presentation is a dynamic, ongoing performance. The identities we perform through CMC are fluid. These identities form within our online relationships, the platforms on which we are active, and the social norms associated with those relationships and platforms at that time.

A variety of perspectives and concepts explain the influences on that identity performance in CMC. Impression management, identity shift, and warranting each describe how identities are socially constructed. The identities of CMC participants form through a combination of social and technological influences on the presentation of self within the CMC context. This social-technological context of CMC influences perceptions of authenticity, warranting, social comparison to others, and privacy management of personal information. Characteristics of the CMC context can make it more difficult to view ourselves as individuals, separate from the CMC environments in which we participate and the dynamically changing influences of those online spaces.

Identity in Practice: Fake News

Fake news, or misinformation that is purposefully inaccurate, has become a major concern for social media users in recent years. People increasingly rely on social media for their news, but social media platforms also serve as the main channels for spreading fake news, increasing the chances that users will encounter it. The dissemination of this fake news provides people with misinformation, decreases trust in the news industry and political system, and arguably has a negative impact on democracy.

Walther et al. (2022) use an identity shift perspective to investigate what happens to people's attitudes toward a politician when they share a fake news story about that politician on their personal Twitter (now known as X) account. Since identity shift theory holds that engaging in a behavior can shift a person's attitude in the direct of that behavior,

Walther et al. reason that sharing a news story, even a fake one, on a public social media site should change a person's attitude in the direction of the story. They also look at the role played by the number of "likes" a shared fake news story receives. Since feedback can increase the effect of a public behavior on a person's sense of self, the number of likes that a retweet receives should lead to a stronger shift in attitude.

In addition, they look at whether the fake news story contains positive or negative information about the politician affects the attitude toward the people in the story. Past research indicates that negative stories lead to stronger responses, so the expected identity shift might be stronger when sharing a negative story than a positive one. Finally, they examine whether the political angle of the story matters. For example, if a Republican shares a fake negative news story about a Democratic politician, does that have a different effect than when that Republican shares a fake positive news story about a Democratic politician?

All the participants in the study read a fake news story created by the researchers. About a fifth of the participants formed a control group who just read the story, reported their attitudes toward the politician, and did so again a week later. The rest of the participants formed the experimental groups. They read the story, saw two tweets about the story, and reported their attitudes toward the politician. Then they were told to retweet one of the two tweets on their personal, public Twitter (X) account. To see if the number of likes matters, the researchers responded to these retweets by liking them different numbers of times. A week later, they measured the participant attitude toward the politician in the story again.

The authors found that simply reading a fake news story and sharing it in a retweet affected people's attitudes to the same degree. This runs counter to a premise of identity shift theory, which holds that the public performance changes a person's attitude. It does, however, align with the "mere thought" premise introduced by Johnson and Rosenbaum (2023) that holds that simply thinking about sharing it is sufficient to induce attitude change.

Additionally, Walther et al. (2022) show that the number of likes that a retweet receives matters, but only for negative stories about politicians from the party a participant does not support. When participants share a negative story about a politician whom they do not like, the more likes their retweet receives, the more negative their attitude toward the politician becomes. When participants share a negative story about a politician from the party they support, the number of likes does not affect their attitude. The number of likes only affects identity shift for retweets of negative stories about disliked politicians. Their study shows the complexity of attitude change, but demonstrates that under certain circumstances, particularly those involving feedback, identity shift can occur.

Illustration of Concepts

Jasmine, Pam, and Sean each manage their CMC presentation of self to be authentic while maintaining a degree of personal privacy. They mention their civic, community, and professional involvement on the appropriate social media sites, such as

LinkedIn, recognizing that this information is relatively public already. They also identify their education and professional accomplishments and areas of expertise on the Home Products store company website. Each of them is discreet about sharing more personal information or saying anything negative about their colleagues. They realize that any relational issues are best addressed in person rather than through CMC.

Looking Forward to Groups

In the next chapter, we discuss how groups form networks of relationships in CMC and the informational and social support implications. Groups use individual expertise and communication to achieve a common goal. Participating in CMC groups can pose both challenges and opportunities.

COMMUNICATION ETHICS CHALLENGE

The Ethics of Social Media Influence

Social media influencers often have multiple loyalties. One is a loyalty to the brands and companies that they recommend and promote. Another loyalty is to their group of followers to provide honest advice and make authentic recommendations that are in that group's best interest.

Imagine that you are an influencer who has been promoting a major brand that is now publicly accused of unethical practices and violations of international child labor laws in their overseas manufacturing plants. In response to these public accusations, the company shares an internal report and video with you that describes the operations at one of their plants. The report contains interviews with several employees and looks legitimate, but because the plant is overseas, you have no way to verify the information. The company asks you to post the report and video for your followers, along with your recommendation. They also inform you that if you choose to not share the post, they will have to reconsider your sponsorship. What do you do? You have spent years building your online reputation, have thousands of followers, and the company sponsorship provides a source of income for you, should you share the report?

1. As an influencer, what is your ethical responsibility to your followers?

2. What do you think the company's purpose is in sharing the report with you and asking you to promote it? How do the concepts of identity shift and warranting inform your decision about whether to share the report?

3. What do you think the repercussions of this decision will be for you, the company, and your followers?

KEYWORDS AND PHRASES

Authenticity defines the perception of an action or communication as real, sincere, or reflecting a person's inner self.

Backstage refers to a more personal, private space where an individual can relax, step out of character, and review any aspects that might offend the audience in the ongoing frontstage presentation.

Calibrated amateurism describes how family influencers purposely add an amateurish look to their videos to create a spontaneous, relatable, yet entirely staged authenticity.

Communication privacy management describes the negotiating process of sharing personal information with close friends, acquaintances, and a broader public.

Context collapse occurs when there are a variety of audiences in the same space. This affects how we present ourselves.

Frontstage presentations involve an individual presenting themselves to a wide audience. This presentation involves a version of self that consciously conceals any perceived personal flaws and accentuates a fit with social role expectations.

Identity shift describes a change in a person's self-concept after observing their online behavior.

Imagined audience refers to the audience people imagine when there isn't a physical audience present.

Impression management is a selective self-presentation that is more common when people become aware of an audience and become concerned about how they appear to other people.

Networked privacy management is a perspective that involves understanding the technological influences of a CMC network on privacy management.

Positivity bias occurs when most social media interactions feel like upward social comparisons due to users' tendency to present highly curated, mostly positive, and generally idealized images of themselves.

Privacy management is about regulating personal informational boundaries. It describes how individuals consider and reconsider who should have access to what information about them under what circumstances.

Self-presentation is a communication activity that conveys who someone is, but it also helps a person construct sense of self.

Social comparison is what happens when people assess their behaviors, abilities, and ideas in comparison to others. This is especially common when there are no objective means by which to assess oneself.

Warrants are online cues, such as a comment, like, or a post, that provide evidence that the online communication is connected to an offline self and thus could be credible.

QUESTIONS FOR FURTHER DISCUSSION

1. How do you see credibility and the use of warrants play out on your social media pages? If you want to appear credible to your social media followers, what kind of cues do you use? Do these cues qualify as having high warranting value? How do you assess whether someone's posts are credible?

2. Have you ever engaged in upward or downward social comparison? Under what circumstances? Do you think that the warranting value of the online cues used in a post impacts whether people will use that post for social comparison? Why (not)?

3. Imagine you are a small company that is trying to increase sales through your social media presence. According to identity shift theory, what steps might be effective in shifting people's brand attitudes?

11

Groups

C heryl, Darius, and Alex form an efficient and effective furniture sales group. They work well together, and customers see them as a team. Darius and Alex are often on the road or at a customer work site, and Cheryl uses multiple forms of CMC to stay in touch with them. At times, she finds it challenging to communicate only using CMC and often feels the need for a face-to-face group meeting to discuss important customer concerns. She likes making decisions through group discussion and continues to consider how to best develop their sales team's efficiency and effectiveness through a combination of CMC and face-to-face meetings.

Group Communication

Group communication occurs in almost every aspect of our daily lives and through every medium that we use. For many of us, our primary group affiliation is a family. Next, we usually connect with friends. Participation in a neighborhood, school, or community group extends that experience beyond family and friends to hobby, sports, work, and social support groups over the course of our lifetime. Through participation in these groups, we

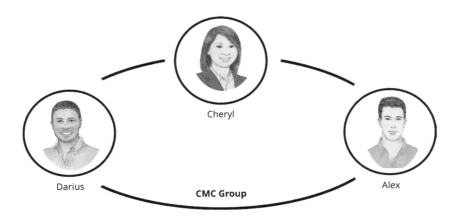

FIGURE 11.1 Cheryl, Darius, and Alex communicate using multiple forms of CMC

develop personal, relational, and professional networks of people and colleagues. These communication networks help us cope with important life decisions and challenges.

Group Size

Groups are networks of individuals who interact for a specific purpose and communicate with a particular style. Harris and Sherblom (2018) define small groups as having between three and 20 participants, who actively communicate with one another, depend on and influence each other, and share a common goal and sense of belonging. Group participants must agree on, and maintain, a common set of rules, standards, and understandings for effective interaction. This definition provides a starting point for discussing group communication.

Group size affects how participants communicate. Two people communicating as a couple often share a connection and understanding of unspoken communication that, at times, appears taken for granted. A couple forms this relationship through their interactions over time. Adding a third person creates a network of three relationships rather than one. This complicates the communication.

Groups of three or more people generally must communicate more explicitly and work at coordinating and managing a common meaning among participants through their verbal communication over time. When the group size exceeds 15 to 20 people, the communication patterns shift once again. The interactive style of interpersonal communication becomes increasingly difficult to maintain, and talk shifts toward more public, one-to-many forms of discourse (Harris & Sherblom, 2018).

Group Interdependence

A second important quality of a group is the sense of interdependence. A gathering of people becomes a group when they develop a shared pattern of relational communication over time. As participants communicate with each other, they begin to (a) identify as members of the group, (b) recognize each individual's abilities and contributions, and (c) share a sense of task interdependence and mutual influence. Through their communication processes, participants develop a sense of commonality around a shared purpose, a common set of goals, and a sense of mutual belonging to the group. Participants take on specialized roles, based on their perceived abilities to accomplish group goals, and they generally conform to a common set of norms, standards, customs, and traditions (Harris & Sherblom, 2018). Table 11.1 list these qualities of group communication.

TABLE 11.1 **Qualities of Group Communication**

SIZE	Three to approximately 20 people in a network of relationships
INTERDEPENDENCE	Mutual influence (recognize, respond to each other)
COMMONALITY	Shared purpose, common goals, mutual belonging, specialized roles
CONFORMITY	Norms, standards, customs, traditions

Managing CMC Work Groups

Many professional work groups today are dispersed geographically. They often consist of a global network of business professionals who have a variety of backgrounds and technical expertise. These networks frequently have few pre-established meeting routines and accomplish their tasks through multiple forms of CMC with little or no face-to-face communication. To be effective, they must combine the knowledge and expertise of the geographically dispersed members to engage in complex work projects that have specific organizational goals (DeRosa et al., 2004).

Working in these physically dispersed groups comes with both difficulties and advantages. Geographic distance and time zone differences mean that group participants perform much of their work independently and communicate their contributions asynchronously. This provides group members with task flexibility. They can work on their own schedules, with relative autonomy and greater independence than conventional office groups. At the same time, the lack of physical interaction in a traditional office workspace reduces the verbal, social, and status cues shared among members. In addition, differences in participant culture, language, and available technology can make group collaboration more difficult.

Furthermore, members also often join or leave these groups during a project according to the need for their expertise. This ability to join and leave a group increases the number of projects any one participant can work on simultaneously but poses a challenge for effective group leadership, supervision, and coordination of the project. Group facilitators must continually monitor member participation, provide feedback, resolve any potential conflicts, and balance member autonomy with the need for interdependent work on the project.

To be productive and meet their project goals, these groups use multiple forms of CMC media to communicate effectively. They often use a combination of texting, email, and social media platforms to achieve their goals. In addition, they use audio or video conferencing so members can ask questions, provide feedback, suggest new ideas, reflect on task progress, review unexpected outcomes, and learn new techniques (DeRosa et al., 2004).

Requirements of Effective Group Communication

Effective group communication that relies on CMC places demands on both the participants and the relationships in a group. Participants must demonstrate cognitive-linguistic-social competencies, self-efficacy, and confidence in communicating through a medium. Group relationships must express an authentic online identity, show social presence, and develop interpersonal trust through the medium.

Participant Competencies

Group CMC requires that participants possess a certain level of cognitive-linguistic-social competencies within a medium. These competencies include the ability of participants to express themselves, show attentiveness to others, and coordinate conversations so that they run smoothly and achieve some level of common understanding. Expressing oneself effectively in conversation relies on the ability to create a message that is easily interpreted and interesting to others. Attentiveness entails showing an interest, concern, affection for others, and willingness to adapt to one's communication style. Coordination means the ability to facilitate smooth transitions that help maintain the conversational flow and sustain the interpersonal relationships. Each of these take practice to achieve in a CMC medium. Participants often feel muted in their ability to be expressive, attentive, and conversationally coordinated in their CMC with others. The reduced nonverbal cues and delayed feedback of an asynchronous CMC medium can hinder the smooth flow of group communication (Bubas et al., 2003; Spitzberg, 2006).

In addition, group communication requires that participants show both self-efficacy and confidence in using the communication medium. Self-efficacy is a participant's ability to communicate effectively through a medium, expressing ideas and emotions in a sensitive way. Confidence is the feeling that one can both express oneself effectively and correctly interpret the meanings and feelings of others. Developing these competencies takes practice in CMC. Feeling self-efficacy in communicating without experiencing undue anxiety or inhibition requires experience with any new medium. Confidence comes with repeated use, experience, and conversational success using a CMC medium (Sherblom et al., 2018; Spitzberg, 2006).

The use of cell phones, social media, and other CMC platforms changes the nature of work group communication. It increases the number of different conversations and networked group interactions people can have in an average day. This changes the nature of relationships within the group, especially the ones formed through CMC (Erhardt et al., 2016; Sashi, 2021).

Relational Competencies

Group relationships also involve the communication of coherent online identities, social presence, and interpersonal trust. An online identity consists of both personal and social-relational components. Personal identity describes people's self-presentation, such as being a kind, helpful, wise, witty, or sarcastic person. This presentation of self becomes apparent through a person's screen name, pseudonym, consistently recognizable appearance, or attitude expressed in language use. How an individual habitually interacts, communicates, and participates with other members builds their social identity in the group. The combination of someone's personal and social identity connects the person to the group (Sherblom et al., 2018).

These relational communication behaviors result in a sense of social presence. Participants express their willingness to be present and engaged with each other through their use of CMC. Group members interpret a participant's responsiveness, involvement, distraction, or apparent preoccupation with other matters as an indication of the person's ability and willingness to interact with the group. Communicating social presence in an online environment includes engaging in self-disclosure and demonstrating an attentiveness, empathy, and rapport with others in a way that makes them feel valued in the communication relationship (Sherblom et al., 2018).

TABLE 11.2 **Requirements of Group Communication**

PARTICIPANT COMPETENCIES

Cognitive-linguistic-social	Ability to communicate effectively; ability to express ideas, emotions, be attentive to others, coordinate conversations
Personal self-efficacy	Communicate in a sensitive way without excessive anxiety, apprehension, or inhibition
Confidence with medium	Communicate effectively through medium; correctly interpret meanings, feelings of others

RELATIONAL COMPETENCIES

Online identities	Personal presentation of self appears in screen name, pseudonym, consistently recognizable appearance, attitudes expressed in group, and online reputation
Social presence	Relational pattern of communication behaviors, responsiveness, involvement, distraction, or apparent preoccupation with other matters
Interpersonal trust	Relational expectation that a person will treat you with respect and benevolence emerges in communication patterns and reputations, and develops more slowly in an anonymous, asynchronous, text-based CMC medium

Interpersonal trust emerges from these communication patterns as well. Trust is the expectation that another person will treat you with respect and benevolence. This trust often develops more slowly in an anonymous, asynchronous, text-based CMC medium but is equally important for maintaining effective group communication as it is in a face-to-face context. Effective communicators build trust through their consistent, specific, and frequent CMC responses to the comments and queries of other group members (Sherblom et al., 2018).

Table 11.2 lists the participant and relational competencies of group CMC. Each of these competencies influences the effectiveness of a CMC work group. Participant and relational competencies within the medium affect how the group communicates and the likelihood of achieving the project goals.

Summary: Facilitating Group Conversational Interaction

Together, these personal and relational competencies facilitate the conversational interaction of the group. This conversational interaction is essential to group formation, maintenance, and productivity. It builds the group communication expectations and norms for conversational turn taking, responsiveness, and feedback timeliness. Each of these affects both the group relationships and productivity.

In text-based CMC conversations, this interaction tends to be slower than in face-to-face conversations. When groups engage in face-to-face discussion, the speaking rate is relatively fast, with rapid turn taking, talk-overs, and interruptions as well as immediate verbal and nonverbal feedback. Members of the group can ask, answer, discuss, clarify, question, reconsider, and respond to each other quickly. In a text-based CMC conversation, group participants type and read slower than they speak and listen. Their turn taking is less rapid, and feedback is slower. Nonverbal cues are subdued, and conversation can become less like dialogue and more like sequential monologues as individuals express their opinions. Despite this, participant interactivity is important, and CMC groups frequently develop either informal or formal rules of interaction to facilitate this group interaction in CMC (Karimi et al., 2014; Sherblom et al., 2018).

Benefits of Group Participation

In addition to making demands on participants, groups also offer member benefits. These benefits exist in the network of connections that groups provide individual members. Through these networks, members are connected to others who may have different expertise, experience, and insights. These connections provide members access to social capital in the form of informational resources and emotional support. Both types of social capital are of value to group members.

Social Capital

Social capital is a resource embedded in the network of group relationships. It represents the investment of time and energy in group relationships and, in particular, the value of these relationships to an individual who may need to access them to solve a problem at a later date. Social capital is a collective network asset that develops in the group relationships through conversational interaction, discussion of topics, and task performance. It is gained and maintained through group participation, communication, and the development of interpersonal trust. The benefits of social capital only become available to group members who have invested time and effort in the relationships of the group (Burt, 1992; Lin, 1999).

By participating in a group, members have access to the informational and emotional resources of the other members who share their knowledge, experience, and expertise with the entire group. This generates an informational and emotional reservoir of social capital for the individual. If a group member needs help with a particular job, another group member might have the expertise to provide that assistance. If a group member is having a tough time at work, another group member might be able to provide guidance and emotional support for dealing with the issue. Both are examples of the informational and emotional resources of social capital (Green-Hamann & Sherblom, 2014; Leonardi et al., 2013; Lin, 1999).

Both weak-tie member acquaintance networks within the group and strong-tie friendship connections provide social capital to participants. The weak-tie acquaintance networks offer access to a wide variety of new and non-redundant information, ideas, advice, and social resources. The strong-tie friendship connections provide the potential for the emotional support of a few, close, personal friends. Access to these weak- and strong-tie networks provide advantages to the individual participants in the availability of informational and emotional social capital (Lin, 1999). Table 11.3 lists these characteristics of group networks that provide social capital in informational and emotional support.

TABLE 11.3 **Informational and Emotional Supportive Social Capital**

Informational Social Capital	Emotional Social Capital
Large network of many acquaintances	Small network of friends, close colleagues
Diverse perspectives, expertise, experiences	Similar background, experience, empathy
Weak-tie acquaintances	Strong-tie friendships
Informational resource	Emotional resource

Informational Social Capital

Individuals can meet a diverse set of acquaintances in any group of which they are a member. These acquaintances may share in the common group purpose, but they bring different types of information, perspectives, personal experiences, innovative ideas, alternative suggestions, and ways of approaching that purpose or common area of interest. These acquaintances form a relatively weak-tie network of connections among individuals who share diverse informational social capital. This network of numerous, relatively weak relationships provides an informational resource that is useful to the group and its participants. The network gives group members access to a wide variety of informational materials, opinions, suggestions, alternatives, and other available options that can be useful in handling a challenging issue. Weak-tie informational networks reduce risky decision-making and facilitate productive group solutions (Granovetter, 1983; Green-Hamann & Sherblom, 2014).

Emotional Social Capital

In addition to connecting with acquaintances, participants also create smaller close-tie networks of friends that can provide emotional social capital. These networks develop through group conversation, discussion, and sharing among participants who express an acceptance and appreciation of each other and who share similar interests, experiences, and views. A feeling of emotional support develops in the expressive action of their communication that facilitates further development of their relationship and feeling of interpersonal trust.

These emotionally supportive networks tend to be smaller, with fewer closer friends who share similar interests and offer relational support, understanding, and encouragement. Over time, these strong-tie connections lead to a relational bonding that generates a sense of shared personal validation and emotional well-being. As a result, participants develop a strong, positive sense of self, self-efficacy, and social presence with others in the group as they reciprocally offer and receive this emotional support. The emotional bonding that occurs through these strong-tie network connections increases feelings of trustworthiness, kindness, supportiveness, and credibility among members (Burt, 1992; Granovetter, 1983; Green-Hamann & Sherblom, 2014).

Figure 11.2 depicts a strong-tie, emotionally supportive network within a larger, weak-tie informational group network. The relationships in work groups often range from a weak-tie network of multiple acquaintances who can provide diverse pieces of useful

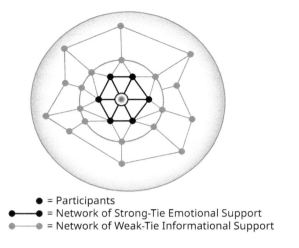

● = Participants
●——● = Network of Strong-Tie Emotional Support
●——● = Network of Weak-Tie Informational Support

FIGURE 11.2 Weak and Strong Tie Networks.

information to a few tightly connected and smaller networks of supportive colleagues. The larger informational network contains this subset of emotionally supportive relationships, and some relationships can provide both informational and emotional support social capital resources. For convenience, we illustrate this often-gradual progression of relationship closeness and support as two identifiable categories of informational and emotional support social capital.

Activating and Mobilizing Social Capital

The potential for informational and emotional social capital exists in an individual's network of relationships in the group. This network contains all the acquaintances, connections, and social contacts that a person has in the larger group. That network, however, represents only the potential informational and emotional social capital resources that are available through those relationships. To become useful as a social capital resource, this network of relationships must be cognitively activated and behaviorally mobilized. Activating and mobilizing this social capital, however, is more challenging than simply establishing and maintaining group relationships (Cao & Smith, 2021; Smith et al., 2012, 2020).

An activated network is the portion of potential connections that a person thinks might provide a useful social capital response to a particular type of need or achievement. Only a subset of the potential network of friends and acquaintances is relevant for any particular informational or emotional need that arises. For example, only certain people in a potential group network are useful to ask for a letter of recommendation. Other members of the network may be helpful with other types of personal assistance or professional advice, but not for a recommendation.

A behaviorally mobilized network is the subset of that cognitively activated network a person is willing to attempt to use for solving a problem or issue. Even if qualified, not everyone who comes to mind in the cognitively activated network is equally useful for a particular purpose. Not all letters of recommendation are equal. There may be five people in the network who could provide a letter of recommendation, but only two of them that an individual is willing to ask. This means that the social capital available to an individual for use in response to a particular event is dependent on a person's ability to activate and mobilize an informational and emotional support resource when needed (Cao & Smith, 2021; Smith et al., 2012).

Activating Social Capital

People maintain an active cognitive perception of their relationships within the group network. They develop beliefs and perceptions not only of their own personal relationships with others, but they also learn who has a connection, acquaintanceship, or close relationship with whom. This influences their activation of the network social capital when needed. A person may remember an interaction with someone in the past that stimulates or reduces the perceived social capital in the relationship with that person. Based on that experience, a person may feel apprehensive and mentally reject reaching out to the person or feel unsafe raising an issue within a portion of the network, such as management or the human resources office. Alternatively, an individual may expect a person or office to be receptive and helpful. In either case, an event activates only a portion of the potential social capital in the network, based on the perception of the relationships (Smith et al., 2012, 2020).

Mobilizing Social Capital

Activating the relevant portions of the potential network is a precondition to mobilizing social capital. The mobilized network represents a further subset of the activated resources. Mobilization is the relational activity of reaching out and interacting with someone in the network about a particular event of importance. It requires that people move beyond their cognitive perceptions to actively seek out responses from other network participants.

The success of the act of mobilization represents the social quality of the relationships in the network. People's perceptions of the individual's social status and value to the group influence their responses to the request for assistance. Thus, the individual's ability to mobilize the social capital in their network is affected by their personal abilities, qualifications, qualities, and demeanor. In addition, socially constructed attributes, such as their group status, socio-economic class, race, ethnicity, and gender, also affect the individual's ability to mobilize that social capital (Cao & Smith, 2021; Smith et al., 2012, 2020).

Figure 11.3 illustrates the availability of informational and emotional support as only one dimension of social capital in a group network. Activating and mobilizing add layers in a second dimension of that social capital. This second dimension varies with the status of a member within the group.

Applying Social Capital: Mobilizing Social Capital in an Online Group

To better understand how social status affects a person's ability to mobilize social capital in an online community, Cao and Smith (2021) examined how social status impacts

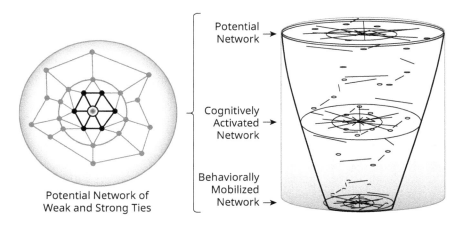

Potential Network

Cognitively Activated Network

Behaviorally Mobilized Network

Potential Network of Weak and Strong Ties

FIGURE 11.3 Activated and Mobilized Networks Form Subsets of Available Social Capital.

people's ability and desire to seek advice in an online group. They conducted multiple experiments involving online interactions. Participants were placed in online groups where they created usernames and then interacted anonymously to complete a series of tasks together. Although participants were told they were interacting with other humans, unknown to them, the other five members of their group were actually computer-generated bots. Participants could interact with these bots to gather specific types of information and expertise useful to completing the task.

Each participant received the title of either master or junior task worker within the group. Their perception of this high or low status in the group affected their advice-seeking behavior during the task. Participants assigned the title of master worker requested help more frequently when they experienced task difficulties. Their perceived high-status positively disposed them to seek assistance from their relatively unknown acquaintances in the newly formed group. The primary deterrent for the junior task worker participants to seeking help was their perception of a potentially negative response to their request because of their lower social status. Cao and Smith (2021) conclude that when faced with a task challenge, participant status within a group affects people's ability to mobilize the social capital benefits of the network relationships.

Mobilizing Social Capital After a Corporate Merger

Woehler et al. (2021) studied a similar real-world effect by examining the behavior of high-ranking employees responding to organizational uncertainty after a corporate merger. They analyzed more than 15 million emails sent between employees over the course of a 2-year period following a corporate merger. The upheaval created by the merger created uncertainty for the employees of the newly formed organization, as noted in their emails.

The perceived power of employees in the organization, as measured by job title and informal status, affected how they used email. Employees with high formal status were more likely to feel job-related demands to forge connections across the newly merged organizations. Their positions required more information throughout the merger process to manage the integration processes, challenges, and changes. Organizational pressures provided an impetus to widen their networks and gain the resources necessary to implement a successful merger.

Employees with high informal status showed a different motivation to broaden their social networks. Their email use demonstrated the perception of a positive relationship between their status in the network, the quality of their work, and their worth to the organization. These high-status employees expressed more optimism, spontaneity, active communication, and confidence when approaching others to seek or offer advice and assistance. They exerted a personal agency, reaching out and communicating more often with their new coworkers during the post-merger integration.

These results indicate a strong relationship between people's beliefs about their status in the network and their communication behaviors providing and receiving informational and emotional social capital during and after a corporate merger. Participant perceptions about their personal worth and place within the network of a new, emerging set of corporate relationships affect their communication decisions about making an offer or request for the social capital resources available in the network.

Six Rules for Effective CMC Work Groups

Walther and Bunz (2005) provide six rules that can help CMC group participants be more productive. These rules encourage communicative dialogue, constructive conflict, and the co-construction of meaning within a group. They facilitate group communication habits that promote strong informational and emotional support networks in relationships.

Rule 1: Start as Soon as Possible

Groups often procrastinate, not fully engaging in gathering information and accomplishing the task until deadlines are looming. This is often a concern for face-to-face work groups but can pose an even bigger problem for CMC groups, particularly those using asynchronous communication. Asynchronous exchanges in CMC take longer. Time delays between message exchanges can slow the group communication process. Successful CMC groups must begin their work quickly. Groups that do not get started right away may not have sufficient time to discuss information and meet deadlines.

Rule 2: Communicate Frequently

Trust is an important aspect of group work. Asynchronous communication, visual anonymity, and a lack of geographic proximity can reduce that sense of trust. Frequent communication builds relational trust and helps participants stay abreast of the group progress. It stimulates member participation as well. Hearing what others have accomplished inspires group members to work on the project. Groups that lack trust have a more difficult time achieving a common understanding, scheduling activities, and meeting deadlines. Frequent communication among members builds trust.

Rule 3: Multitask

Face-to-face groups often begin by organizing the process, defining goals, and allocating chores to specific members before engaging in the actual work of retrieving information and accomplishing the task. This approach increases efficiency of effort by reducing unnecessary work and redundant efforts. In CMC groups, however, this takes too long to be efficient. Working in a careful linear, sequential manner may take too much time to allow for the collaborative discussion necessary for a successful project. Not all tasks need to be fully planned out before beginning. The need to accomplish tasks earlier in the process is more important. Even if this leads to a duplication of effort, this can actually produce beneficial results such as recognizing alternative perspectives. Begin working on tasks immediately rather than negotiating all the details first. Simultaneous discussion and presentation of early results can build group trust and social presence.

Rule 4: Let Others Know You Have Read Their Messages

Participants in face-to-face groups use nonverbal facial expressions, head nodding, attentive body posture, and other forms of informal verbal feedback to indicate they have received and understood a message. For visually anonymous CMC groups that communicate asynchronously, knowing whether others have received and read a message is difficult. It is easy to assume common knowledge within a group, even when it does not exist. A distribution error or receiver neglect may create a lack of information for some group members. Explicitly showing reception and support for a message with a short response can enhance the group communication process.

Rule 5: Be Explicit About Thoughts, Ideas, and Activities

Even in a videoconference, group members may miss the visual feedback of head nods, facial frowns, and surprised expressions. It can be difficult to know if others agree, disagree, or wish to modify a proposal unless they state that verbally. When members of a CMC group are quiet and do not explicitly state agreement or disagreement with a statement or proposal, a group does not know if it has achieved a common agreement. A group may move forward in its discussion, falsely assuming agreement, or it may hesitate unnecessarily, waiting to arrive at consensus. Recognize that different members of the group may respond differently to the social capital available in the group relationships. Therefore, being supportive and explicitly encouraging other group members to offer and request informational and emotional support helps group success. Explicit verbal feedback allows the group to move forward with further discussion, decision-making, and effective action.

Rule 6: Set Deadlines and Adhere to Them

Participants often experience greater uncertainty and perceive less accountability in CMC groups than in a face-to-face meeting. The asynchronous communication, geographic distance, and lack of physical contact among group members can make it difficult to know what others are doing. Setting specific deadlines, assigning members explicit tasks, and

TABLE 11.4 Virtual Group Communication Participation Rules

1.	Start as soon as possible.
2.	Communication frequently.
3.	Multitask: Organize group activities and work simultaneously.
4.	Let others know you have read their messages.
5.	Be explicit about thoughts, ideas, and activities.
6.	Set deadlines and adhere to them.

eliciting agreement to accomplishing those tasks can reduce interpersonal uncertainty and increase relational trust. When members successfully complete assigned tasks early on in the group process, participants gain interpersonal trust and develop a sense of accountability to each other. Demonstrated trustworthiness and perceived commitment to the group facilitates group satisfaction. Table 11.4 lists these six rules.

Perspective in Context

Analysis and Critique

Analyses of group networks and social capital often provide just a snapshot of their communication interaction. This can be insightful but does not account for changes in group communication patterns over time. Newly formed groups do not have the established communication patterns, reputations, and common understandings of groups with more history. These zero-history groups generally do not have a system for learning, storing, and retrieving social capital that is commonly shared by the members of the group. Nor do they have the communication habits of complementary participation based on recognized member knowledge, expertise, and proficiency. Both of these group characteristics can affect the social capital that members are able to activate and mobilize when in need of information or emotional support. For example, participants who offer informational support early in a group discussion and receive positive feedback are more likely to provide additional information in the future, which is beneficial to the group accumulation of social capital.

The six group rules are probably most useful for newly formed, zero-history groups. Experienced work groups, for better or worse, have developed communication patterns relying on particular member expertise, knowledge, work habits, and task proficiency. Other approaches, such as theories of group memory, do a better job of predicting these group learning processes (Littlepage et al., 2008).

Many groups use multiple forms of CMC to accomplish their tasks. Some forms may facilitate informational or emotional support more than others. Recent analyses by Cao and Smith (2021) and Woehler et al. (2021) suggest there is a communication medium–social support interaction. It would be interesting to know if group participants are more likely to provide each other informational support in one medium, such as email, while simultaneously offering emotional support to each other through another, such as social media. Many work groups use texting, emails, videoconferencing, social media, and occasional face-to-face meetings to communicate. Describing the informational and emotional support social capital sharing of these groups across the multiple CMC platforms and occasional face-to-face meetings is important to fully understand their communication patterns.

Computer-Mediated Groups in Practice: Online Health Care Advice

Does flossing really help prevent tooth decay? Should I get the flu shot this year, or is that just for old people? Does frequent handwashing prevent illness or just chap my hands? People often turn to relatively anonymous online group networks to answer questions such as these and get personal health care advice.

Saran et al. (2018) analyzed the effects of this type of anonymous advice on the decision-making behavior of 679 participants. The participants played a computer game in which they made a series of personal health care decisions. Each session of the game ran through 15 rounds of decision-making. Each round required a participant to make a decision about a common health care issue, including personal hygiene and annual vaccination shots. Participants then saw the consequence of their personal choice, based on statistical averages. Participants earned $10 in each round that they stayed healthy. They received no money if they fell ill. Choosing a preventive health care measure reduced their probability of falling ill but costs them $1.

The game ran through three sessions. In the first two sessions of the game, participants made independent personal health care decisions. For the third session, researchers randomly assigned participants to an anonymous virtual group of four people. Participants could share their personal decisions and the health consequences with the other group members. In this study, participants exchanged 2,806 messages within these groups; approximately 70% of their messages contained information about current or previous health care decisions and the consequences.

Results show that participants are more likely to communicate when they choose a preventative health measure than when they do not. In addition, participants tend to adopt the prevention choices suggested by the other group members. They give less weight to whether the adoption of the prevention or the decision to take a risk and not opt for the prevention was successful in preventing illness.

In summary, participants are significantly more likely to select a preventive measure when they receive a message from one of their group members about choosing that health care measure, regardless of that member's explicitly stated outcome experience. They are less likely to choose a preventative measure when others in their group report not choosing it, regardless of the consequences of that choice. The participants appear to rely on the perception of social capital embedded in the informational relationships they have with the three other anonymous group members, with whom they have no relational history.

Illustration of Concepts

Cheryl, Darius, and Alex form a professional work group network that consists of informational and emotional support ties. Cheryl has the most experience with carpeting and floor coverings. Darius knows office furniture. Alex is more knowledgeable about lighting. Together they form a professional group with the necessary expertise and product information to achieve their product sales objectives. Each relies on the others for expert advice and accurate, detailed, and complete information on their product lines. This represents the informational social capital of the group.

They are also friends. When Alex and Darius are out of the office traveling, they primarily use texts or email to communicate with each other, Cheryl, their customers, and suppliers. They also meet face-to-face on a weekly basis to discuss business. Before and after these meetings, they tell jokes, talk about their families, and share personal stories, strengthening their strong-tie emotional bonding connections. The emotional support expressed in these meetings facilitates the openness of their informational exchanges through CMC the rest of the week.

In addition, they are connected to the employees of the Home Products store, Pam, Jasmine, and Sean. They exchange information about products and logistics with them. Pam and Cheryl are also relatively close friends and rely on each other for emotional support when needed. They reach out to each other when they have nonwork-related challenges as well. Figure 11.4 illustrates their activated and mobilized informational and emotional support networks.

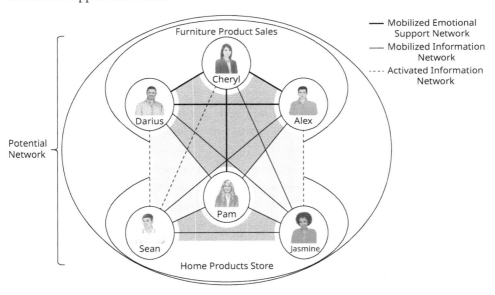

FIGURE 11.4 Activated Informational and Emotional Support Networks.

Looking Forward to CMC Communities

CMC communities have many of the same qualities as groups but tend to be larger and more immersive in participation. Connecting, belonging, sharing, and immersion are the communication characteristics of CMC communities. We discuss these characteristics in the next chapter.

Participation and Social Loafing in a Virtual Group

Working together using CMC can be complicated. When some members do not contribute much to the group conversation, they may be accused of social loafing. Social loafing describes a perceived lack of contribution of a member to the group's goals. This perception may cause other members to feel that they are being unfairly required to contribute more time and energy to accomplish the shared group task. This can reduce the informational and emotional supportiveness of a communication network and decrease the productivity of a task-oriented work group.

Social loafing occurs in face-to-face groups too, but it is a particular concern for virtual groups and networks. When group members communicate only using CMC, particularly text- or audio-based platforms, they lack a physical presence and have a perceived visual anonymity. This may allow some members to be less invested in the group task and related conversations, focusing their energies on other activities and only contributing occasionally to the shared group conversation. Other group members, however, may feel less competent about the task at hand, or be less comfortable about working in groups, and be reticent to contribute to the conversation.

The perceived unfairness of social loafing can reduce a group's cohesion and task performance. Effective communication networks and task groups must solicit full member participation in decision-making, as this helps to clarify group goals and accomplish tasks. Whose communication responsibility is it to develop group cohesion, enhance productivity, and reduce social loafing?

1. How is the responsibility of achieving open and relatively equal communication among participants shared by the group members? Can a group function well without a facilitator or leader?

2. Does a group member who experiences communication apprehension, reticence, or anxiety about the group task have a responsibility to make an effort to contribute equally to the group conversation?

3. Do members who feel more communication competence working in groups through the medium have more responsibility for the communication process?

4. How should a virtual group effectively negotiate issues of perceived social loafing within the group communication?

KEYWORDS AND PHRASES

Activated network is the portion of potential connections that a person thinks might provide a useful social capital response to a particular type of need or achievement.

A **behaviorally mobilized network** is the subset of that cognitively activated network a person is willing to attempt to use for solving a problem or issue.

Emotional social capital refers to emotional support that generates a sense of shared personal validation and emotional well-being.

Groups are networks of individuals who interact for a specific purpose and communicate with a particular style. They usually have between three and 20 participants.

Informational social capital refers to different types of information, perspectives, personal experiences, innovative ideas, alternative suggestions, and ways of approaching an issue.

Interdependence refers to the development of a shared pattern of relational communication over time. As participants communicate with each other, they begin to (a) identify as members of the group, (b) recognize each individual's abilities and contributions, and (c) share a sense of task interdependence and mutual influence.

Social capital is a resource embedded in the network of group relationships. It is a collective asset that develops in the group relationships and includes the informational and emotional resources of the other members.

Strong-tie friendship connections provide the potential for the emotional support of a few, close, personal friends.

Weak-tie acquaintance networks offer access to a wide variety of new and non-redundant information, ideas, advice, and social resources.

QUESTIONS FOR FURTHER DISCUSSION

1. Look at your online networks of acquaintances, friends, and family members. Would you consider most of them to be weak-tie informational, strong-tie emotionally supportive relationships, or both? Why?

2. Do you think that having a large, virtual network of friends and acquaintances could be more helpful for certain types of things, such as searching for a new job, than having a physical network of friends and acquaintances? Why? What about when you need emotional support?

3. Consider your online networks again. Imagine you had a question about finding an internship. Which part of your network would you activate? Which part would you mobilize? What if you had a question about a fight you had with a friend?

4. Have you ever worked in a virtual group? Describe the experience.

5. Which of the virtual group rules do you think are the most important? Are there any that you think are not important? Explain why.

12

Communities

Cheryl identifies as a member of several professional communities. She enjoys working with Darius and Alex and frequently interacts with Sean, Pam, and Jasmine. She belongs to a larger community of commercial furniture professionals, as well. She shares a set of professional values, interests, and experiences with the members of this community. She knows who can provide informational support and whom she can trust for confidential emotional support, when needed. This sense of community with coworkers, clients, and professional colleagues helps Cheryl achieve both her personal and professional goals.

Conceptualizing Community

Communities are "ways of being together" (Willson, 2006, p. 85). They represent a sense of shared values, characteristics, and commonalities among members. Common qualities are a sense of social interaction, sociability, solidarity, shared identity, shared

FIGURE 12.1 Professional Video Conference.

stories, and emotional connection among members. Community members generally experience a sense of belonging and attachment to one another and a feeling of being involved together in events of common importance. These feelings of belonging, attachment, and involvement both arise from, and give rise to, people behaving as members of a community (Blanchard & Markus, 2004; Gruzd et al., 2011; McMillan, 1996; Willson, 2006).

In the past, the idea of community implied a shared geographic location. In these place-based communities, members depended on one another to survive and prosper. The commonality of location and perceived destiny formed the foundation for a community. In recent years, however, it has become clear that sharing a geographical location is not the defining characteristic of community. Physical proximity alone is not sufficient. For a neighborhood to form a community, for instance, the people living there must perceive and perform interdependent functions that provide each member a sense of social, emotional, and economic support. In addition, communities can form around other types of shared interests and commonalities as well (Blanchard & Markus, 2004; Farahani, 2016; Jordan, 2005).

A Social Communitarian Perspective on Community

Willson (2006) uses a social communitarian perspective to define a community as an underlying connection between and among people bonded together by common processes of culture, emotion, and values. Four criteria underlie this social communitarian definition of community. The first is the need for social interaction, or sociability. This shapes members' identities as well as the community as a whole. Second is a set of shared conceptions of what constitutes a "good life" as expressed through members' ethics and worldviews (p. 120). The third criteria is made up of the shared norms and practices that members enact and incorporate into the structure of the community. Finally, the fourth is a sense of reciprocity between the community and its members. The community provides the members with benefits, and in turn members have recognizable obligations and responsibilities within the community. Table 12.1 lists these four social communitarian criteria of community.

TABLE 12.1   **Social Communitarian Criteria for Community**

SOCIABILITY	The social interaction shapes members' individual identities as well as of the community as a whole.
SHARED ETHICS, VALUES	A common conception of what constitutes a good life as expressed through a shared set of ethics, values, and worldviews.
COMMON NORMS, PRACTICES	Members enact and incorporate a common set of norms and practices into the structure of the community.
RECIPROCITY OF MEMBERS	Community provides member benefits. Members have responsibilities to community, building reciprocity between community and members.

A Sense of Community

Virtual communities differ from geographically located, place-based ones but have many of the same characteristics. Rather than being placed based, what draws people into these virtual communities is a set of common interests, relational interactions, or social ties. Virtual communities refer to gatherings of people who use CMC to interact and develop relationships. This means that most virtual communities are relational in nature and not bound by the physical proximity of members. People join and participate in a virtual community because of a common interest, life experience, or set of values. Participants may share a craft, hobby, political orientation, religious faith, social support group, or fan club interest (Koh & Kim, 2004).

As a result, most virtual communities form through participant choice. They often are self-organizing and informal. They may have a leader, or a hierarchical structure, but the fact that these virtual communities are the result of member choice often renders these virtual communities more ephemeral. Individual participants have more say over when and how they want to participate in a virtual community and on setting the boundaries of whom to include or exclude from that community. Members can create, sustain, or abandon a virtual community with relative ease as well. The ability of participants to transition easily to a new community that better meets their needs also makes membership less predictable, however, and often less sustainable over time (Jiménez et al., 2010; Song, 2009; Wellman, 2001; Willson, 2006).

Belonging, Sharing, and Immersion

Virtual communities differ from geographically placed-based ones, but the sense of community among members remains much the same. Several CMC scholars seek to describe this sense. Koh and Kim (2004) conceptualize the sense of virtual community as the dimensions of membership, influence, and immersion. Blanchard and Markus (2004) describe the sense of virtual community as an experience of support, identification, emotional connection, and trust. Both of these perspectives indicate that a sense of community is more than a relational connection. Community, whether physical or virtual, requires a sense of membership and belonging, enhanced by a mutual influence and the sharing of identities, as well as an immersive emotional engagement among participants.

Belonging

Koh and Kim (2004) describe membership as the sense of belonging to a virtual community. This sense of belonging is more than simply connecting to other people. It is also a recognition of community boundaries and sense of belonging to, identification with, and involvement in a common system of symbols, values, and norms. This sense of belonging and identification develops through interpersonal discussion, exchange of personal experiences, and feeling of support by the other members (Blanchard & Markus, 2004). Participation is a necessary component (Milton et al., 2023).

Sharing

Koh and Kim (2004) add a second dimension to the sense of virtual community, namely influencing other members and the community at large through the sharing of personal ideas, beliefs, and experiences. This sharing builds on the sense of belonging and adds a sense of recognition and influence. Participants must feel that others recognize them as a member of the community and are willing to respond to them. This process of recognition and response creates an interaction through which participants can influence each other and make a difference in the community.

Virtual community members create identities for themselves through their posts. They develop an understanding of other members through their responses. This reciprocal process of member identification goes beyond recognizing names to anticipating the responses others will provide to particular topics, issues, and posts (Blanchard & Markus, 2004). Milton et al. (2023) report that their respondents describe this type of interaction as increasing the sense of belonging to the virtual community, helping participants feel seen and not alone in their sharing of experiences and interests with like-minded people.

Immersion

Koh and Kim (2004) describe the third dimension of virtual community as immersion. This is what happens when people feel involved in and absorbed into a community. Immersion builds on belonging and sharing as an emergent quality, providing a sense of holistic involvement, participation, absorption, and flow within the experience of the virtual community. Blanchard and Markus (2004) find this immersion in the shared emotional connections and development of trust among participants. Their respondents report that the feelings of relationship and friendship developed through sharing personal histories and the exchange of informational and socio-emotional support are important contributors. Developing meaningful personal relationships with other members over time produces interpersonal trust and reinforces the sense of virtual community. Milton et al. (2023) report that their respondents view participation, engagement, shared experience, and expression of feelings of support as important contributors to their sense of community as well.

Summary: Belonging, Sharing, Immersion

A sense of virtual community requires more than connecting to participants online or being together in a virtual space. Feelings of belonging, sharing, and immersion are important to that sense of community. Participants can, and often do, experience the sense of belonging, sharing, influence, identification, and shared emotional support within a virtual community. Actively engaging in an online community and feeling a reciprocity with others in thought and emotion can produce the sense of community immersion and flow, yet not all online gatherings facilitate this experience to the same degree (Blanchard, 2007; Blanchard & Markus, 2004; Ch'ng, 2015; Koh & Kim, 2004). Table 12.2 summarizes this sense of virtual community.

TABLE 12.2 **Sense of Virtual Community**

CONNECTING	Necessary, but not sufficient to create sense of virtual community
BELONGING	Recognized boundaries, membership, who belongs (and who doesn't), identification with other members and the community as a whole
(Koh & Kim, 2004)	More than connecting, membership, sense of belonging
(Blanchard & Markus, 2004)	Boundaries, membership, belonging, identification, investment in common set of symbols, values, norms, personal experiences, support
SHARING	Mutual influence among members, community influence on members
(Koh & Kim, 2004)	Influential interactions, recognition, and response as community members, ability to influence others, make a difference in community
(Blanchard & Markus, 2004)	Sharing identities through posts, responses, beyond recognizing names, anticipating responses to posts, topics, issues
IMMERSION	Emotional bonds shared through conversation, personal investment, social interaction, feeling that community meets needs
(Koh & Kim, 2004)	Emergent, holistic quality, sense of involvement, absorption, experience of community flow
(Blanchard & Markus, 2004)	Emotional connection, trust, relationships, friendships developed over time through information exchange, shared history, emotional support

Networked Individualism, Settlements, and Permeable Communities

Not all online gatherings of individuals form virtual communities. Individuals use CMC to connect and develop a sense of belonging, sharing, and engaging in relationships with others online in a variety of ways. Networked individualism, virtual settlements, permeable communities, and virtual communities form a rough continuum that describes how the different ways connections and relationships can form in online environments.

Networked Individualism

The combination of high-speed internet access, mobile connectivity, and multiple types of social media sites create an environment in which people do not need to connect to a specific community for informational and emotional support. Technology connects individuals to a myriad of fragmented, often disconnected, personal networks. These network clusters can change constantly, based on the time constraints, needs, and immediate interests of the individual involved. Networked individualism recognizes that many people use the internet to find information, emotional support, and a sense of connection to like-minded others.

Unlike communities to which members belong, networked individuals are just people who connect to each other to meet immediate personal needs, not to share a sense of belonging in a membership with a common set of goals, values, and identities. The members of a person's network often know each other only vaguely, if at all. However, being the center of one's own unique network can provide a valuable resource for problem solving, as well as a sense of control, and even intimacy. These networked connections make a wide and diverse variety of informational and emotional resources available to an individual, which allows a person to reach outside the bounds of a tight social circle or community to experience multiple, different perspectives, interests, and ways of thinking (Komito, 2011; Quan-Haase et al., 2018; Rainie & Wellman, 2019).

Although networked individualism provides connectivity to a large and diverse collection of people, it does not preclude the existence of virtual communities or render them obsolete. In fact, the connectivity provided by networked individualism can, and often does, lead to virtual settlements, and even the creation of communities. Over time, people can forge connections between their personal networks, creating a space for sharing and a sense of community in the process. In a virtual settlement, participants can begin developing a sense of relational trust and affective bonds that are missing from networked individualism. Virtual communities build on these sentiments to provide the sense of membership boundaries, participant belonging, identification sharing, and reciprocal engagement indicative of virtual communities (Gruzd, et al., 2011; Milton et al., 2023; Rainie & Wellman, 2019).

Virtual Settlements

Virtual settlements describe shared online spaces where participants interact with a variety of other people over time. These virtual settlements exist in online spaces where messages, public comments, active membership, and continuity of participation develop into a sustainable form of CMC. Continued participation in these spaces, over time, with the same group of participants, is what distinguishes these virtual settlements from networked individualism. Not all of these settlements become virtual communities. Only those settlements in which members develop affective bonds qualify as communities (Blanchard & Markus, 2004; Jones, 1997).

A virtual settlement becomes a community when its participants begin sharing emotional bonds and develop a shared sense of community. This goes beyond the feeling of connection among participants to a sense that members matter to each other and the group and share a commitment to information sharing, social interaction, and companionship. Participants enjoy being together and share a sense of belonging to a community (Blanchard & Markus, 2004; Blight et al., 2017; Gruzd, et al., 2011; Jones, 1997; Milton et al., 2023).

Permeable Communities

The word *community* describes a quality of having something in common. This quality can be the ownership of physical goods, an interest, a social interaction, or an emotional bonding. Virtual communities vary in the commonality of this quality shared among participants. The dimensions of profitability, regulation, and permeability affect this sense of commonality (Plant, 2004).

The first dimension is profitability. There are some for-profit virtual communities, placed behind firewalls and accessed only by user subscription, ID, and password. These often are located within a large organization or a professional association. These for-profit business communities of practice provide participants a place to engage in private, member-only, business-to-business transactions. In these communities, professionals with complimentary backgrounds or expertise can meet, share ideas, form partnerships, and engage in cooperative business ventures.

A second dimension is the regulation and control of the information within a virtual community. Nonprofit and not-for-profit educational, research, development, and community outreach organizations often use social media sites as a location to host moderated discussions on specific topics, such as physical or mental health concerns. Hospitals or community health organizations support, manage, and regulate the topic and informational content on these virtual community sites. The virtual community that forms may be open to any interested participant or only by invitation, but in either case the health services organization facilitates, guides, and manages the information and discussion.

A third dimension, and perhaps the most important influence, is the permeability of a virtual community. Permeability describes the openness of a virtual community to membership and control of discussion topics. A permeable community is open and allows anyone who wishes to join or simply access its content. Participants can voice their opinions and feelings or just listen and observe. Alternatively, a community can be non-permeable, closed, private, and open only to those invited to participate. A leader may guide and facilitate the discussion with a prescribed set of rules (Milton et al., 2023; Plant, 2004).

The more permeable a community is, the less clearly defined its boundaries and the more transparent the discussion to outsiders. This permeability allows the presence of lurkers, which can challenge the very sense of virtual community itself. Permeable communities can become less stable but often still provide a sense of belonging and support to participants (Milton et al., 2023; Plant, 2004).

In addition, these virtual communities can change over time. An open, unregulated community may come into existence when a set of participants begin interacting on a common site or social media location. If the interaction on the site is of interest to others, the community may evolve and grow in the number of active participants. It is likely to either then fracture into multiple, smaller, unregulated communities or move to a more regulated environment with a facilitator and rules of conduct.

Permeable boundaries and the degree of openness in sharing is a concern for many virtual community participants. Milton et al. (2023) report that although their respondents all acknowledge the importance of their mental health discussions on TikTok, only some view these discussions as occurring within a virtual community. Others acknowledge TikTok as a place to connect to mental health discussion topics but do not view it as a virtual community. The difference in opinion stems from a person's perspective on the permeability, or loose discussion boundaries that allow ease of access to their content, which is outside of a participant's control and preferences.

Participants who perceive a sense of community in these TikTok mental health discussions describe more than a connection to others. They discuss their sense of belonging and feeling seen and understood by others who are like-minded and who share similar interests. This sense of belonging to a community facilitates a sense of social support for self-discovery and the development of mutual understanding through discussion.

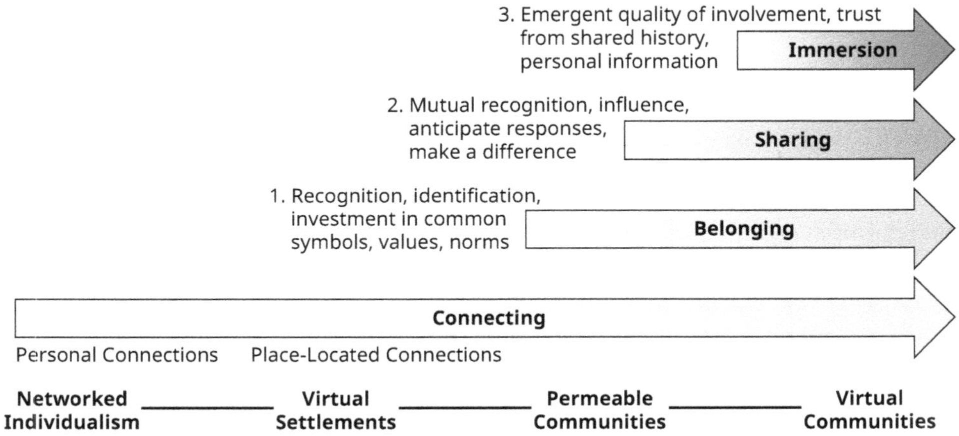

3. Emergent quality of involvement, trust
from shared history,
personal information — **Immersion**

2. Mutual recognition, influence,
anticipate responses,
make a difference — **Sharing**

1. Recognition, identification,
investment in common
symbols, values, norms — **Belonging**

Connecting

Personal Connections   Place-Located Connections

Networked _____ **Virtual** _____ **Permeable** _____ **Virtual**
Individualism   **Settlements**   **Communities**   **Communities**

FIGURE 12.2 Connecting, Belonging, Sharing, and Immersion in a Virtual Community.

Participants who question the sense of community cite the permeability of the platform structure that allows lurking and voyeurism and the inability to question misinformation as diminishing their feelings. The permeability of community boundaries and accessibility to silent lurking audiences reduces the participant sense of belonging, trust in sharing, feeling of mutual influence, and ability to engage in truly reciprocal relationships (Milton et al., 2023).

Figure 12.2 illustrates the continuum of connection among participants in online spaces and the features that characterize a virtual community. Personal connections are an indication of networked individualism. Virtual settlements form when connected individuals are co-located in the same online space. Permeable communities form as participants begin to recognize each other; invest in common symbols, values, and norms; and feel a sense of belonging. As that sense of belonging grows with mutual recognition, influence, anticipated responses, and sharing in a way that makes a difference, a sense of virtual community grows. Eventually, participants feel a sense of immersion in the virtual community from a sharing of history, personal information, involvement, and trust in others. Figure 12.2 illustrates this multistep process.

Virtual Communities: Personal Narratives

Virtual communities are communication spaces in which participants can continually shape and transform their own and each other's identities and relationships. Participants often do this by sharing personal narratives. These personal narratives place conversation at the center of the ongoing relational communication processes out of which communities emerge. The sharing of personal narratives in conversation with others provides the meaning base through which relationships develop. Over time, these relationships form the virtual community, built on the personal narratives shared by multiple participants, across multiple conversations (Orgad, 2005).

Through these multiple conversations, participants engage in simultaneous relationships that build the virtual community. The personal narratives exchanged within these conversations help participants explore their own personal identities, connect with the experiences of others, achieve a sense of closure with personal issues, and engage in meaningful social processes. A virtual community not only provides a space for sharing these authentic personal narratives with supportive others who have similar thoughts, experiences, and emotions, but emerges out of this sharing. The private–public nature of these conversations can transform the meanings and identities held by the individual participants, the virtual community as a whole, and the larger, dominant, society-wide narratives as well.

The creation of a virtual community through storytelling is especially important to people who feel isolated, are part of a minority group, and are unlikely to have otherwise found each other. This is especially true for those communities of people who are isolated from other social contact due to, for example, severe illness. These communities of relationships build on the sharing of personal experiences to produce experiential knowledge valued by the community members. When centered on a specific experience, such as an illness or a health-related experience, these personal narratives form virtual communities of experience (Akrich, 2010; Orgad, 2005).

Advantages and Challenges of Virtual Communities

Accessibility

Virtual communities have several advantages over physically located communities. The available bandwidth and interconnectivity provided by the Internet, social media, and cell phone technologies allow users to communicate through text, voice, and video and to provide feedback almost instantaneously across long distances, with a global audience, 24 hours a day, 7 days a week. A local community center may only be open 3 to 5 days a week. A physical library may close at 9:00 p.m. every night. A virtual community, especially an unmoderated one, may be available whenever an individual desires or needs it.

The mobile portability of cell phones and tablets further increases the accessibility of a virtual community to the average person. Personalized messages, information, and newsfeeds tailored to a person's individual interests, preferences, needs, and desires further promotes awareness of like-minded communities of people. Interconnectivity, portability, and personalization work together to increase the functional accessibility of virtual communities (Wellman et al., 2003).

Participant-Driven Community Practices

Participants often shape their virtual communities. On platforms that do not provide formalized structures for community building, such as Facebook, users form interest groups to create communities. In other forms of CMC, people can use symbols such as hashtags to create a sense of virtual community. The hashtag, first popularized on Twitter (now known as X), facilitates the formation of virtual communities on many social media sites by providing a symbolic space in which people can connect, interact, and receive emotional support (Berry et al., 2017; Lee & Lee, 2023).

When platforms ban specific hashtags, for safety or health concerns, users often resort to using misspelled versions of the banned words to connect with others (substituting *anorexiaa* for *anorexia*, for example, in a pro-eating disorder community). The production and recognition of their post by others shows that they are part of a larger community of users. This indicates not only a desire of users to connect and find support, but also their ability to use the features of social media platforms to create and maintain communities of interest (Chancellor et al., 2016).

Likes, Shares, Comments, and Online Leadership

Likes, shares, and comments are another popular way to create communities in online spaces. These features allow users to recognize other like-minded individuals and connect with them. With the rising popularity of video-based platforms, such as TikTok, online users increasingly rely on the use of the "stitch" and "duet" feature to respond and connect with other posts, creating affect-based communities (Lee & Lee, 2023).

Users can also restrict their virtual community. Some social media users actively control who sees which posts. This allows them to be more open when it comes sharing personal narratives with a more select virtual community of friends. Not all of their friends or followers see these posts (Petersen et al., 2020).

In addition, many virtual communities have one or more informal leaders whose comments and contributions are more influential than those of other community members. Their posts receive more attention and more feedback. Their ideas are more likely to affect community norms. These individuals may be social influencers or simply people perceived as experts on a particular topic. Communities often form around such individuals, rendering the virtual community less group centered and more focused on an individual network (Gruzd et al., 2011; Vicari, 2021).

Lurking: Challenge or Advantage?

Active participation helps to create the relationships that form the sense of virtual community. This means that online participants must work together to create the shared sense of belonging, support, social identity, norms, and values. Members need to be active participants rather than just show up to create that sense of community (Wellman, 2001; Zhong & Frey, 2022).

Many online spaces, however, allow people to engage in lurking and merely observe what others do and not actively participate in the community by posting or commenting. In some virtual communities, the majority of members are said to be lurkers. In many virtual communities, users are mostly anonymous, posts and conversations are stored and retrievable later, and users can observe without taking part or anyone noticing. Although permeable boundaries and lurking can have a detrimental effect on the sense of community that a participant experiences, opinions diverge on how and what a lurker contributes or gains. Lurkers can benefit from the community interactions by learning important information and experiencing emotional support, and just by observing people talk to one another (Dai & Shi, 2022; Milton et al., 2023; Sun et al., 2014).

Social Implications of Virtual Communities

Participation in a virtual community can change the physical spaces in which people interact socially by transforming, decreasing, or supplementing physical communities. Virtual communities can facilitate communication among family and friends who are geographically dispersed, connect people with shared interests who do not share the same physical location, and provide an opportunity for people to build a community that is not tied to geographical proximity. At the same time, they can maintain face-to-face communities by providing a means of communication that builds on existing social relationships and civic engagement. Virtual communities can sometimes outperform face-to-face communities for generating social activism and task performance. Finally, virtual communities can provide better opportunities for building social connections, foster civic engagement, and form an extension of face-to-face communities.

Alternatively, virtual communities can draw people away from family, friends, and local communities. They can reduce an individual's desire to engage in offline socializing, activities, interactions, and face-to-face relationships. Furthermore, the global popularity of social media sites may be cultivating a reclusive, solitary generation by discouraging people from pursuing social interactions in their everyday physical lives. In addition, a virtual community can dissipate quickly and is limited in how much emotional support and meaningful interaction it can offer members. This is particularly true of the durability of virtual communities created by a hashtag in social media, which often represents no more than a group formed around an ad hoc sentiment (Li, 2004; Li et al., 2017; Wellman et al., 2003).

Creating Transformative Relationships

The relationships formed in a virtual community can be transformative. Virtual communities offer a new environment and a new set of conditions for the formation of human relationships. Consequently, participation in a virtual community can change how people think about themselves, their interpersonal relationships, social responsibilities, and public life (Song, 2009).

A virtual community offers many relational benefits with few burdens or obligations. Participants can speak openly, share secrets, and still maintain a great deal of personal privacy. Virtual communities are always available and easy to join if one is interested, leave if they become boring, and join again when desirable. One can be personally anonymous while relationally connected. This allows individuals to share their deepest personal secrets while maintaining anonymity. They offer a sense of connection, belonging, public agreement, and social solidarity while allowing members to maintain a personal independence and individuality.

Once formed, these virtual communities connect people who have a common interest, similar experiences, and shared perceptions. Participants who might otherwise have been alone, dispersed across considerable distances, and never realized they shared a common vision or purpose with others are now able to engage and mobilize. These virtual communities provide a new source of personal information, social identity, emotional support, relational solidarity, and social activism (Bliuc et al., 2019; Ch'ng, 2015; Lee & Lee, 2023; Zhong & Frey, 2022).

For virtual communities to continue to exist, however, they require continuous contributions from active members. In addition, communities persist longer if they have users who function as leaders. Virtual communities appear to have few burdens, but keeping them functioning does require member contributions (Ch'ng, 2015; Lee & Lee, 2023; Milton et al., 2023; Song, 2009).

Applying Virtual Communities: Social Support and CMC

People increasingly use CMC to gain access to informational and emotional support provided by virtual communities. Participants often identify privacy, confidentiality, ease of accessibility, and sense of personal empowerment as the reasons for participating in virtual communities. They can remain relatively anonymous while discussing personally sensitive topics about their health, relationships, or addictions with people who understand their situation. This sense of anonymity reduces the risk of personal embarrassment, social stigma, and marginalization (Green-Hamann et al., 2011; Kim et al., 2022).

These virtual communities vary in the type of support that they provide participants. Some provide information, advice, and feedback. Others offer emotional support, expressing empathy, sympathy, understanding, and concern. The type of support varies with the issue or concern under discussion within the community (Cutrona & Russell, 1990; Cutrona & Suhr, 1992).

Alcoholics Anonymous

A number of Alcoholics Anonymous support communities meet through CMC. They provide members access to an informational and motivational support network 24/7. Participants build relationships expressing shared values and expectations through regular meetings. Participants achieve sobriety goals by participating in meetings with others who share similar life experiences. Within these communities, participants generally also develop a relationship with an individual who acts as a sponsor. Through regular meetings and conversations, participants build cohesion and trust and internalize a set of values common to the community (Green-Hamann & Sherblom, 2014).

Cancer Caregivers

Cancer caregivers, people who take care of a family member or friend with cancer, also meet through CMC. The demands of caregiving are complex and stressful for the caregiver. Caring for someone with cancer can disrupt a caregiver's daily life, require emotional adjustments, and negatively affect both physical and mental well-being.

Cancer-caregiving participants often feel frustrated with their life situation, unable to make medical decisions, and sometimes angry about the lack of support from other family members. Seeking emotional support is a primary coping strategy. Participants often have difficulty attending meetings in person because of their caregiving duties, and the CMC community provides that emotional support from others who understand their situation.

The cancer caregiver community provides an emotionally supportive place where participants can express their feelings. It is a safe place to express anger, fear, and depression. Participation in the community can reduce feelings of social isolation, personal sorrow, emotional distress, loneliness, and helplessness. It increases feelings of self-efficacy, self-worth, and coping abilities. The virtual community participation alleviates feelings of tiredness, physical weakness, and poor health, and mitigates the sense of emotional turmoil and of having life disrupted (Green-Hamann & Sherblom, 2014).

Postpartum Depression

Kim et al. (2022) describe the emotional bonding between participants sharing stories in a virtual community of mothers suffering from postpartum depression. Sharing personal stories helps participants cope with psychological distress, shame, and postpartum depression. The reciprocity among participants in this storytelling builds an emotional bonding within the virtual community.

Kim et al., however, express concern that this expression of emotional support exceeds the amount of informational sharing in the community. They suggest that this imbalance in type of support offered may not adequately address participant needs to seek professional help or find other means of resolving a serious issue such as postpartum stress and depression. This raises a concern for matching of the informational and emotional social support needs of community participants (Cutrona & Suhr, 1992; Kim et al., 2022).

Perspective in Context

Analysis and Critique

Participants use their personal networks, virtual settlements, and virtual communities to meet a wide variety of personal, professional, and relational needs. Virtual communities provide a place to connect, belong, share in an identity, and engage in the mutual expression of reciprocal feelings and responsibility with others. They provide information, emotional support, and a shared social identity. The social communitarian and personal narrative perspectives both highlight the ability of a virtual community to construct and change personal and social meaning through communication.

Networked individualism describes how people connect to meet their informational and emotional needs without becoming part of a virtual community. This perspective raises the question whether a sense of community is as central to our social life as it once was. Virtual settlements describe another alternative, with many of the benefits of a community without the burdens of membership. Permeability raises additional questions about the membership boundaries and sense of belonging, sharing, and engaging that virtual communities need to exist. Each of these alternatives raise questions about the extent to which virtual communities exist as an ideal versus a practical reality in CMC.

Ideally, virtual communities serve similar purposes as place-based face-to-face communities, but perhaps with more ease of access. They are, however, often more fleeting, with people joining and leaving virtual communities as their needs, interests, desires, and relationships change. Both the existence and the fleeting transience of virtual communities may have negative implications if the global popularity of social media sites is truly cultivating a more reclusive, solitary generation of people and discouraging everyday social interactions. Positive benefits exist as well, in the informational and social support participants, particularly members of social minority groups, find in virtual communities. It is useful to consider both the positive and negative implications for both virtual and place-based community interaction.

Virtual Community in Practice: Breast Cancer Support Forums

Virtual communities play an especially important part in providing support and information for those affected by illnesses such as cancer. Online health communities provide patients, families, and friends essential information and emotional support. Jo et al. (2023) examined the shared content and relational connections made by participants in a virtual breast cancer community.

They collected posts from a U.S.-based, nationwide online breast cancer–related forum (community.breastcancer.org) to determine whether the different needs that accompany various types of breast cancer lead to the creation of different kinds of virtual communities. They examined the posts from four forums that center on the four stages of breast cancer, looking at what people write about, the words they use, and who replies to which posts.

They found that the forum means the most to those with the most advanced forms of breast cancer. These users are the most active; they post the most and have the highest level of reciprocity in replies. In addition, the content of the posts in the four forums, representing the four breast cancer stages, differ. Forum posts in the earlier stages focus on informational support, discussing the practical aspects of breast cancer diagnosis and treatment. Words like *chemo* and *node* are most commonly used. Posts in the later stage forums focus on the sharing of emotions. Emotional support words like *hope*, *love*, and *hug* are the most commonly used words in the stage 4 breast cancer forum. Jo et al. (2023) found that people access and use these virtual communities to meet different needs. The virtual communities serve different needs for different memberships.

The conversations and relationships people form in these communities look different because of the differing needs of its members. In the early stage forum, people express a higher need for information seeking and sharing. In the stage 4 breast cancer forum, participants seek and share emotional support and connection. Both the content of the posts and the reciprocity of responses in this forum indicate this emotional support. People with different needs construct different virtual communities, with different conversations, values, and shared perspectives, based on their commonalities.

Illustration of Concepts

Cheryl relies on her virtual professional community for both informational and emotional support on the job. Beyond her daily conversations with Darius and Alex and frequent interactions with Pam, Sean, and Jasmine, she looks at professional websites and virtual community conversations for the latest information on new products and the experiences of colleagues with customers. She often gets a chuckle when colleagues describe their less-than-stellar workday experiences. It helps her maintain her sense of professional expertise, perspective, and demeanor when things happen in the office or on work sites.

Looking Forward to the Proteus Effect

In the next chapter, we will explore the Proteus effect. This effect represents one of the most frequently replicated cognitive and behavioral implications of participating in a virtual environment. We will discuss some specific research findings on the influence that participating in a virtual environment has on a person's cognitive, behavioral, and relational communication.

A COMMUNICATION ETHICS CHALLENGE

Lurking in a Virtual Community

Virtual and physical communities are formed through reciprocal communication, participation, and interaction. The visual anonymity of virtual communities, however, allows participants to engage in lurking. Lurking can be defined as being present, paying attention, observing, and listening but remaining hidden by only minimally participating in a virtual community while carefully not revealing personal information about oneself.

Many people find this kind of relational communication behavior ethically questionable, arguing that relational communication should be open and reciprocal, not a one-way process of observation and data collection.

1. How much communication openness and participation is necessary for ethical participation in a virtual community?

2. Does my communication intent matter? Is it ethical for me to gather information about a person or community as long as I do not intend to cause them any harm?

3. Can I ethically participate in a virtual community without personal disclosure to gather psychological, medical, or gender-identity information about which I have a personal concern but about which I am not yet comfortable openly sharing my personal thoughts or feelings in communication with others?

KEYWORDS AND PHRASES

Communities represent a sense of shared values, characteristics, and commonalities among members. Community members generally experience a sense of belonging and attachment to one another and a feeling of being involved together in events of common importance.

Lurking happens when CMC participants merely observe what others do without actively participating in the community by posting or commenting.

Networked individualism recognizes that many people use the internet to find information, emotional support, and a sense of connection to like-minded others.

Networked individuals are people who connect to each other to meet immediate personal needs, not to share a sense of belonging in a membership with a common set of goals, values, and identities.

Permeability describes the openness of a virtual community to membership and control of discussion topics. A permeable community is open and allows anyone who wishes to join or simply access its content.

Reciprocity occurs when the community provides the members with benefits, and in turn members have recognizable obligations and responsibilities within the community.

Sense of virtual community refers to a sense of membership and belonging, enhanced by a mutual influence and the sharing of identities, as well as an immersive emotional engagement among participants.

Sociability is the need for social interaction.

Social communitarian perspective defines a community as an underlying connection between and among people bonded together by common processes of culture, emotion, and values.

Virtual communities refer to gatherings of people who use CMC to interact and develop relationships.

Virtual settlements describe shared online spaces in which participants interact with a variety of other people over time.

QUESTIONS FOR FURTHER DISCUSSION

4. Consider the various forms of CMC that you use. Where do you see yourself participating in virtual settlements? Virtual communities? Networked individualism? How do you differentiate between the three?

5. What virtual communities are you a part of? How does participation in these virtual communities impact you? Do you think you gain the same benefits from participating in a physical community?

6. To what extent does participation in a virtual community affect physical communities?

7. Many people lament the disappearance of physical communities (e.g., book clubs, language learning groups). Do you think that virtual communities will one day be the only kind of community available? Why (not)?

Implications

Goal of this approach: To compare and contrast the multiple perspectives on and influences of CMC and their implications for individuals, relationships, and society. This final approach considers the implications of participating in CMC. The chapters consider how CMC use affects individual beliefs, feelings, and behaviors as well as its potential effects on broader social trends.

Proteus Effect examines how the visual presentation of self in a CMC environment can affect a person's cognitions and communication. These effects include the influence of gender, race, and body image stereotypes on communication and behavior in physical-world relationships.

Actor-Networks analyses how the assemblage of technological and social influences affect the communication practices and social meanings of participant groups, whether family, friends, colleagues, business associates, organizations, communities, or society in general. An actor-network perspective integrates the use of technology within the social implications of its practice. Technology not only facilitates communication; its use shapes the social context, which has broader implications for the constitution of human relationships.

13

Proteus Effect

Alex is mindful of the pictures he shares of himself online. He takes care to only use professional-looking profile pictures and he carefully curates the images others share of him, in both his professional and personal online spaces. He knows that how he presents himself matters. It is not just about looking professional and presentable. He recognizes that the images he posts can affect both his profession relationships and his own self-image.

FIGURE 13.1 Alex and His Virtual Identity.

Defining the Proteus Effect

In Greek mythology, Proteus is a god who can change his appearance at will. In CMC, the Proteus effect describes how an online presentation of self can affect a person's conceptual, behavioral, and communication relationships with others, both on- and offline. This Proteus effect has been demonstrated to be a "reliable phenomenon, with [an] effect size [that] is relatively large compared to other digital media effects" (Ratan et al., 2020, p. 651).

Numerous studies examine how modifying one's appearance in a CMC environment affects a person's beliefs, communication, and offline relationships. Research shows that altering the visual presentation of participants in an online environment influences their communication with others. This influence often affects their face-to-face communication and relationships, as well (Navarro et al., 2022; Ratan et al., 2020; Stavropoulos et al., 2020; Verhulst et al., 2018; Yee & Bailenson, 2007; Yee et al., 2009).

Avatar Appearance and Social Stereotypes

Early research examines the Proteus effect as an influence of a participant's avatar appearance in multiplayer games such as *World of Warcraft*. These games continue to be a part of contemporary life and, for many people, constitute a daily activity. Large numbers of gamers play simultaneously, and participation is growing worldwide. (Buisine & Guegan, 2020; Peña et al., 2016; Stavropoulos et al., 2020).

Within these games, which are often played using head-mounted virtual reality (VR) goggles, players engage in self-representation through the visual appearance of an avatar. This self-representation provides the individual with a social identity that includes such visible characteristics as gender, race, ethnicity, physical appearance, and age. Research into the Proteus effect examines the influences of the social stereotypes associated with these characteristics on a participant's virtual and offline communication and behaviors (Hawkins et al., 2021; Lin & Wu, 2021; Lin et al., 2021; Navarro et al., 2022; Reinhard et al., 2020).

Early Research

The influence that an individual's avatar appearance has on a participant's behavior in both the virtual and physical worlds was first demonstrated in two studies, carried out in 2007 and 2009 respectively. This early research laid the groundwork for future analyses of the Proteus effect. In one study, participants who were given attractive avatars stood and walked closer to others in the virtual environment (within 3 feet). They also talked more; displayed more confidence, friendliness, and extroversion; and shared a greater amount of personal information. Participants with less attractive avatars stood farther apart from others in the virtual environment and shared fewer self-disclosures. These differences in avatar appearance affect participant physical-world behaviors, as well. Thirty minutes after leaving the virtual environment, participants who had embodied the attractive avatars show more confidence in choosing potential dates from photographs presented in a face-to-face context (Yee & Bailenson, 2007).

In a second study, Yee et al. (2009) analyzed the effect of avatar appearance on bargaining behaviors. First, they assigned avatars with different appearances to participants in a virtual environment and then asked those participants to negotiate how to split $100. Following this virtual world negotiation, they asked the same participants to engage in the same negotiation face-to-face. They found that avatar appearance affected the participant's negotiation behaviors in both the virtual and subsequent face-to-face contexts, regardless of the physical appearance of the participant. Yee and Bailenson (2007) called this influence of a digital self-representation on a person's behavior the Proteus effect.

Proteus Effect of Presence, Identity, Deindividuation, and Transference

This Proteus effect relies on an immersive presence in the medium, the embodiment of a virtual identity, deindividuation, and transference of these effects into the physical world. We described virtual identity in Chapter 5, presence in Chapter 6, and deindividuation in Chapter 9. Here, we apply those concepts to the Proteus effect and describe the research evidence showing the transference of these effects into physical-world communication and behaviors.

Presence

An immersive presence within the CMC medium is a prerequisite for the Proteus effect. Stavropoulos et al. (2021) describe three levels of presence: engagement, engrossment, and immersion. Engagement represents the time spent learning to navigate an environment. Engrossment occurs when participants become more involved, less aware of their physical surroundings, and more emotionally attached to their experiences in the virtual environment. An immersive presence follows as a participant spends more time, focuses more attention, and expends more effort in the environment. This immersive presence involves an awareness and adoption of the characteristics of a virtual identity within the environment.

Stavropoulos et al. (2020) report that the degree of immersive presence in a game affects the extent to which participants experience a Proteus effect. Participants who experience the least amount of presence report little effect of their avatar appearance on their subsequent cognitions, perceptions, and behaviors in either the virtual or physical environments. Participants who are more engaged with the game report that their in-game cognitions and experiences affect their subsequent physical-world perceptions, behaviors, and relationships. Gamers who experience high levels of immersion in the game report subsequent physical-world feelings, behaviors, and communication relationships attributable to that feeling of immersive presence.

Similarly, Ash (2016) found that people who were immersed in their avatar, that is, those who felt like they *were* their avatar and were truly present in an online competitive boxing game, experienced an increased Proteus effect. Participants who experienced this high level of embodiment in their avatar, as measured in agreement to statements such as "I literally had the feeling I was in the character's skin" and "I almost had the feeling of actually being the character" during the boxing game often expressed feelings of being furious with their opponent during the game (Ash, 2016, p. 4). These aggressive feelings often continued after the end of game as well. The immersive presence in their avatar was a significant predictor of aggression expressed in their thoughts, mood, and communication both during and after the online boxing game.

Navarro et al. (2022) found similar immersive presence effects in the behavior of participants they provided with an avatar displaying their face and dressed in sports clothes. These participants engaged in more activity and showed a greater increase in heart rates during their physical exercise workouts than those with avatars who did not look like them. Participants having an avatar displaying a stranger's face and wearing formal clothes showed a decrease in both physical and cardiac activity. These results indicate that user–avatar similarity increases presence, which increases the likelihood of a Proteus effect.

Identity

The immersive presence of embodying an avatar creates associations between participant self-identity and the demographic characteristics of the avatar. As a result, social stereotypes associated with the demographic characteristics of the avatar become salient to the participant. When asked to act or communicate, participants tend to do so in accordance with these perceptions of those social stereotypes. The more a person embodies the avatar and its demographic characteristics, the more they adopt those stereotypes and behave accordingly (Hawkins et al., 2021; Ratan et al., 2020; Yee & Bailenson, 2007).

The social norms and stereotypes associated with the avatar further influence the Proteus effect. The presence of social identity cues affect how that Proteus effect operates. When an avatar contains social cues, such as membership identification in a specific group, this shifts the person's identity salience from personal to social, priming the person to behave more in line with the social expectations associated with that group. The Proteus effect follows this shift in the influence of cultural stereotypes on personal self-presentation and relational communication responses (Buisine & Guegan, 2020).

These social expectations also can temper the Proteus effect. Kocur et al. (2020) show a Proteus effect of avatar muscularity in male participant physical exertion and perceptions of performance. They find that male participants who embody the muscular avatars exert greater physical grip strength when lifting weights during an isometric exercise. These participants also report lower perceived exertion and do not consider the task as difficult as those who embody non-muscular avatars. Female participants embodying the muscular avatars perceive the task as easier but do not increase their grip strength. The researchers suggest this indicates that exercising with a muscular avatar conforms to male but not female perceptions of being athletic and physically strong. Identification with the social stereotype is thus necessary to foster the motivation and behavioral performance of the Proteus effect. In this case, identification with the social norm is more salient for the male participants.

Similarly, the Proteus effect is tempered by the social norms associated with the avatar. These are shown to affect a person's perceptions of self, their ideas of what others might think of them, and their subsequent social interactions. Van der Heide et al. (2012) find that when people embody an unattractive avatar, they engage in compensating behaviors and act more positively toward others.

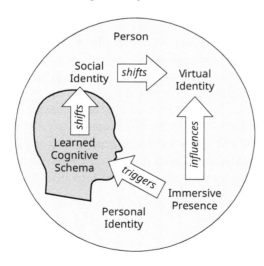

FIGURE 13.2 Immersive Presence Triggers a Social Identity That Shifts to a Virtual One in Alignment With Social Stereotypes.

Figure 13.2 illustrates this process of immersive presence and virtual identity as an avatar. The immersive presence activates the social stereotypes associated with the virtual identity and shifts a person's social identity to a virtual one that aligns with those stereotypes. This sets the stage for deindividuation.

Deindividuation

As individuals shift their cognitive salience from a personal to a social identity and immerse themselves in the social demographic cues of the virtual environment, a sense of deindividuation can occur. This deindividuation facilitates the Proteus effect. Deindividuation decreases self-awareness and self-evaluation. It shifts identity salience from the personal toward the social, increasing sensitivity to the environmental cues and social influences while decreasing an awareness of oneself as a unique individual. As this deindividuation process takes place, it facilitates the Proteus effect with participants behaving in ways they think others expect them to, based on their avatar appearance (Yee & Bailenson, 2007).

This deindividuation leads to the Proteus effect. Buisine et al. (2016), for example, showed the effects of deindividuation on creative thinking. They randomly assigned participants to one of two groups. One group embodied avatars with the social identity of inventors. The other group resembled the users of a public transportation system. Each group discussed creative solutions to help a public transportation system meet user needs. The participants who embodied avatars with the identity of inventors generated more technologically oriented solutions. Those participants whose avatars resembled public transportation customers developed more user-centered, needs-oriented solutions.

Peña et al. (2016) extended the analysis of deindividuation beyond cognition to physical exertion in virtual tennis matches. They randomly assigned 96 male participants to avatars appearing to have either a normal body weight or an obese appearance. The participants playing as normal-weight avatars engaged in greater physical activity than those having the obese avatars. When participants perceived themselves to be members of the obese group, they made less effort. Actual participant body mass index showed little effect on this activity. These results show how personally held stereotypes affect people's physical exertion when their self-identity becomes deindividuated and they perceive themselves to be a member of an obese group.

Buisine and Guegan (2020) found that when people are deindividuated, the identity cues they associate with their avatar impacts their ideas and behavior. Participants brainstorming as the creative inventor avatars generated a greater number of ideas and more unique ideas than the participants having the ordinary, noncreative avatars. This difference disappeared, however, when Buisine and Guegan introduced an explicit, physical-world social identity cue in the form of avatars dressed in the participants' school colors. When they did this, the avatar's inventor identity cues no longer affected participant behavior. This suggests the interference of a group identity that overrides the participant's stereotype of the creative inventor and demonstrates that deindividuation represents a complex process of social identities interacting.

Transference

Once activated, the Proteus effect can influence communication in the physical world. This transference to the physical world requires that the deindividuated social identity that people take on as a result of the Proteus effect becomes more cognitively salient than their personal identity. Then the effect transfers from a virtual environment to the cognitions, behaviors, and communication enacted in the physical world. This is especially true when the avatar is perceived as similar to oneself. This transference to the physical world, however, also occurs when people use an avatar from a different demographic group if that avatar behaves in alignment with the social expectations for that group (Ash, 2016; Hawkins et al., 2021; Lee et al., 2014; Lin & Wu, 2021; Ratan & Dawson, 2016).

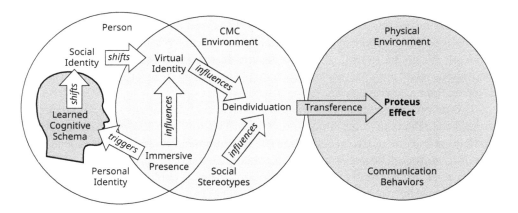

FIGURE 13.3 Identity Shift, Deindividuation, Transference to Physical Environment: Proteus Effect.

Guegan et al. (2016) looked at the transference of creative thinking from online brainstorming sessions to face-to-face brainstorming sessions. First, they asked participants to engage in 15-minute brainstorming sessions in one of three conditions. A control group met face-to-face and recorded their ideas through an instant messaging system. The other two groups met as avatars in a virtual environment. One of these groups met as creative-looking, inventor avatars. The other group appeared as normal-looking, non-inventor avatars.

The participants who embodied the inventor avatars produced a greater number of ideas, generated more unique ideas, and felt more creative during the virtual meeting than either of the face-to-face or non-inventor groups. The benefit of embodying the inventor avatars in the first meeting carried over to a subsequent face-to-face brainstorming session as well. In the subsequent face-to-face brainstorming sessions, participants who had met as inventor avatars continued to perform better, generating both a greater number of ideas and more unique ideas than either the non-inventor or control groups. This demonstrates the transference of a Proteus effect from virtual to face-to-face meetings.

Figure 13.3 illustrates the deindividuation and transference processes. Deindividuation decreases the cognitive salience of self, increases the awareness of a social group stereotype, and indicates the appropriate actions within that stereotype. Subsequent transference of this state of mind from the virtual to the physical environment produces the Proteus effect. The immersive presence, identity shift, deindividuation, and transference to the physical environment are all necessary steps to achieve a Proteus effect. When they co-occur, the effect can be profound.

Applying the Proteus Effect: Gender, Race, and Body Image Stereotypes

Several studies examine the activation of the Proteus effect in commonly accepted social stereotypes surrounding gender, race, and body image. Research into these effects produces a set of nuanced results, showing an interaction between personal identity and social stereotypes. These studies suggest important implications for the potential consequences of Proteus effects.

Gender

Lee et al. (2014) randomly assigned 120 students (60 males, 60 females) to either a female or a male avatar. While embodying these avatars, the students mentally solved a series of 20 math problems. Regardless of participant gender or SAT math score, both female and male participants who had male avatars performed better on the math assignment than those embodying female avatars.

In another study, Fox et al. (2013) asked 86 female participants to engage in a brief virtual conversation with a research assistant. Approximately half of the female participants embodied a highly sexualized avatar. The other half participated as non-sexualized avatars. Following the conversation, the participants left the virtual environment. They then completed a short paper-and-pencil measure that asked about body-related thoughts and a rape myth acceptance scale that assesses the degree to which participants accept rape myths, such as victim blaming. Women who participated in the virtual conversation as highly sexualized female avatars reported more body-related thoughts afterward and scored significantly higher on the rape myth acceptance scales than those who embodied the non-sexualized avatars. Having embodied a highly sexualized avatar, even for a short time, appears to activate social stereotypes that induce a propensity to blame a rape victim for the assault.

Race

Researchers find similar effects regarding the influence of racial stereotypes on cognitive thinking and behavior. Hawkins et al. (2021) invited 248 White participants (170 female, 78 male) to play a newly created M-rated video game. The objective of the game is to progress through a virtual territory and reach a goal by shooting and killing various enemies along the way. Participants played as either an African American or a White avatar, with either African American or White avatar enemies. The participants who scored high on embodied presence with their avatars demonstrated the influence of racial stereotypes in both the game and subsequent behavior. During the game, they demonstrated a greater desire to hurt enemies appearing as a different race than their avatars.

Following the video game, participants engaged in a separate exercise of selecting plastic shapes for a partner to use in creating an outlined form. Each shape has a difficulty level labeled as easy, medium, or hard, which makes a partner's task easier or more difficult in assembling the pieces. Results show that participants assigned a higher number of difficult shapes to a partner from a different racial background than their avatars. This indicates the transference of a racial bias to the physical-world exercise.

Body Image, Food Choices, and Exercise

Several studies investigate the Proteus effect of body image stereotypes on behavior. These studies examine the effect of virtual embodiment on physical exercise and food choices. They suggest some positive outcomes as well as negative effects.

Verhulst et al. (2018) investigated the effect that virtual embodiment and the social stigma associated with obesity have on people's food perceptions and purchasing behaviors They assigned participants, all of whom had "normal" body weights as measured by body mass index (BMI between 18 and 25), to two groups of avatars. One avatar group appeared to have a normal virtual body weight and the other appeared to be obese (with a BMI appearance greater than 30). Participants then selected products to purchase in a virtual store and rated the tastiness, healthiness, and price of each food product.

Participants in both groups scored the same on ratings of immersive presence. Obese group participants, however, perceived their virtual avatar body to be significantly heavier and older. Results show that the obese avatar participants assessed soda as tastier and apples as healthier than the normal group. However, there were no differences in shopping and purchase behaviors between the two groups. The results suggest that embodying an obese avatar may influence a person's perception of food. The researchers conclude that there is a subtle relationship between the acceptance of social stereotypes and the activated cognitive schema.

Lin and Wu (2021) investigated the use of a virtual gym to encourage real physical exercise among older adults. They assigned participants to either an older or younger avatar and asked them to do a series of physical exercises while watching their avatar perform the same routine in a virtual gym. After completing the routine, participants were given additional time to practice on their own. Results show that avatar age does not affect the actual physical effort exerted, as measured in step counts. Neither male nor female participant groups produced more effort when represented by a younger or older avatar. Both groups, however, perceived that they exert more effort when they embody the younger avatars. This perceptual difference is particularly strong for the female group. Females who embodied older avatars reported significantly less physical activity than the males who embodied the older avatars. The females who embody the younger avatars, however, report greater self-efficacy and likelihood of continuing the physical activity in the future than any of the other groups. This points to the salience of the social expectation of females to aspire to an ideal, thin body type, one that is activated by the use of a younger avatar.

In a similar study with young adults, Lin et al. (2021) examined the effect of avatar body shape on perceived physical exertion in a virtual gym. They gave participants either a very muscular or a normal-looking avatar. Participants then completed an exercise routine in a virtual gym, followed by some free exercise time. Those participants who embodied a normal-looking avatar were more physically active than those in the muscular, six-pack avatar group. This difference holds for both male and female participants. In addition, the female participants in the normal avatar group reported a significantly higher sense of self-efficacy. They reported feeling confident in their ability to continue the exercise program on their own and maintain this confidence when asked again the next day.

Finally, Reinhard et al. (2020) investigated the Proteus effect of age perceptions on actual walking speeds. They asked young adult participants to complete a vision test using either a physical or a virtual environment screening. Participants had to walk to and from the testing room, and their walking speeds were recorded. A control group and a group who embodied young avatars did not differ in their walking speeds to and from the testing room A third group of participants who embodied older avatars for the virtual screening, however, took significantly longer to walk back from the testing room. Their slowness, however, only occurred in walking the first half of the hallway. There were no measurable differences in the group walking times along the second half of the hallway, indicating a rapid decay in the observed behavioral Proteus effect.

Summary: The Proteus Effect

Taken together, these results indicate a pattern of Proteus effects that transfer from the virtual to cognitions and physical behaviors. Appearance as a gendered avatar affects math skills and attitudes toward rape victims. The apparent race of an avatar in a video game influences participant aggressive behaviors in socially stereotypic ways in both the virtual and subsequent physical environment. Avatar body image affects perceptions of food, induces physical activity, and stimulates self-efficacy for continuing an exercise program. Avatar age can improve the likelihood of continuing a program of physical activity. Finally, when measured carefully enough, avatar age shows a physical effect on a participant's actual walking speed, but only for a short time.

Perspective in Context

Analysis and Critique

The results of these multiple studies show that the Proteus effect is complicated but consistent. These studies show cognitive, attitudinal, and behavioral effects in participants across a broad range of contexts. The specific effects differ from one study to the next, but the Proteus effect is recurrent across the studies and contexts (Ratan et al., 2020).

The Proteus effect captures the influence of social stereotypes on a participant's perceptions, attitudes, and relational communication, both on- and offline. This Proteus effect occurs when the salience of a participant's personal identity characteristics is subsumed by the social stereotypes that are associated with the virtual demographics of an avatar. The avatar appearance activates a set of inferred thoughts, attitudes, and behaviors that are consistent with accepted social stereotypes. Seeing oneself in the virtual identity of an avatar stimulates a social role in which to participate. The increased salience of group membership over personal uniqueness facilitates a deindividuation that actualizes a potential self-identity built on the social stereotypes of that role. The Proteus effect occurs when this social role affects self-identity and behavioral choices that transfer to the physical environment.

The Proteus effect relies on the salience of self-perception. When people perform a task as an avatar, they engage in a process of self-perception to determine how they should act. Self-perception involves acknowledging the avatar as a manifestation of a potential self, which influences self-perception so that it is in alignment with the avatar's apparent physical and demographic characteristics. The embodiment of the avatar's apparent physical and demographic characteristics influences their self-perception and conformity to the stereotypical behaviors associated with them. The process requires an immersive presence in the virtual environment and an avatar that expresses a potential self-identity, followed by the experience of deindividuation. All of these, occurring together, facilitate the transference of a self-identity, within a set of perceived social stereotypes, from the virtual environment to physical-world communication behaviors (Ratan et al., 2020).

The Proteus effect is stronger the closer the user feels to the avatar, supporting the argument that the phenomenon is facilitated by a process of both self-perception and cognitive social schema activation. People tend to emulate the behaviors and attitudes that they associate with their avatars' identity characteristics. These perceptions can persist, even after leaving the virtual environment, and transfer to physical-world behavior.

This Proteus effect has important implications for CMC. The virtual environment enhances the salience of certain social identity cues and deindividuation of self-perception. Participants often focus more attention on external identity cues, such as the avatar's height, weight, skin color, and similarity in appearance to oneself. The salience of these cues and acceptance of the avatar appearance as one's self-identity leads to the conceptual, attitudinal, and behavioral changes of the Proteus effect.

Proteus Effect in Practice: Helping in Stroke Recovery

Buetler et al. (2022) investigated the potential of using virtual reality (VR) solutions to help stroke victims recover their physical abilities through neuro-rehabilitation training. Stroke is a major cause of long-term disability among adults, with one third of stroke patients needing assistance with daily activities. Following a stroke, a patient often requires neuro-rehabilitation interventions to regain even partial bodily motor functionality. This neuro-rehabilitation training is intensive, repetitive, and costly. If effective, a VR Proteus effect could provide a patient the ability to mimic task-specific body motions and facilitate effective individualized training programs that match a patient's specific needs, lower costs, and optimize motor recovery.

The healthy participants in this study viewed their avatars from a first-person perspective in a virtual environment. Participants were gender matched to their avatars and sat at a table during an experiment that took approximately 60–70 minutes. They rested their right hand on an armrest in front of them. Their avatar sat in a similar position, with the right hand lying on a virtual table. The participants could see the upper body, arms, and shoulders of the avatar sitting in a chair at the virtual table.

Researchers slowly transformed the avatar arm, changing its appearance from a soft pliable human skin texture into stone. They reinforced the effect of this changing visual impression by repeatedly touching the real arm of the participant while simultaneously striking the arm of the avatar with a virtual hammer. They progressively replaced the sound of the hammer touching skin with that of a hammer hitting stone.

Participants had to perform a simple motor task. They had to move their arm, as fast and accurately as possible, from the resting position up to touch a vertically appearing sphere. Results show that when the avatar arm appeared as stone, participants were slower in performing this motor task than when the arm had a human appearance. Participants also rated their arm as heavier, colder, stiffer, and more insensitive when the avatar arm appeared as stone.

After the VR test, participants rated their arm as relatively less heavy, stiff, and insensitive than they did before the experience. In addition, physical measures of their neurological responses and physical movements indicated that participants compensated for the appearance of a stone arm. This finding suggests that immersive VR training can stimulate the motor networks of the brain in ways that are helpful to stroke recovery.

Illustration of Concepts

Alex takes great care in maintaining a professional-looking online presence. He makes sure any pictures he shares of himself are appropriate for anyone to see and takes special care in sharing only professional work-related pictures on his public social media platforms and the business website. Whenever he looks at his profile picture on the corporate website, in which he wears a suit and tie, he feels proud of his achievements and feels he could continue to be highly successful in his career.

Looking Forward to Actor-Networks

Participation in CMC is relatively unavoidable in the 21st century. The Proteus effect highlights the importance of understanding some of the influences of CMC participation. In the next chapter, we examine the constraints, experience, relationships, interactions, and implications of participation in CMC. A communicator can become more effective by understanding these multiple influences and taking them into account when using CMC.

COMMUNICATION ETHICS CHALLENGE

What Are the Communication Ethics of Knowing About the Proteus Effect?

Some people are concerned that the ability to make an avatar as attractive as possible can have negative impacts on people's body image and related eating behaviors. Some are concerned that participating in virtual war games can lead a person to become physically violent and callous toward human life. Still others think that being virtually connected too much of the time detracts from interpersonal relationships and negatively affects developing appropriate social behavior. There may be other issues surrounding the virtual expression of health, violence, and relationships that affect the physical world as well. Can you identify some more?

1. If my participation in a virtual environment can affect my thoughts and behavior in the physical world, what is my ethical responsibility to reflect on my virtual world activities and presentation of self?

2. Given the research evidence of a Proteus effect, how would you respond to the concerns surrounding the virtual expression of online sexuality and violence and their potential influence on physical-world communication and relationships?

3. How do we create virtual identities that promote positive physical world effects?

KEYWORDS AND PHRASES

Deindividuation is a state of decreased cognitive salience of oneself as a person and increased awareness of a social identity within a specific group context. The deindividuation process shifts identity salience from the personal to the social, increasing sensitivity to the environmental cues and social influences while decreasing an awareness of oneself as a unique individual.

Engagement represents the time spent learning to navigate an environment.

Engrossment occurs when participants become more involved, less aware of their physical surroundings, and more emotionally attached to their experiences in the virtual environment.

Immersive presence follows as a participant spends more time, focuses more attention, and expends more effort in the environment. This immersive presence involves an awareness and adoption of the characteristics of a virtual identity within the environment.

Proteus effect describes how an online presentation of self can affect a person's conceptual, behavioral, and communication relationships with others, both on- and offline.

Social cues are signs that indicate someone's social identity, such as membership identification in a specific group.

Transference occurs when the Proteus effect influences communication and/or behaviors in the real world.

QUESTIONS FOR FURTHER DISCUSSION

1. Do you play any online games? How do you design your avatar? Have you ever experienced something like the Proteus effect in that you feel more like your avatar after playing?

2. Do you think that participation in social media changes how you think about social relationships, political issues, and life in general? Why (not)?

3. When selecting and curating images of yourself that you share online, do you find that viewing good pictures of yourself makes you feel different about yourself than pictures that you consider less than flattering?

4. Some of the research presented in this chapter provides evidence that playing certain games can make it more likely that people will racially stereotype or hold negative beliefs about certain genders or body shapes. What could be done to prevent this from happening?

Image Credits

14

Actor-Networks

C ommunication is a symbolic system of processes and interacting influences. People create personal, relational, and social meaning in their lives through this communication. The CMC perspectives we have reviewed describe some of influences on communication when it is carried out through a technological medium. Figure 14.1 illustrates an actor-network showing the multiple, interacting influences of CMC constraints, experience, relationships, and opportunities.

Approaches and Perspectives

Each of the CMC perspectives that we describe in this book investigates a particular aspect of communication. Media richness, naturalness, and affordances examine the constraints of communication. Presence, social presence, and propinquity describe the

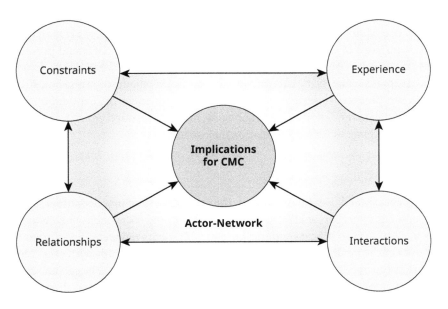

FIGURE 14.1 An Actor-Network of technical and social CMC Influences.

communication experience. Social information processing, hyperpersonal, and the social identity model of deindividuation discuss how communication informs relationship building. Virtual identities, groups, and communities examine interactions. Finally, the Proteus effect identifies some of the implications. We summarize these perspectives here.

Constraints

The media richness perspective focuses attention on the constraints of the technology that might hinder the relational communication process: (a) the ability to provide feedback, (b) the ability to utilize multiple nonverbal cues, (c) language variety, and (d) personal focus. These constraints hinder people's ability to convey informational and relational content in a message. Media naturalness shifts attention away from the technological constraints toward to the cognitive schema, effort, and adaptation constraints of the human mind. This perspective argues that humans have evolved to communicate face-to-face in co-located, spoken, synchronous, conversation that contains verbal and nonverbal cues of expressiveness, excitement, sincerity, and intimacy. The media synchronicity perspective adds the constraints created by the communication context in which relationships are built, with a focus on the information conveyance and meaning convergence. Affordances shift the perspective to the participant perception and use of the medium. The affordances approach identifies the communication opportunities for developing successful relationships as existing in the interaction between the user and the characteristics of a CMC environment.

Experience

Exploring the experience moves the discussion away from the constraints of the medium to a consideration of how individuals use CMC to construct a sense of self in relationship to others. The examination of presence and social presence focuses on how people create a sense of closeness with those others through CMC. It recognizes that some of the characteristics of CMC can adversely affect the experience of social presence, but focuses on the relational connections people develop through the medium. In addition, CMC participants make relational communication choices about when and how to connect to others. Propinquity describes the relational consequences of these communication choices. It indicate how choices made about the medium through which to communicate can have consequences for future relational closeness.

Relationships

These perceptions and uses further inform the communication practices of social information processing, hyperpersonal relationship formation, and social identity deindividuation effects in CMC. These processes describe how CMC users navigate the affordances and constraints of the medium to communicate and build relationships with others and how this relationship building can differ from face-to-face interactions. The social information processing perspective describes how relational closeness develops and changes through CMC. Participants use active, passive, interactive, and extractive information-gathering strategies to reduce interpersonal uncertainty. The hyperpersonal perspective flips the influence of text-based communication on this communication process by suggesting that within certain CMC contexts, relationships can develop more quickly and become more personal than in face-to-face conversation. The social identity of deindividuation effects (SIDE) model describes how personal and social identity function in an online environment. The model depicts some of the potentially negative implications of an over awareness of the social identity cues embedded in CMC and offers a note of caution about deindividuation and stereotyping.

Interactions

Through these communication practices, CMC users construct and participate in individual, group, and community interactions. Individuals represent, redefine, or embellish a presentation of self through CMC. Visual anonymity allows CMC users to experiment with a self-expression that may differ from their physical characteristics. CMC groups provide participants with the potential for forming weak-tie informational and strong-tie emotional networks of support. The accrued social capital of these networks can provide participants with important sources of informational and emotionally support. Virtual communities offer access to others who have similar interests, experiences, and values.

Implications

Finally, the Proteus effect illustrates a potential implication of CMC participation. Participation in a virtual environment may have cognitive and relational consequences. This participation can affect a person's identity, thoughts, attitudes, and relational behavior. The Proteus effect examines some of the consequences, describing both potentially positive and negative effects of participating in CMC.

An Actor-Network Perspective

The actor-network perspective includes all these influences on CMC, from the technological constraints of the richness of a medium to the social experience of participating in an online community and the potential for Proteus effects. Actor-networks include and describe all these technological and human influences on the constitution of CMC. In an actor-network, these multiple technological and social stimuli interact to form an assemblage of influences that collectively work together to allow for the creation of CMC identities, relationships, groups, and communities, influencing the process of creation as well as the eventual outcome. No single influence, or additive set of influences, produces this outcome; it is the interaction between the human and nonhuman influences that make up the network that constitutes the resulting effect. An actor-network perspective provides an inclusive view of the interaction of these multiple social and technological influences affects CMC.

The actor-networks perspective originates in the analysis of the influences of science and technology on society. The perspective considers how using an available technology not only facilitates communication, but also plays a role in shaping its use within the social context. It moves beyond an examination of the technological constraints and opportunities provided to include social influences and implications. This perspective describes the use of technology as playing an active role in the social constitution of human relationships, groups, organizations, and communities. Rather than separating the technology of a media platform from its use, the actor-network perspective includes user engagement in the use of that technology and the resulting social implications for group communication (Bencherki, 2017; Nimmo, 2011).

Actor-Networks

The actor-network perspective does not capture how people, objects, or technologies connect to each other. It does not explain, for example, how the Internet, cell towers, or other networks carry information. It also does not explain how participants use CMC networks to accumulate social capital or to provide informational and emotional support. Actor-networks are larger than that. Instead, the actor-network perspective examines how the use of a technology mediates the communication of meaning in groups of people across an assemblage of social-technological influences that shape those participant interactions, understandings, and relationships (Bencherki, 2017).

An actor-network is thus an assemblage of technological and social influences that shape the communication practices and social meanings of the participants, whether family, friends, colleagues, business associates, organizations, or communities. Email, texting, social media sites, and videoconferencing conversations all involve these assemblages of technological and social entities that occur together to form a collectivity of influences.

For example, one technological feature of CMC is the ability to carry text and speech from one location to another, across time and space. This allows groups to coordinate their action beyond the specific moment and location of expression. A CMC network does not just provide a passive, constrained, or opportunistic medium for the group's communication; it also serves as a mediating influence in that the communication facilitates and shapes the social group action across time and space in a way that can bring families and communities closer together or push them apart, depending on their use of available technologies.

This represents an example of how social and technological influences work together to mediate and modify the communication that takes place in a network. Each specific combination of social and technological characteristics forms a relatively unique and somewhat unpredictable set of influences on the communication that takes place. Subsequently, the resulting group communication may not align closely with the original intent of any one participant, or of the group as a whole, as the technological and social influences on each node in the network modify and transform the communication passing through.

A social media site, for example, consists of multiple mediating technological and social influences. Adding or removing a participant or a technological capability can change the communication on that site significantly. The objective of an actor-network analysis is to observe and describe how the action of the network comes into being, achieves stability, maintains its functioning, and becomes unstable again, and through this process, influences and shapes the communication on this social media site. An actor-network analysis does this by carefully describing the combination of technological and social influences and tracing the multiple associations and transformations across the network that produces the observed outcome (Bencherki, 2017; Cresswell et al., 2010; Nimmo, 2011).

Actors and Agency

Actors are any element of a network that can influence communication practices. While this obviously includes humans, technologies also affect how people communicate. Actor-networks make little distinction between the intentional agency of human participants and the nonhuman technological influences of the network. In addition, human participants within an actor-network may act with intent, but their actions can often produce unintended social consequences (Bencherki, 2017; Latour, 2005).

Agency in actor-networks takes place when technologies affect how users and societies at large interact and engage with the world around them. To understand how agency operates inside these networks, one has to know who uses what technology (and who doesn't), why, and how that usage is influenced by the characteristics of the people using it, as well as the nature of the technology itself (Latour, 2005).

This broader understanding of agency, as located in the network-mediated effects of social-technological influences, goes beyond the intentionality of any one human being and forms a central premise of the actor-network perspective. The interaction of technology with human social habits affects the resulting CMC. These cognitive, technological, and social influences, rather than acting separately, interact within each other to form the assemblage of mediated influences on CMC (Bencherki, 2017; Law, 2009).

In other words, people may communicate with a personal intent, but within an environment of cognitive, social, technological, and physical influences that shape their identities, interpersonal relationships, groups, and communities. CMC occurs within this complex network of social and technological influences. The network assemblage of these influences mediates the human intent, shaping its expression and interpretation. The actor-network perspective describes the transformative process of this mediation of human intent and communicative action (Law, 2009).

For example, an individual may express an authentic personal identity using CMC, but the action of that expression includes social, relational, and even nonhuman components such as the technology they use for their self-expression. People present personal identities within social roles and physical expressions of self that involve clothing, status, and relationships with others. These personal, social, and virtual identities occur within physical and mediated environments of expression. These environments mediate and transform the communication of that identity within the relationships and communities of its expression.

Action: Actants, Mediators, and Figuration

Three terms describe the action of influences that occur in an actor-network: *actants*, *mediators*, and *figuration*. Each term describes something specific about the nature of the technological and social influences in an actor-network and the interaction among them (Latour, 2005).

An **actant** is any individual person, technology, set of social relationships, or combination of assembled influences that produces an effect. The concept of an actant eliminates the distinction between human intent and nonhuman influences and focuses attention instead on the effects of the combined action of a network assemblage (Latour, 2005).

These actants interact as mediators in the actor-network. **Mediators** form in the interaction among the influences in an actor-network and transform the effect of an action as it moves through that network. Each network consists of a variety of these influences that interact to change the effect of an action as it moves through it. Together, the collection of technological and social mediators transform the action of the network in ways that constitute a relatively unique resulting social communication action and meaning. An actor-network analysis focuses on this mediation process as it shapes the ongoing communication practices, relationships, and social meanings in the network (Latour, 1994).

Figuration describes the observable pattern of effects produced by an actor-network. It shifts the focus to implications rather than intents, to the collective outcome rather than the origination. No single social or technological influence or set of influences affects CMC in isolation. It is the configuration of these influences, together, that influences the communication in a medium. The configuration of these influences has implications that transform the resulting communication practices. Figuration describes this combined set of influences that shapes a communication outcome (Latour, 2005; Leonardi, 2011).

Actor-Network Analysis

Actor-networks describe the social relationships that develop among individuals through the use of technologies. Communication scholars increasingly use actor-network analyses to study the implications of CMC. They examine the complexity of social relationships and the active role of technology in shaping them. An actor-network analysis provides a lens through which to view the role that technology plays in shaping human communication processes and a way of understanding the social implications.

Changes in technology interact with human social practice to affect the ongoing communication in relationships, groups, organizations, and human society. Actor-network analyses focus on how changes in the user-generated content and communication practices affect both the technological development and ongoing human social community. A careful analysis of the action of each network mediator, and of their collectivity, provides an understanding of the dynamics that shape both technology and human society (Bencherki, 2017; Cresswell et al., 2010).

Summary: Actor-Networks

Table 14.1 summarizes these actor-network terms and propositions. Action in an actor-network focuses on the implications rather than the intentions of actors. Agency defines those influences, human and non-human, social and technological, which affect outcomes. Intent is inadequate to capture the concept of agency. There is no agency without a resulting action. The actor-networks perspective represents the assemblages of technological and social influence coalitions that produce these actions. These technological and social agents, and their assemblages, function as actants within the actor-network. The actants

TABLE 14.1 Summary of Actor-Network Terms and Propositions

ACTION	Outcomes, implications of action, not intentions of actors, create agency
AGENCY	Coalitions of technological and social influences form an actor-network
ACTOR-NETWORK	Assemblage of technological and social coalitions of become influential actants
ACTANTS	Influences, acting and acted upon by each other, in a network of mediators
MEDIATORS	Intermediary influences that transform network action, affecting outcome figuration
FIGURATION	Configuration of influences that constitute the outcome of a CMC social environment

act, and are acted upon, and in doing so become mediators that modify the influence of the action across the network. Each mediator modifies and transforms the action of the network, affecting the resulting outcome. Figuration describes the configuration of this mediated actor-network of influences and the implications of a resulting outcome. This figuration of technological and social influences and implications becomes constitutive in shaping the present understandings, relationships, and shared social reality of a CMC group.

Constraints, Experience, Relationships, and Interactions in Actor-Networks

The multiple perspectives of CMC describe an assemblage of technological and social influences that affect the methods and content of communication as well as the interpretation of social-relational meaning. Some of these influences are technological, such as those captured by the media richness perspective that introduces constraints on the use of nonverbal cues, feedback, symbolic expression, and personal focus. Others are human, such as the recognition of cognitive effort, ambiguity, alignment, arousal, and learning as discussed by the media naturalness perspective. The media synchronicity perspective adds the communication influences of function, phase, familiarity, and communication goal (i.e., information conveyance and meaning convergence). Affordances contribute the influence of participant perceptions and uses of the technology. The experience of personal, social, and virtual identity; presence and social presence; and the relational closeness of propinquity provide network influences as well. These influences, however, are not additive. They interact and are transformative of the resulting CMC.

The actor-networks perspective recognizes these as an assemblage of influences on CMC. Each modifies and transforms the others. The perspective of perceived media richness described in Chapter 1 provides a simple example of this. Perceived media richness describes richness not as an attribute of the medium, but as the perception and use of nonverbal cues, feedback immediacy, symbolic expression, and personal focus in a medium. Actor-networks expands this perspective to include all the technological, human cognitive, personal identity, and social-relational influences of CMC as they occur within a medium at a particular point in time.

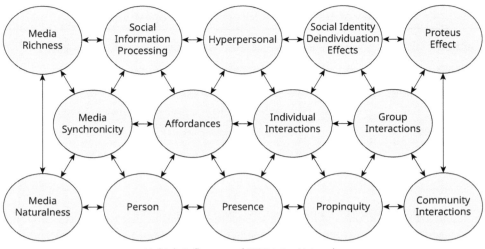

Multiple Influences of CMC Actor-Networks

FIGURE 14.2 Actor-Networks in Practice.

Figure 14.2 depicts an example of this interaction of influences on CMC. Each of the influences is bidirectional and modifies the influence of the others on CMC. Media synchronicity, for example, can increase a participant's perception of affordances and experience of naturalness and facilitate an ease in personal expression. Each of these also shares a bidirectional influence with social information processing, the hyperpersonal, social information deindividuation effects, propinquity, and group interactions that mediate the CMC. These interacting, mediating influences exist across the network. Each influence, when present, modifies and transforms the effect of the others on the resulting CMC.

Actor-Networks in Practice: Email, Reddit, WhatsApp

Email, Organizational Culture, and Communication

To better understand how CMC technologies interact with social practices, Turnage (2016) analyzed the use of email at the now defunct Enron Corporation. Enron was a highly successful energy commodities corporation run by CEO Ken Lay. In 2001, it was revealed that Enron's financial situation was far worse than their annual reports had made it seem, and that this was the result of large-scale accounting fraud and corruption.

Turnage analyzed email traffic during two distinct time periods: The first set was during Enron's heyday, when it was one of the most successful corporations in the United States. The second set was collected after news about the fraud and corruption had gone public. The analysis provides an actor-network illustration of the mediating influences of technology and corporate culture before and during a time of organizational crisis.

Given the large size of the organization, Enron employees used email as the main way to communicate with each other and with the CEO, Ken Lay. Enron valued email as it allowed employees to express their feelings directly to the CEO. Email is also a relatively non-personal, text-based medium that has persistence and broadcast-like characteristics. At Enron, this combination of technological features at first helped maintain a stable corporate culture and then, later on, facilitate a rapid change in the expression of workplace values.

Analysis of the email exchanges during the first period reveals a volume of congratulatory email from employees that reinforced and reified corporate norms and business practices. These emails emphasize a corporate culture of greed and ideology of employee rivalry. Examples include the following: "I ... will speak for so many in saying THANK YOU for your hard work, great planning, and sacrifice made in the early years long before we came here to enjoy all the extra benefits provided" and "I can tell you without hesitation, that since you took over our company in the late 80's, it has been the most challenging and exciting time that I have spent in my work life" (Turnage, 2016, p. 210).

The tone of the emails changed during the second period, when Enron was in crisis. Employee emails become more unrestrained, hostile, nonconformist, and even vitriolic: "Thanks Ken You Piece of _____" and "Thanks for everything knob head" (Turnage, 2016, p. 211). This shift reveals how the distance from face-to-face interaction makes it easier for a person to be critical, and email often is associated with the disinhibited expression of feelings.

The existing organizational reliance on email as the primary means of communication makes broadcasting an emotional expression across the organization possible. At first, this helped to maintain the corporate Enron culture. Even as the continued existence of the organization became problematic, employees were slow to respond. Once the crisis became apparent, however, the number of Enron employees involved in the email exchanges increased, and previously disconnected people engaged in a larger quantity of mutual email exchanges. The language in employee emails shifted from echoing a corporate ideology of greed that prioritizes monetary gains and the importance of competition to an expression of personal ethics and a conflict between the two. Email facilitated a sense of coalition and political strength among employees that was not present before, and a new group of email participants formed around the expression of this changing value system.

The existing organizational practice of email use at Enron facilitated this rapid change to a communication of dissent, just as it had earlier helped maintain adherence to the corporate culture. This, combined with the email's asynchronous but persistent communication, as well as its broadcast and rebroadcast distribution characteristics, facilitated a rapid change in the employee expression of values and culture at Enron. Hearing others articulate criticisms and alternative values emboldened their expressions and sense of political power within the organization. The technological affordances of email are actants that, combined with the employees' dissatisfaction, come together to serve as mediators that disrupt company culture (Turnage, 2016).

Reddit Construction of Social Reality

Pantumsinchai (2018) used an actor-network perspective to investigate two cases wherein communities of social media users attempted to utilize collective intelligence to solve real-life terrorist attacks. The first is a community of Reddit social media sleuths who investigated the 2013 Boston marathon bombing. The second is the social media community response to the 2015 bombing of the Erawan Shrine in downtown Bangkok.

In 2013, Reddit became a major source of information for people interested in following the Boston marathon bombing. In an attempt to solve the case, the FBI shared surveillance camera photos of the Boston bombers with the public and asked for help in identifying the men. Redditors combed through the photos and videos to find the bombers and quickly targeted individuals who looked similar to the men in the photos. They posted comments, opinions, and ideas to several news sub-Reddits and quickly created their own thread: r/findbostonbombers. This subsequently led to criticism of r/findbostonbombers as Redditors named and harassed numerous innocent people by sharing their private information.

At one point, Redditors believed they had identified the suspect, an innocent college student who had been reported as missing by a Redditor. This belief was further augmented when an old high school classmate tweeted that he physically resembled one of the men in the FBI photos. Other statements about this individual on Reddit took on a life of their own. Word of his name mentioned on a police scanner spread from Reddit to Twitter (now known as X), the interconnected networks constituting a nonhuman actant that moved his name beyond the person and platform of creation.

The Reddit community celebration of having identified the suspect before the FBI did not last long. After a police shootout in Watertown, Massachusetts, the FBI identified the Tsarnaev brothers as the real bombing suspects. The revelation of this fact undermined the circular network of posted comments, opinions, ideas, and expressed concerns and demolished the socially constructed reality that the Reddit network had once believed to be robust. The discovery of Tripathi's body not long after provided further proof of his innocence, with his death ruled a suicide.

The social media sleuthing of the 2015 Bangkok bombing followed a similar pattern of social construction that mediated the collected empirical evidence with the social reality of an online networked community. On August 17, 2015, a bomb explosion at the Erawan Shrine in downtown Bangkok killed 20 and injured 125 people. As the Thai police began their investigation, a group of Thai citizens posted photos, discussed facts, and constructed theories about the bombers in Facebook groups and on Pantip, a Reddit equivalent.

From the outset, these online citizens believed that the bomber was not Thai. Despite a long history of political coups, many people in the online community believed that a Thai person could not hurt another Thai. In addition, citizens argued that since all "true" Thais are Buddhist, the bomber was not Thai, since Buddhists would not attack a religious shrine.

Eventually, the Thai police arrested two of the bombers. They were Uyghurs protesting Thailand's handling of asylum-seeking Uyghur Muslims from China. Before their arrests, Pantip and Facebook users had generated "mounds of misinformation", produced numerous false leads, and shamed many innocent people, but had failed to identify the perpetrators (Pantumsinchai, 2018, p. 762).

Both online communities used the technology of the internet, cell phones, surveillance cameras, and social media to engage in their CMC investigations. Participants uploaded evidence from their cell phones and security cameras, posting and reposting photos, screenshots, and surveillance videos. Without these technologies, the online sleuthing communities could not exist. Through these technologies, social media sites enable the human connections of an actor-network. Interested individuals turn to them for the latest, most accurate and updated news. Participants within these sites also engage in personal speculation, rumor generation, and the social construction of a reality that expresses personal concerns and interpretations as well as material facts and empirical evidence. Within a mixture of these concerns and evidence, each community constructs a social reality, engages in false accusations and harassment of innocent people as suspects, and fails to find the real perpetrators. This is not their intent, but often the outcome.

These examples illustrate how actor-networks mediate information rather than transmit it. Each post and repost transforms the information shared across the network, interpreting the facts, making social claims, and mixing social concerns with empirical evidence. Each community construes claims made about the facts in a way that transforms them from empirical evidence to social knowledge. However empirically accurate or false that knowledge is, these communities accept them as constituting a social reality.

WhatsApp Silence, Relationship, Culture, and Power

CMC applications such as WhatsApp are becoming increasingly popular in the workplace. These text-based platforms are generally used for immediate and shorts bursts of communication. So how do people respond to and make sense of those instances wherein a communication partner does not respond immediately? Asynchronous digital communication tools, such as WhatsApp, allow for delays in response. The perception of these delays socially constructs the network of working relationships and use of CMC within an organization. Pihlaja (2020) analyzed the use of silence, or lack of response, in two WhatsApp exchanges, one between a manager and an employee and the other between the manager and a customer.

The company that Pihlaja investigated uses numerous forms of CMC, including phone conversations, email, and Google Docs. They recently added WhatsApp to help staff handle the challenges of communicating in the cross-border environment in which they operate. WhatsApp texting is a relatively stable and increasingly important form of CMC within the organization, for both employees and customers.

WhatsApp usage by the individual staff members, however, tends to be ad hoc and based on individual preferences. The manager whom Pihlaja interviewed uses it to oversee the product movement between the company job sites across the U.S.–Mexico border and troubleshoot as necessary. He uses WhatsApp to text the company truck driver at least once a day to check in, see how things are going with moving materials, ensure that he has the correct documents, and ask when he plans to arrive at the company delivery site. The driver, however, does not always respond to the message right away, soliciting a second and sometimes third message from the manager, to which the driver eventually responds.

While the silence from the driver frustrates the manager, the manager uses digital silence in his communications with customers too. Sometimes this is the result of competing obligations; other times it is because the manager did not want to not respond until he had more details on the production process himself.

The interpretation of the driver's and the manager's silence and eventual response depends on the weak informational and strong relational ties between the two CMC participants as well as the larger organizational cultural expectations. These social network bonds between the participants mediate the informational interpretation of the silence. Cell phone signal strength, employee habits, past practices, and cultural expectations within the organization form some of the actor-network of influences on this use of CMC.

The use of silence in asynchronous, written, mobile CMC is open to personal, social, and cultural influences and interpretations. It represents implicit understandings in the technology, interpersonal relationships, and organizational power dynamics, in one case between the manager and driver, and in the other between the company and customer. Any particular text exchange invokes these influences in a different way, as when the manager needs information from the driver or needs to respond to the request from a customer. Digital silence serves as a tool to influence the communication patterns or send a message about a communication partner's importance.

Each participant responded to the silence by sending another text, calling, or waiting, based on their social interpretation of the personal working relationship, shared history, organizational culture, positional power, economic reality, and urgency of the need to know. Actor-networks describe all of these as mediating technological and social influences on the perception and use of CMC technologies in an organization.

Perspective in Context

Analysis and Critique

Treating technology as a passive, inflexible entity that simply responds to human intent and purpose does not adequately describe the communication that occurs through CMC. The actor-network perspective provides a more complex and nuanced analysis of the multiple, collective, technological, and social influences of the CMC expression and interpretation of identities, relationships, groups, and communities that emphasizes the influential interaction patterns of the technological, social, and human use of technology on CMC (Leonardi, 2011).

It is important to view technologies as more than something that people use. Technologies have become an intrinsic part of human communication practices. An actor-network analysis provides a useful perspective for recognizing how technologies interact with and affect our lives and relationships (Hall et al., 2021).

Critiques of the actor-networks perspective often revolve around the conception and placement of agency in technological innovations, platforms, and material objects. Human agency represents the ability to state an intent and achieve a desirable goal. Agency implies a sense of responsibility, ethics, and meaning to the actions taken. We do not often think of technological innovations and material objects as having these characteristics. Nonhuman agency, formed without intentionality, is difficult to conceive. The actor-networks perspective describes but does not critically evaluate the ethics and meaning of human–technology interactions or the resulting constituted social realities (Bencherki, 2017).

There is, however, often a substantial difference between the stated intent of a human agent and the goal achieved. The actor-network perspective focuses on the observable outcomes and the multiple interacting influences upon them. It does not deny the concept of human agency but recognizes that technological artifacts often affect the resulting communication practices as much as the original human intent does. Recalcitrant objects in the natural, social, and technological environment intervene, affecting that intent through nonhuman, material, as well as social influences, producing a distinctly different outcome. Human agency is thus realized through the use of technological capabilities and within their constraints. That is, humans enact agency in conjunction with physical, social, and technological influences that are separate from and affect the accomplishment of that human intent (Cooren, 2020; Latour, 2005; Leonardi, 2011).

COMMUNICATION ETHICS CHALLENGE

Social Media and Societal Implications

Many users of Twitter (now known as X) and other social media sites inflate their perceived social influence by creating or buying fake or automated followers. This type of social media fraud increases the appearance of popularity in order to enhance a person's real-world entertainment career, political endeavors, or social influence. In response to mounting skepticism from advertisers and users about the accuracy of its numbers, Twitter (X) acknowledged that easy access to creating fake accounts and the company's slow response had devalued the influence of legitimate users on the platform. In July of 2018 Twitter (X) began removing tens of millions of suspicious accounts in an effort to restore trust in their social media platform. Many celebrities found their numbers reduced by 2–3 million followers overnight. Politicians from both political parties lost hundreds of thousands of followers (Confessore & Dance, 2018).

Despite these efforts, this type of fraud continues to be an ongoing concern for social media platforms. Even more disturbing than artificially inflated numbers are fake profiles created by using people's real personal information. Many of these are created by stealing profile information from real users, including minors. One teenage girl, for example, discovered that her photo and biographical information were used for a fake account that tweeted ads for cryptocurrency (Confessore & Dance, 2018; Harris et al., 2018).

1. Do you think that the creation of fake accounts on Twitter (now known as X) or other social media sites is a serious social ethical concern? Why or why not?

2. Do you think that social media companies have an ethical responsibility to put measures in place that guard against the use of fake or automated accounts on their sites?

3. What type of ethical responsibility does a social media site have to maintain the integrity of its user accounts?

4. What type of ethical responsibility does a social media site have to ensure that an individual's personal information is not used by others for profit without their consent?

KEYWORDS AND PHRASES

An **actant** is any individual person, technology, set of social relationships, or combination of assembled influences that produces an effect.

The **actor-network** perspective examines how the use of a technology mediates the communication of meaning in groups of people, across an assemblage of social-technological influences that shape those participant interactions, understandings, and relationships.

Actor-network analysis provides a lens through which to view the role that technology plays in shaping human communication processes and a way of understanding the social implications.

Actor-networks include and describe all the technological and human influences on the constitution of CMC.

Actors are any element of a network that can impact communication practices.

Agency takes place when technologies affect how users and societies at large interact and engage with the world around them.

Figuration describes the observable pattern of effects produced by an actor-network. It shifts the focus from intents to implications and to outcomes rather than original intent.

Mediators are the interactions among a variety of influences that transform the effect of an action as it moves through the network.

QUESTIONS FOR FURTHER DISCUSSION

1. What do you think is the best description of the influential relationships among human agency, constraints, and communication?

2. To what extent is communication free personal expression, socially constrained, or strategically constituted within the medium or within a relationship?

3. The actor-networks perspective argues that technologies can hold agency just as humans can. What do you think about this idea? Do you agree with the critics of this perspective?

Conclusion: Implications

Concerns and Benefits of CMC

Computer-mediated communication has become a common alternative to face-to-face communication. A great deal of our everyday interaction takes place via CMC; and that interaction is inherently social. How we use CMC shapes our identities and our social relationships (Baym, 2015). Understanding how our communication and relationships, both on and offline, are affected by CMC is important. CMC has become a part of our everyday lives. Figure I.1 illustrates the interaction of CMC technology, interpersonal relationships, and social practice.

When considering the implications of CMC, it is important to note that the use of CMC and "social media ... is not inherently beneficial or harmful" (American Psychological Association, 2023, p. 3). Social media use can be psychologically beneficial, particularly for members of marginalized groups. It provides an opportunity for developing positive interactions and relationships with a diverse group of peers who can provide social support that buffers the effects of stress, especially among those who have been historically marginalized by society. It can create new opportunities for online companionship and emotional intimacy, and it can facilitate access to information and support. Both of these protect against the negative consequences of psychological stress (U.S. Surgeon General, 2023a, 2023b).

At the same time, some uses of CMC can have negative consequences. The use of social media for social comparison, for example, particularly around issues of physical appearance, with attention focused on self-photos and the feedback to those photos, can lead to poorer body image, disordered eating, and depressive symptoms. In addition, inappropriate and harmful material can spread through social media quickly and easily.

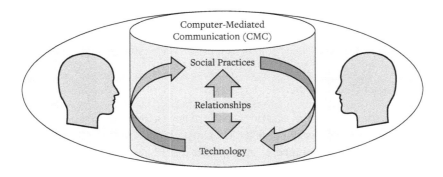

FIGURE I.1 CMC Technology, Relationships, and Social Practices.

This can occur as a consequence of unwanted content exchanges or the algorithmic designs of the platform. In some cases, the deaths of individuals have been linked to the self-harm, suicide materials, or risk-taking challenges that appeared on a social media platform (American Psychological Association, 2023; U.S. Surgeon General, 2023b). Numerous scholars explore how CMC affects our relationships, both online and offline. They highlight both the concerns with and the opportunities provided by CMC.

Concerns With CMC and Social Media

Scholars have identified several areas of concern with CMC and social media use. The concerns with CMC range from the for-profit motive of social media corporations to personal data privacy, the compulsive or additive behaviors of users, cyberbullying, and mental health issues.

Algorithms and Profiting From Personal Data

Most social media platforms and applications are created and maintained by for-profit corporations. This means that the social practices carried out through CMC are eventually used to generate corporate profits. These social media corporations typically make money in two ways. One way is by ensuring users see as many ads and sponsored posts as possible. This means that the longer a user stays online, the more profitable the social media platform becomes. Thus, platforms design algorithms to try to keep users online for as long as possible, presenting them with posts and updates that they expect the users will like. These algorithms also shape the user experience, personalizing the information that a user sees about family, friends, community, and society in general. This can become a concern when users get most of their news from social media (Baym, 2015; Eslami et al., 2015; Pew Research Center, 2022).

A second way that social media companies make money is by selling personal user data to advertisers or other interested parties. Many CMC users express concern for the loss of control over the personal information they inadvertently share through Google searches, on social media sites, or the use of cell phone apps (Marwick et al., 2017). Khati et al. (2022), for example, found that their research participants in Malaysia were very willing to use an app-based strategy for HIV prevention but expressed privacy and confidentiality concerns. They found that participants were interested in learning about the app for HIV prevention, but were less willing to use the app, expressing concern over what the app might do with their personal data, the security of that data, and the possibility of third-party data breaches. These concerns reduced their trust and use of the app.

Addictive and Compulsive Behaviors

In addition to the for-profit motivations and privacy issues, a number of scholars raise concerns about addictive or compulsive CMC user behavior. Users sometimes appear unable to stop using a social media, smartphone, or VR gaming platform, even when it has a negative effect on their lives. This is of particular concern, given the active use of computer algorithms designed to make compulsive use more likely and that this addictive behavior often is associated with negative psychological and relational consequences, such as feelings of lower self-esteem and fewer physical interactions with friends (Barreda-Àngeles & Hartmann, 2022; Bhargava & Velasquez, 2021; Huang, 2022; Yang et al., 2022).

To examine this phenomenon, Young et al. (2017) reviewed a number of internet addiction studies and analyzed Facebook user behaviors, experiences, and potential for addiction. They found that even though participants often use Facebook as a form of escape, there is no association between this type of Facebook use and addiction. Likewise, Barreda-Àngeles and Hartmann (2022) examined the addictive potential of VR. They found compulsive behaviors in 2% to 20% of users, depending on the specific measurement criteria used. They report that these estimates are similar to those previously found for the use of social networking sites and other activities, suggesting that VR applications do not present a higher addictive potential than other types of CMC-based activities. Their results do indicate, however, a concern that the feeling of immersive embodiment within a virtual reality while playing the game may predict a potential for addiction.

Cyberbullying

A larger concern is cyberbullying. Online acts of cyberbullying, aggression, and victimization are gaining an increasing amount of attention among researchers and with the general public. Direct cyberbullying involves a perpetrator attacking a victim without an audience. Indirect bullying describes the same types of aggression, but in acts that take place across multiple online platforms and in front of one or more audiences. Other examples of cyberbullying include aggressive acts of victimization that only take place in online settings, such as hacking into someone's social media accounts. The prevalence of these types of online aggressive behaviors vary widely between countries, with only 5% of 11–14 year olds in countries like Australia and Germany reported being a victim of cyberbullying to 23% of that same age group in North America and China (Marciano et al., 2020). These types of cyberbullying are most often perpetrated against women, members of historically marginalized ethnic or racial groups, and LBGTQ+ youth. They are linked to a variety of negative outcomes, including increases in levels of anxiety, depression, and suicide (Kowalski et al., 2019; Marciano et al., 2020).

Mental Health Concerns

A final concern is the connection between CMC and the mental health of users. These potential mental health concerns include poor body image, low self-esteem, higher anxiety depression symptoms, being pressured to act in a certain way, being harassed, or bullied. Social media use can perpetuate a negative body image social comparison, dissatisfaction, and disordered eating behaviors. In addition, extensive social media use can increase feelings of anxiety, loneliness, and depression. The use of social media can worsen any existing mental health issues, such as poor body image, low self-esteem, and disordered eating; deactivation of a social media platform for 4 weeks often improves an individual's subjective sense of well-being, self-reported happiness, life satisfaction, and reduced anxiety and depression (Thai et al., 2023; U.S. Surgeon General, 2023b).

Benefits of CMC and Social Media

The use of social media and CMC in general also provides numerous benefits in the potential for social connection, social support, and social change. Through CMC, some people, particularly those marginalized from mainstream society, can make connections and build community. Others, such as the breast cancer caregivers and members of Alcoholics Anonymous, find social support in times of need. Finally, many people use CMC as a medium for the advocacy of social change.

Social Connection

The use of CMC often is blamed for a decrease in the social connection experienced across society, but the technology of CMC also enables people to stay in touch with friends and family more easily. Sending a text message, email, or sharing a story on Instagram takes less time and effort than writing a letter or even placing a phone call (U. S. Surgeon General, 2023a). Social media benefits include a "positive [sense of] community and connection with others who share [similar] identities, abilities, and interests. It can provide access to important information and create a space for self-expression. The ability to form and maintain [these] friendships online and develop social connections are among the positive effects of social media use" (U.S. Surgeon General Social, 2023b, p. 6).

Social media gives people whose voices have been silenced in mainstream discussions a digital space to find like-minded folks, connect with others, share stories, seek advice, offer emotional support, and feel safe. This is especially important for historically marginalized groups, such as people with disabilities, racial and ethnic minorities, and members of the LGBTQ+ communities. In addition, social media provides access to political information and potential for collective action that might otherwise remain outside their reach (Rosenbaum, 2018; Trevisan, 2020).

Social Support

In addition, people often turn to CMC for social support. Recently, technology has enabled this social support to extend beyond the connections made with other people to support provided by a chatbot using AI. This provides a particularly interesting perspective on the perception of social support. Yang (2020) cites an example of a user response to an AI bot saying "I know you are not real but I just wanted to send these pictures of my family out at Disneyland having a great time. I'm doing better now. Thank you" (p. 35).

Communicating with AI chatbots allows people to talk about socially awkward feelings; deeply held private emotions such as loneliness, fear, and depression; and socially unacceptable practices such as opioid use in a relatively anonymous context, away from human judgment. The bots encourage these vulnerable people to talk about their issues in a safe space. They allow people to "say something to something that wouldn't judge them" (Yang, 2020, p. 35).

Meng and Daie (2021) report that a chatbot can build as much rapport with an individual using CMC as a human being can, providing both share their worries with the individual. Sharing concerns, whether by a human being or a chatbot, increases the sense of supportiveness that reduces stress and worry. Lew and Walther (2023) find that participants rate humans as more socially attractive than chatbots, but the results of these studies suggest some interesting possibilities for AI chatbots providing mental health support through CMC.

Social Change

Finally, CMC also allows people to connect more easily with their elected representatives. Rather than needing to call, write, or visit your U.S. senators or representatives, you can now submit an online query, send an email, or tag them in a social media post. Although this does not always lead to the desired change, it allows citizens to communicate more directly with their representatives.

CMC also provides spaces for individuals to discuss important social issues and organize and activate groups in response to a social issue. For example, social media facilitated the growth and effectiveness of the #MeToo movement. In addition, historically marginalized groups can now more easily join mainstream discussions of issues that affect them directly, connecting with likeminded others to provide the strength in numbers needed to make a difference in a public debate and policy decision (Freelon et al., 2016; Jackson et al., 2020; Rosenbaum, 2018).

A Final Word

CMC has both positive and negative social implications. Advances in CMC technology means we are able to write using a word processing program, share our work using a cloud-based server, send a quick email, text questions, and meet using videoconferencing. The existence of CMC, however, does not mean that we necessarily will engender positive outcomes through its use, bring about more just societies, reduce people's suffering, or generate goodness in the world. Our use of CMC, even with the assistance of AI, does not necessarily increase our "ability to comprehend our place in the universe [which] remains not just incomplete but inadequate" (Damasio, 2018, p. 230).

CMC provides an opportunity for more social connection, support, and positive change. It also holds the negative potential of personal data exploitation, compulsive and addictive user behavior, cyberbullying, and the aggravation of mental health concerns. As the actor-networks perspective indicates, our intent does not affect what CMC will become as much as our ongoing social practices in the use of its technologies.

Image Credit

Glossary

An **actant** is any individual person, technology, set of social relationships, or combination of assembled influences that produces an effect.

Activated network is the portion of potential connections that a person thinks might provide a useful social capital response to a particular type of need or achievement.

Active information gathering strategies involve finding out information about a person without interacting with them. This can include asking a shared network of friends about the person.

The **actor-network perspective** examines how the use of a technology mediates the communication of meaning in groups of people, across an assemblage of social-technological influences that shape those participant interactions, understandings, and relationships.

Actor-network analysis provides a lens through which to view the role that technology plays in shaping human communication processes and a way of understanding the social implications.

Actor-networks include and describe all the technological and human influences on the constitution of CMC.

Actors are any element of a network that can impact communication practices.

Actualized selves are the external material identity and social roles that the person enacts in life.

Affordances describes features of the environment that are perceived and used by a participant in that environment to behave in a specific manner.

Agency takes place when technologies affect how users and societies at large interact and engage with the world around them.

Ambient presence describes the sense of presence that is the result of two people in geographically different locations using CMC.

Anonymity is the degree to which a source is unknown or unspecified.

Appropriation occurs when participants adapt the capabilities of a medium so that they can reach their communication goal.

Authenticity defines the perception of an action or communication as real, sincere, or reflecting a person's inner self.

Backstage refers to a more personal, private space where an individual can relax, step out of character, and review any aspects that might offend the audience in the ongoing frontstage presentation.

A **behaviorally mobilized network** is the subset of that cognitively activated network a person is willing to attempt to use for solving a problem or issue.

Budgeted social presence assumes an audience that allocates and manages its social presence across a number of interactions and platforms.

Calibrated amateurism describes how family influencers purposely add an amateurish look to their videos to create a spontaneous, relatable, yet entirely staged authenticity.

Cognitive adaptation describes a person's ability to learn through experience, develop expertise, and adopt new cognitive schema to communicate effectively in a medium.

Cognitive effort describes the amount of time and energy needed transfer information from one person to another through a communication medium.

Cognitive schema help us efficiently interpret the meaning of a message by simultaneously evaluating the patterns of verbal, vocal, facial, and physical body cues. They provide efficient cognitive short cuts for quickly interpreting the most likely meaning of a message.

Collective affordances allow the members of a specialized work team to use the CMC medium in complementary ways.

Colocation permits participants to see and hear each other within the same communication context and environment.

Communal frame places the individual identity within the group to which the individual belongs.

Communication is the symbolic system of human expression through which individuals share information, create personal identities, connect with others, develop relationships, participate in groups, and construct communities. It has both a content and a relational aspect.

Communication accommodation describes how changes in language use expresses both a conscious and unconscious affiliation with or difference from a group.

Communication affordance refers to the interaction between a person's perception of the communication potential of a medium and its desired use.

Communication ambiguity is the degree to which the meaning of a message can be misinterpreted. As the nonverbal cues available in a medium decrease, communication ambiguity, and that probability of misinterpretation, increase.

Communication function–medium fit aligns the purpose of a communication to the richness of a medium.

Communication functions refer to the purposes of communication. There are two general communication functions: a production function that contributes to the accomplishment of a task and building and maintaining social relationships.

Communication privacy management describes the negotiating process of sharing personal information with close friends, acquaintances, and a broader public.

Communication task efficiency–medium fit balances the efficiency of transmitting the message content with the effective interpretation of its meaning.

Communities represent a sense of shared values, characteristics, and commonalities among members. Community members generally experience a sense of belonging and attachment to one another and a feeling of being involved together in events of common importance.

Competitive social presence is a strategy used to describe when communicators make their message more interesting, stimulating, exciting, or provocative to stand out from a background of CMC noise.

Complementarity refers to a style of communication that appears divergent but represents a reciprocal pattern of communication behaviors that recognize and reinforce social status differences in group member relationships.

Computer-mediated communication (CMC) describes communication expressed and interpreted using a technological medium. We use the term to describe any communication that is technologically mediated, in part, in whole, or across multiple platforms.

Connected presence describes the extent to which the sense of being together in a relationship is mediated by CMC. It describes how people use multiple platforms and devices to maintain their sense of closeness to others and maintain patterns of relational communication.

Context collapse occurs when there are a variety of audiences in the same space. This affects how we present ourselves.

Convergence (in media synchronicity) is the process through which people achieve a common understanding of the meaning of transmitted information. **Convergence** (in communication accommodation) means using a communication style that is similar to a person or group with whom someone identifies.

Conveyance (in media synchronicity) describes the transmission of information through one or more messages to accomplish a communication task.

Copresence refers to CMC participants being aware of each other. It has a bidirectional meaning and is not about a single participant's awareness of another person's presence but about both people being aware of each other.

The **cues filtered-out** perspective suggests that the lack of nonverbal cues common to CMC may reduce a communicator's interpersonal awareness and affect their ability to form an accurate impression of the other person.

Deindividuation is a state of decreased cognitive salience of oneself as a person and increased awareness of a social identity within a specific group context. The deindividuation process shifts identity salience from the personal to the social, increasing sensitivity to the environmental cues and social influences while decreasing an awareness of oneself as a unique individual.

Depersonalization is the tendency to perceive oneself and others not as unique individuals with multiple idiosyncratic characteristics, talents, behaviors, and ways of communicating but as defined only by membership in a group, community, or social category.

Divergence in language style distances participants from people and groups with whom they do not identify.

Electronic propinquity is the experience of a psychological closeness and feeling of connectedness to another person through CMC.

Emotional social capital refers to emotional support that generates a sense of shared personal validation and emotional well-being.

Enacted frame describes how identity comes into being through the dynamic performance of that identity in conversation with others.

Engagement represents the time spent learning to navigate an environment.

Engrossment occurs when participants become more involved, less aware of their physical surroundings, and more emotionally attached to their experiences in the virtual environment.

Entitled social presence describes when communicators attempt to promote social presence by limiting the number and variety of CMC sources available to the audience.

Expressive–perceptual dimension builds on the space-time dimension and argues that the ability to observe vocal inflections of speech, facial expressions, and physical body cues facilitates the expression and interpretation of meaning.

Extractive information gathering strategies include looking up information about the person in the newspaper, library, or searching the internet.

Facial expressions show frustration, distaste, enthusiasm, fear, and excitement, adding to the emotional content of the voice and words.

False perception refers to a potential that an individual perceives but that the medium does not provide.

Feedback describes the immediacy of response to a communicated message. In a synchronous medium, such as face-to-face conversation, participants can simultaneously speak, listen, provide verbal and nonverbal feedback, and respond to questions and comments.

Figuration describes the observable pattern of effects produced by an actor-network. It shifts the focus from intents to implications and to outcomes rather than original intent.

Frontstage presentations involve an individual presenting themselves to a wide audience. This presentation involves a version of self that consciously conceals any perceived personal flaws and accentuates a fit with social role expectations.

Generalized other describes the influences that parents, family, social groups, community, and the broader cultural environment have on personal identity.

Generative role taking is a third form of conversation control. Participants can alternately take on leadership roles and engage in behaviors that sustain productive group dialogue.

Groups are networks of individuals who interact for a specific purpose and communicate with a particular style. They usually have between three and 20 participants.

Hyperpersonal perspective describes how these feelings of intimacy can develop in less time and with more intensity in a CMC medium.

Identity represents a person's sense of self. A person constructs that identity through an iterative process of communication, feedback, and cognitive reflection.

Identity shift describes a change in a person's self-concept after observing their online behavior.

Imagined audience refers to the audience people imagine when there isn't a physical audience present.

Immersive presence follows as a participant spends more time, focuses more attention, and expends more effort in the environment. This immersive presence involves an awareness and adoption of the characteristics of a virtual identity within the environment.

Impression management is a selective self-presentation that is more common when people become aware of an audience and become concerned about how they appear to other people.

Individual affordance represents an ability one member may have due to a particular role in the group or technical expertise

Influences on electronic propinquity refer to (a) existing relational closeness, (b) the ability to provide and receive feedback (or the mutual directionality of communication), (c) bandwidth, (d) information complexity, (e) communication rules, (f) communicator skill, and (g) amount of choice in the selection of a medium through which to communicate

Informational social capital refers to different types of information, perspectives, personal experiences, innovative ideas, alternative suggestions, and ways of approaching an issue.

Interactive information gathering strategies include engaging a person in conversation, asking questions, listening to statements of self-disclosure, and paying attention to any apparent enhancements, evasive responses, omissions, distortions, falsifications, or contradictory statements.

Interactivity identifies the turn taking, immediacy of feedback, and rate of conversational exchange.

Interdependence refers to the development of a shared pattern of relational communication over time. As participants communicate with each other, they begin to (a) identify as members of the group, (b) recognize each individual's abilities and contributions, and (c) share a sense of task interdependence and mutual influence.

Invitational social presence means that communicators focus on one specific audience and work to relate to them.

Language–medium fit describes the extent to which the medium's capacity meets the language demands of intended communication. This method considers the verbal, visual, and numeric information demands of a communication task and the ability of a medium to meet those demands.

Language variety describes the range of meaning that can be conveyed through a medium using the linguistic symbols available in and appropriate for that medium.

Lean medium is a medium that is efficient for making simple requests, exchanges of routine information, official documents, and noncontroversial directives.

Lurking happens when CMC participants merely observe what others do without actively participating in the community by posting or commenting.

Material element of identity refers to physical attributes such as clothes, property, and places to which a person attributes meaning and that contribute to their sense of self.

Media naturalness is a perspective holds that the more CMC reflects face-to-face communication, or the more "natural" this communication is, the less effort it requires from its participants to engage in collaborative activities.

Media richness refers to the extent to which a CMC medium allows people to communicate effectively, sharing both content and relational information.

Media synchronicity perspective builds on both the richness and naturalness perspectives, but it shifts attention from the constraints of the medium and the effects of human cognitive schema to the fundamental processes of communication.

Mediators are the interactions among a variety of influences that transform the effect of an action as it moves through the network.

Metavoicing describes engaging in the ongoing conversation by commenting on the presence and participation of others.

Networked individualism recognizes that many people use the internet to find information, emotional support, and a sense of connection to like-minded others.

Networked individuals are people who connect to each other to meet immediate personal needs, not to share a sense of belonging in a membership with a common set of goals, values, and identities.

Networked privacy management is a perspective that involves understanding the technological influences of a CMC network on privacy management.

Nonverbal cues are the vocal inflection, facial expressions, hand gestures, and bodily movements that facilitate the interpretation of verbal information.

Numeric symbols use formulas to communicate important information about budgets, program costs, sales commissions, profit sharing, pay increases, retirement benefits, or other types of statistical relationships.

Parallelism refers to the number of simultaneous transmissions that a medium allows. It refers to how many people can send and receive multiple messages simultaneously.

Passive information gathering strategies include quietly watching how someone interacts with others in a social setting or on social media, observing the person's responses to particular situations, and drawing comparisons to the behaviors of friends or people we know.

Permeability describes the openness of a virtual community to membership and control of discussion topics. A permeable community is open and allows anyone who wishes to join or simply access its content.

Persistence describes the extent to which communication remains accessible after its original presentation.

Personal element of identity references the mostly unchanging collection of traits, goals, beliefs, and values that an individual holds.

Personal focus is the extent to which a message conveys personal feelings and emotions. A personal focus establishes a connection and relationship, shares feelings, emotional support, trust, and friendship.

Personal frame is the meaning that people attribute to themselves, their motivations, perceptions, and expectations.

Personal identity means viewing oneself as a unique individual. This identity becomes salient in thoughts about personal ambitions, motivations, accomplishments, satisfactions, desires, regrets, relationships, and meaning.

Personal presence is the degree to which an individual is involved in a virtual environment.

Physical body cues in the gestures and bodily stance further contextualize the meaning of a particular communication.

Physiological arousal is a heightened state of attention and emotion, whether happy, sad, angry, or joyous, that participants experience when together in face-to-face conversation.

Positivity bias occurs when most social media interactions feel like upward social comparisons due to users' tendency to present highly curated, mostly positive, and generally idealized images of themselves.

Presence means being in the moment, focused, and not distracted. It describes the experience of immersion in a conversation, relationship, narrative, or mediated experience.

Privacy management is about regulating personal informational boundaries. It describes how individuals consider and reconsider who should have access to what information about them under what circumstances.

Private self-consciousness reflects the inner feelings, emotions, beliefs, and thoughts of an individual. It connects a person with the inner aspects of identity.

Propinquity means physical proximity or closeness in time and space.

Proteus effect describes how an online presentation of self can affect a person's conceptual, behavioral, and communication relationships with others, both on- and offline.

Public self-consciousness pays attention to the social aspects of identity, such as appearance, behaviors, and style.

Reciprocity occurs when the community provides the members with benefits, and in turn members have recognizable obligations and responsibilities within the community.

Rehearsability is the ability to practice and edit a message before sending. A medium that supports rehearsability, such as texting and email, allows the sender to review the message, and, if need be, change it to express the intended meaning more precisely before transmission. Perceiving this affordance allows adjustments to a message that may reflect an initial response from a "test" audience. This ability varies with medium and is more difficult when speaking live to an audience face-to-face.

Relational frame refers to the individual identity created in relationship with others.

Reprocessability is the persistence of a message over time. It describes the ability of both sender and receiver to access, reflect on, reprocess, and reinterpret a message after it was initially sent.

Rich medium is a medium that is more effective for (a) relaying non-routine, complex, or controversial content information; (b) showing a personal interest or concern; (c) building trust in an interpersonal relationship; and/or (d) implementing a new plan or strategy that requires commitment and involvement of participants.

Schema alignment identifies achieving a relative sameness between the cognitive schema of two or more people who, over time, reduce their communication ambiguity and develop a common way of thinking about a problem or issue.

Self-presence refers to an individual's awareness of, and personal-emotional involvement in, a virtual identity and self-presentation.

Self-presentation is a communication activity that conveys who someone is, but it also helps a person construct sense of self.

Sense of virtual community refers to a sense of membership and belonging, enhanced by a mutual influence and the sharing of identities, as well as an immersive emotional engagement among participants.

Shared affordances provide all group members common access to a CMC medium characteristic.

Sociability is the need for social interaction.

Social affordance describes the relationship between a person and the medium in a way that changes social practice.

Social capital is a resource embedded in the network of group relationships. It is a collective asset that develops in the group relationships and includes the informational and emotional resources of the other members.

Social communitarian perspective defines a community as an underlying connection between and among people bonded together by common processes of culture, emotion, and values.

Social comparison is what happens when people assess their behaviors, abilities, and ideas in comparison to others. This is especially common when there are no objective means by which to assess oneself.

Social cues are signs that indicate someone's social identity, such as membership identification in a specific group.

Social element of identity emphasizes group membership, ethnicity, religion, nationality, gender, and family norms and expectations, all of which might influence a person's identity.

Social identity means seeing oneself within a social role, as a member of a group or community, and behaving in accordance with the social norms appropriate to that role. It becomes salient in the awareness of social roles, activities, responsibilities, and obligations to others, such as family, friends, colleagues, professional and social groups, or communities to which someone belongs.

The **social identity of deindividuation effects (SIDE)** perspective describes the tendency of people to identify with a group when engaged in CMC.

Social information processing argues that people will strategically use whatever social cues are available as a substitution for the missing nonverbal information.

Social penetration provides a social psychological perspective on relationship development. It describes relationship formation as a process of peeling back layers to get to know increasing levels of personal information about someone.

Social presence is a feeling of psychological proximity, closeness, connectedness, and intimacy with another person.

Speech conveys the vocal qualities of anxiety, excitement, hesitation, qualification, and overall expressiveness.

Strong-tie friendship connections provide the potential for the emotional support of a few, close, personal friends.

Symbol sets refer to the diverse ways a medium allows people to communicate. When people communicate, they use a variety of symbols, from words to facial expressions, body language, written language, vocal tones, and charts, graphs, and visuals.

Synchronicity describes a pattern of coordinated communication among participants who share a common focus.

Synchronous communication allows participants to speak and listen simultaneously and to provide interactive feedback.

Synchronous conversation assumes that participants are in the same space at the same time.

Technological affordance refers to an adaptation of the technical characteristics of a medium to a particular communication purpose or goal. It emerges through the interaction of technology and sociocultural uses.

Telepresence is a general term that describes a person's psychological state and subjective perception of reality as filtered by a technology.

Textual paralinguistic cues are cues that people use to communicate facial expressions, gestures, and other nonverbal cues. These cues include misspelling words, the use of specific symbols, punctuation, emojis, emoticons, and gifs.

Third place references public spaces where identity development can occur without the social hierarchies implicit in family gatherings or at work. These include informal social gatherings at neighborhood pubs, cafés, or community centers and groups meeting through CMC.

Time and space structure our perceptions of reality and make it accessible to us through our sensory awareness and cognitive interpretations. Time and space spent together define the basic dimensions of human relationships.

Transference occurs when the Proteus effect influences communication and/or behaviors in the real world.

Transmission velocity is the speed at which a medium transmits information. This refers to more than just passing on information. It includes the rapidity of transmission, immediacy of feedback, and synchronicity of turn taking in communication.

Triggered attending allows a participant to be part of an online conversation but remain relatively uninvolved until alerted to a topic of interest.

Uncertainty reduction describes the interpersonal motives and strategies for seeking that information about another person with whom we plan to develop a relationship.

Verbal information refers to the use of words. This kind of information can convey a broad range of abstract ideas and concepts, as well as concrete meanings.

Virtual communities refer to gatherings of people who use CMC to interact and develop relationships.

Virtual settlements describe shared online spaces in which participants interact with a variety of other people over time.

Visibility recognizes the relative ease with which information can be located.

Visual anonymity means that participants cannot see each other while they interact and may not know what each other looks like.

Visual representations show spatial relationships and geometric information in a picture, chart, graph, map, or diagram. These representations may show a spatial relationship in two or three dimensions, or a sequence through time.

Warrants are online cues, such as a comment, like, or a post, that provide evidence that the online communication is connected to an offline self and thus could be credible.

Weak-tie acquaintance networks offer access to a wide variety of new and nonredundant information, ideas, advice, and social resources.

References

Abidin, C. (2017). #familygoals: Family influencers, calibrated amateurism, and justifying young digital labor. *Social Media + Society*, *3*(2). https://doi.org/10.1177/2056305117707191

Abidin, C. (2018, April 16). *Layers of identity: How to be "real" when everyone is watching*. Real Life. https://reallifemag.com/layers-of-identity/

Adams, A., Miles, J., Dunbar, N. E., & Giles, H. (2018). Communication accommodation in text messages: Exploring liking, power, and sex as predictors of textisms. *The Journal of Social Psychology*, *158*, 474–490. https://doi.org/10.1080/00224545.2017.1421895

Akrich, M. (2010). From communities of practice to epistemic communities: Health mobilizations on the Internet. *Sociological Research Online*, *15*. https://minesparis-psl.hal.science/hal-00517657

Altman, I., & Taylor, D. (1973). *Social penetration: The development of interpersonal relationships*. Holt, Rinehart, and Winston.

American Psychological Association. (May 2023). *Health advisory on social media use in adolescence*. https://www.apa.org/topics/social-media-internet/health-advisory-adolescent-social-media-use

Anders, A. (2016). Team communication platforms and emergent social collaboration practices. *International Journal of Business Communication*, *53*, 224–261.

Antheunis, M. L., Schouten, A. P., & Walther, J. B. (2020). The hyperpersonal effect in online dating: Effects of text-based CMC vs. videoconferencing before meeting face-to-face. *Media Psychology*, *23*(6), 820–839. https://doi.org/10.1080/15213269.2019.1648217

Appel, H., Gerlach, A. L., & Crusius, J. (2016). The interplay between Facebook use, social comparison, envy, and depression. *Current Opinion in Psychology*, *9*, 44–49. https://doi.org/10.1016/j.copsyc.2015.10.006

Ash, E. (2016). Priming or Proteus effect? Examining the effects of avatar race on in-game behavior and post-play aggressive cognition and affect in video games. *Games and Culture*, *11*, 422–440.

Banks, J., & Carr, C. T. (2019). Toward a relational matrix model of avatar-mediated interactions. *Psychology of Popular Media Culture*, *8*, 287–295. https://doi.org/10.1037/ppm0000180

Baron, N. S. (2004). See you online: Gender issues in college student use of instant messaging. *Journal of Language and Social Psychology*, *23*, 397–423.

Barreda-Ángeles, M., & Hartmann, T. (2022). Hooked on the metaverse? Exploring the prevalence of addiction to virtual reality applications. *Frontiers in Virtual Reality*, *3*. https://doi.org/10.3389/frvir.2022.1031697

Barta, K., & Andalibi, N. (2021). Constructing authenticity on TikTok: Social norms and social support on the "fun" platform. *Proceedings of the ACM on Human-Computer Interaction*, *5*(430), 1–29. https://doi.org/10.1145/3479574

Bastiaensens, S., Vandebosch, H., Poels, K., Van Cleemput, K., DeSmet, A., & de Bourdeauduji, I. (2015). "Can I afford to help?" How affordances of communication modalities guide bystanders' helping intentions towards harassment on social network sites. *Behaviour & Information Technology*, *34*, 425–435. https://doi.org/10.1080/0144929X.2014.983979

Baumeister, R. F., & Hutton, D. G. (1987). Self-presentation theory: Self-construction and audience pleasing. In B. Mullen & G. R. Goethals (Eds.), *Theories of group behavior* (pp. 71–87). Springer-Verlag. https://doi.org/10.1007/978-1-4612-4634-3

Baxter, L. A., & Wilmot, W. W. (1984). "Secret tests": Social strategies for acquiring information about the state of the relationship. *Human Communication Research*, *11*, 171–201.

Baym, N. K. (2015). Social media and the struggle for society. *Social Media + Society*, 1–2.

Bem, D. J. (1967). Self-perception: An alternative interpretation of cognitive dissonance phenomena. *Psychological Review*, *74*(3), 183–200.

Bencherki, N. (2017). Actor-network theory. In C. Scott & L. Lewis (Eds.), *The international encyclopedia of organizational communication* (pp. 1–13). Wiley.

Berger, C. R., & Calabrese, R. J. (1975). Some explorations in initial interaction and beyond: Toward a developmental theory of interpersonal communication. *Human Communication Research, 1,* 99–112.

Berry, N., Lobhan, F., Belousov, M., Emsley, R., Nenadic, G., & Bucci, S. (2017). #WhyWeTweetMH: Understanding why people use Twitter to discuss mental health problems. *Journal of Medical Internet Research, 19,* e107. https://doi.org/10.2196/jmir.6173

Bhargava, V. R., & Velasquez, M. (2021). Ethics of the attention economy: The problem of social media addiction. *Business Ethics Quarterly, 31*(3), 321–359. https://doi.org/10.1017/beq.2020.32

Biocca, F. (1997). The cyborg's dilemma: Progressive embodiment in virtual environments. *Journal of Computer-Mediated Communication, 3*(2). https://doi.org/10.1111/j.1083-6101.1997.tb00070.x

Blanchard, A. L. (2007). Developing a sense of virtual community measure. *CyberPsychology & Behavior, 10,* 827–830. https://doi.org/10.1089/cpb.2007.9946

Blanchard, A. L., & Markus, M. L. (2004). The experienced "sense" of a virtual community: Characteristics and processes. *The DATA BASE for Advances in Information Systems, 35,* 65–79.

Blight, M. G., Ruppel, E. K., & Schoenbauer, K. V. (2017). Sense of community on Twitter and Instagram: Exploring the roles of motives and parasocial relationships. *Cyberpsychology, Behavior, and Social Networking, 20,* 314–319. https://doi.org/10.1089/cyber.2016.0505

Bliuc, A. M., Betts, J., Vergani, M., Iqbal, M., & Dunn, K. (2019). Collective identity changes in far-right online communities: The role of offline intergroup conflict. *New Media & Society, 21*(8). https://doi.org/10.1177/1461444819831779

Boghrati, R., Hoover, J., Johnson, K. M., Garten, J., & Dehghani, M. (2018). Conversation level syntax similarity metric. *Behavioral Research, 50,* 1055–1073. https://doi.org/10.3758/s13428-017-0926-2

Bourdon, J. (2020). From correspondence to computers: A theory of mediated presence in history. *Communication Theory, 30,* 64–83. https://doi.org/10.1093/ct/qtz020

boyd, d. (2008). Why youth (heart) social network sites: The role of networked publics in teenage social life. In D. Buckingham (Ed.), *MacArthur Foundation series on digital learning: Youth, identity, and digital media volume* (pp. 119–142). The MIT Press.

boyd, d. (2010). Social network sites as networked publics: Affordances, dynamics, and implications. In Z. Papacharissi (Ed.), *A networked self: Identity, community, and culture on social network sites* (pp. 39–58). Routledge. https://doi.org/10.4324/9780203876527

Bubas, G., Radosevic, D., & Hutinski, Z. (2003). Assessment of computer mediated communication competence: Theory and application in an online environment. *Journal of Information and Organizational Sciences, 27,* 53–71.

Buetler, K. A., Penalver-Andres, J., Özen, Ö, Ferriroli, L., Müri, R.M., Cazzoli, D., & Marchal-Crespo, L. (2022). "Tricking the brain" using immersive virtual reality: Modifying the self-perception over embodied avatar influences motor cortical excitability and action initiation. *Frontiers in Human Neuroscience, 15.* https://doi.org/10.3389/fnhum.2021.787487

Buisine, S., & Guegan, J. (2020). Proteus vs. social identity effects on virtual brainstorming. *Behaviour & Information Technology, 39,* 594–606. https://doi.org/10.1080/0144929X.2019.1605408

Buisine, S., Guegan, J., Barre, J., Segonds, F., & Aoussat, A. (2016). Using avatars to tailor ideation process to innovation strategy. *Cognition, Technology & Work, 18,* 583–594.

Burke, M., Cheng, J., & de Gant, B. (2020). Social comparison and Facebook: Feedback, positivity, and opportunities for comparison. *Proceedings of the 2020 CHI Conference on Human Factors in Computing Systems,* (355), 1–13. https://doi.org/10.1145/3313831.3376482

Burt, R. S. (1992). *Structural holes: The social structure of competition.* Harvard University Press.

Buunk, A. P., & Gibbons, F. X. (2007). Social comparison: The end of a theory and the emergence of a field. *Organizational Behavior and Human Decision Processes, 102,* 3–21. https://doi.org/10.1016/j.obhdp.2006.09.007

Campbell, K., & Wright, K. B. (2002). On-line support groups: An investigation of relationships among source credibility, dimensions of relational communication, and perceptions of emotional support. *Communication Research Reports, 19,* 183–193.

Cao, J., & Smith, E. B. (2021). Why do high-status people have larger social networks? Belief in status-quality coupling as a driver of network-broadening behavior and social network size. *Organization Science, 32*, 111–132. https://doi.org/10.1287/orsc.2020.1381

Carr, C. T. (2021) Identity shift effects of personalization of self-presentation on extraversion. *Media Psychology, 24*(4), 490–508. https://doi.org/10.1080/15213269.2020.1753540

Carr C. T., & Foreman, A. C. (2016). Identity shift III: Effects of publicness of feedback and relational closeness in computer-mediated communication. *Media Psychology, 19*, 334–358. https://doi.org/10.1080/15213269.2015.1049276

Carr, C. T., & Hayes, R. A. (2019). Identity shift effects of self-presentation and confirmatory and disconfirmatory feedback on self-perceptions of brand identification. *Media Psychology, 22*, 418–444. https://doi.org/10.1080/15213269.2017.1396228

Carr, C. T., Kim. Y., Valov, J. J., Rosenbaum, J. E., Johnson, B. K., Hancock, J. T., & Gonzales, A. (2021). An explication of identity shift theory: Getting our shift together. *Journal of Media Psychology, 33*, 202–214. https://doi.org/10.1027/1864-1105/a000314

Chancellor, S., Pater, J., Clear, T., Gilbert, E., & De Choudhury M. (2016). #thyghgapp: Instagram content moderation and lexical variation in pro-eating disorder communities. *Proceedings of the 19th ACM Conference on Computer-Supported Cooperative Work & Social Computing*, 1201–1213. https://doi.org/10.1145/2818048.2819963

Child, J. T., & Petronio, S. (2011). Unpacking the paradoxes of privacy in CMC relationships: The challenges of blogging and relational communication on the Internet. In Wright, K. B. & Webb, L. M. (Eds.), *Computer-mediated communication in personal relationships* (pp. 21–40). Peter Lang.

Ch'ng, E. (2015). The bottom-up formation and maintenance of a Twitter community. *Industrial Management & Data Systems, 115*, 612–624. https://do.org/10.1108/IMDS-11-2014-0332

Collins, N., Vaughan, B., Cullen, C., & Gardner, K. (2019). GaeltechVR: Measuring the impact of an immersive virtual environment to promote situated identity in Irish language learning. *Journal of Virtual Worlds Research, 12*, 1–16.

Collins, R. L. (1996). For better or worse: The impact of upward social comparisons on self-evaluations. *Psychological Bulletin, 119*(1), 51–69.

Comello, M. L. G. (2009). William James on "possible selves": Implications for studying identity in communication contexts. *Communication Theory, 19*, 337–350.

Confessore, N., & Dance, G. J. X. (2018, July 11). Battling fake accounts, Twitter to slash millions of followers. *The New York Times*. https://www.nytimes.com/2018/07/11/technology/twitter-fake-followers.html

Cooren, F. (2020). A communicative constitutive perspective on corporate social responsibility: Ventriloquism, undecidability, and surprisability. *Business & Society, 59*, 175–197. https://doi.org/10.1177/0007650318791780

Couture Bue, A. C. (2020). The looking glass selfie: Instagram use frequency predicts visual attention to high-anxiety body regions in young women. *Computers in Human Behavior, 108*(106329). https://doi.org/10.1016/j.chb.2020.106329

Cozolino, L. (2006). *The neuroscience of human relationships.* Norton.

Cramer, H., de Juan, P., & Tetreault, J. (2016). Sender-intended functions of emojis in US messaging. *Mobile HCI '16: Proceedings of the 18th International Conference on Human-Computer Interaction with Mobile Devices and Services*, 504–509. https://doi.org/10.1145/2935334.2935370

Cresswell, K. M., Worth, A., & Sheikh, A. (2010). Actor-network theory and its role in understanding the implementation of information technology developments in healthcare. *BMC Medical Informatics and Decision Making, 10*(67). https://doi.org/10.1186/1472-6947-10-67

Cutrona, C. E., & Russell, D. W. (1990). Type of social support and specific stress: Toward a theory of optimal matching. In B. Sarason, I. Sarason, & G. Pierce (Eds.), *Social support: An interactional view* (pp. 319–366). Wiley.

Cutrona, C. E., & Suhr, J. A. (1992). Controllability of stressful events and satisfaction with spouse support behaviors. *Communication Research, 19*, 154–174.

Daft, R., L., & Lengel, R. H. (1986). Organizational information requirements, media richness, and structural design. *Management Science, 32*, 554–571.

Daft, R. L., Lengel R. H., & Trevino, L. K. (1987). Message equivocality, media selection, and manager performance: Implications for information systems. *MIS Quarterly*, *11*(3), 355–366.

Dai, M., & Robbins, R. (2021). Exploring the influences of profile perceptions and different pick-up lines on dating outcomes on Tinder: An online experiment. *Computers in Human Behavior*, *117*, 1–9. https://doi.org/10.1016/j.chb.2020.106667

Dai, Y., & Shi, J. (2022). Vicarious interactions in online support communities: The roles of visual anonymity and social identification. *Journal of Computer-Mediated Communication*, *27*(3). https://doi.org/10.1093/jcmc/zmac006

Damasio, A. (2018). *The strange order of things*. Pantheon.

Darr, C. R., & Doss, E. F. (2022). The fake one is the real one: Finstas, authenticity, and context collapse in teen friend groups. *Journal of Computer-Mediated Communication*, *27*(4), https://doi.org/10.1093/jcmc/zmac009

DeAndrea, D. C. (2014). Advancing warranting theory. *Communication Theory*, *24*, 188–204. https://doi.org/10.1111/comt.12033

DeAndrea, D. C., & Carpenter, C. (2018). Measuring the construct of warranting value and testing warranting theory. *Communication Research*, *45*(8), 1193–1215. https://doi.org/10. 1177/00903650216644022

Dennis, A. R., Fuller, R. M., & Valacich, J. S. (2008). Media, tasks, and communication processes: A theory of media synchronicity. *MIS Quarterly*, *32*, 575–600.

Dennis, A. R., & Kinney, S. T. (1998). Testing media richness theory in the new media: The effects of cues, feedback, and task equivocality. *Information Systems Research*, *9*, 256–274.

Dennis, A. R., Wixom, B. H., & Vandenberg, R. J. (2001). Understanding fit and appropriation effects in group support systems via meta-analysis. *MIS Quarterly*, *25*, 167–193.

DeRosa, D. M., Hantula, D. A., Kock, N., & D'Arcy, J. (2004). Trust and leadership in virtual teamwork: A media naturalness perspective. *Human Resource Management*, *43*, 219–232.

de Vries, D. A., Möller, A. M., Wieringa, M. S., Eigenraam, A. W., & Hamelink, K. (2018). Social comparison as the thief of joy: Emotional consequences of viewing strangers' Instagram posts. *Media Psychology*, *21*(2), 222–245. https://doi.org/10.1080/15213269.2016.1267647

Douglas, W. (1994). The acquaintanceship process: An examination of uncertainty, information seeking, and social attraction during initial conversation. *Communication Research*, *21*(2), 154–176.

Downing, N. R., Bogue, R. J., Terrill, P., & Tucker, S. (2021). Development and test of a text-messaging follow-up program after sexual assault. *Violence Against Women*, *27*, 2111–2128. https://doi.org/10.1177/10778012211014567

Dings, R. (2018). Understanding phenomenological differences in how affordances solicit action: An exploration. *Phenomenology and the Cognitive Sciences*, *17*, 681–699.

Duguay, S. (2017) Dressing up Tinderella: Interrogating authenticity claims on the mobile dating app Tinder. *Communication & Society*, *20*(3), 351–367. https://doi.org/10.1080/1369118X.2016.1168471

Emmers, T. M., & Canary, D. J. (1996). The effect of uncertainty reducing strategies on young couples' relational repair and intimacy. *Communication Quarterly*, *44*(2), 166–182. https://doi.org/10.1080/01463379609370008

Erhardt, N., Martin-Rios, C., Gibbs, J., & Sherblom, J. (2016). Exploring affordances of email for team learning over time. *Small Group Research*, *47*, 243–278.

Eslami, M., Rickman, A., Vaccaro, K., Aleyasen, A., Vuong, A., Karahailos, K., Hamilton, K., & Sandvig, C. (2015, April 18–23). *"I always assumed I wasn't really that close to [her]": Reasoning about invisible algorithms in news feeds* [Paper presentation]. CHI 2015, Seoul, Korea.

Evans, S. K., Pearce, K. E., Vitak, J., & Treem, J. W. (2017). Explicating affordances: A conceptual framework for understanding affordances in communication research. *Journal of Computer-Mediated Communication*, *22*, 35–52. https://doi.org/10.1111/jcc4.12180

Fägersten, K. (2010). Using discourse analysis to assess social copresence in the video conference environment. In L. Shedletsky & J. E. Aitken (Eds.), *Cases in online discussion and interaction: Experiences and outcomes* (pp. 175–193). IGI Global.

Fairweather, J. E. (2022). *Media richness and the relationship between direct reports and supervisors* (AAI29394843) [PhD dissertation, Johnson & Wales University]. Dissertation & Theses Collection. https://scholarsarchive.jwu.edu/dissertations/AAI29394843

Farahani, L. M. (2016). The value of the sense of community and neighbouring, housing. *Theory and Society*, *33*, 357–376. https://doi.org/10.1080/14036096.2016.1155480

Farmer, S. M., & Hyatt, C. W. (1994). Effects of task language demands and task complexity on computer-mediated work groups. *Small Group Research*, *25*, 331–366.

Feaster, J. C. (2010). Expanding the impression management model of communication channels: An information control scale. *Journal of Computer-Mediated Communication*, *16*, 115–138. https://doi.org/10.1111/j.1083-6101.2010.01535.x

Festinger, L. (1954). A theory of social comparison processes. *Human Relations*, *7*(2), 117–140. https://doi.org/10.1177/001872675400700202

Fox, J., Bailenson, J. N., & Tricase, L. (2013). The embodiment of sexualized virtual selves: The Proteus effect and experiences of self-objectification via avatars. *Computers in Human Behavior*, *29*, 930–938.

Fox J., & Holt, L. F. (2018). Fear of isolation and perceived affordances: The spiral of silence on social networking sites regarding police discrimination. *Mass Communication and Society*, *21*, 533–554. https://doi.org/10.1080/15205436.2018.1442480

Fox, J., & McEwan, B. (2017). Distinguishing technologies for social interaction: The perceived social affordances of communication channels scale. *Communication Monographs*, *84*, 298–318. https://doi.org/10.1080/03637751.2017.1332418

Freelon, D., McIlwain, C. D., & Clark, M. D. (2016). *Beyond the hashtags: #Ferguson, #BlackLivesMatter and the online struggle for offline justice.* Center for Media and Social Impact. https://papers.ssrn.com/sol3/papers.cfm?abstract_id=2747066

Fullwood, C., & Attrill-Smith, A. (2018). Up-dating: Ratings of perceived dating success are better online than offline. *Cyberpsychology, Behavior, and Social Networking*, *21*, 11–15. https://doi.org/10.1089/cyber.2016.0631

Gasiorek, J., & Giles, H. (2015). The role of inferred motive in processing nonaccommodation: Evaluations of communication and speakers. *Western Journal of Communication*, *79*, 456–471. https://doi.org/10.1080/10570314.2015.1066030

Gaver, W. W. (1991). Technology affordances. *Proceedings of the SIGCHI Conference on Human Factors in Computing Systems*, 79–84. https://dl.acm.org/doi/pdf/10.1145/108844.108856

Gibbs, J. L., Ellison, N. B., & Heino, R. D. (2006). Self-presentation in online personals the role of anticipated future interaction, self-disclosure, and perceived success in internet dating. *Communication Research*, *33*, 152–177.

Gibson, J. J. (1986). *The ecological approach to visual perception.* Psychology Press.

Giles, H. (1973). Accent mobility: A model and some data. *Anthropological Linguistics*, *15*, 87–109.

Giles, H., Linz, D., Bonilla, D., & Gomez, M. L. (2012). Police stops of and interactions with Latino and White (Non-Latino) drivers: Extensive policing and communication accommodation. *Communication Monographs*, *79*, 407–427.

Giles, H., Mulac, A., Bradac, J., & Johnson, P. (1987). Speech accommodation theory: The first decade and beyond. In M. L. McLaughlin (Ed.), *Communication yearbook* (Vol. 10, pp. 13–48). SAGE.

Giles, H., & Ogay, T. (2007). Communication accommodation theory. In B. B. Whaley & W. Samter (Eds.), *Explaining communication: Contemporary theories and exemplars* (pp. 293–310). Erlbaum.

Goffman, E. (1959). *The presentation of self in everyday life.* Penguin.

Granovetter, M. (1983). The strength of weak ties: A network theory revisited. *Sociological Theory*, *1*, 201–233.

Green-Hamann, S., Eichhorn, K. C., & Sherblom, J. C. (2011). An exploration of why people participate in Second Life social support groups. *Journal of Computer-Mediated Communication*, *16*, 465–491.

Green-Hamann, S., & Sherblom, J. C. (2014). The influences of optimal matching and social capital on communicating support. *Journal of Health Communication*, *19*, 1130–1144.

Green-Hamann, S., & Sherblom, J. C. (2016). Transgender transitioning: The influence of virtual on physical identities. *The Electronic Journal of Communication*, *26*. https://www.cios.org/EJCPUBLIC/026/3/026344.html

Gruzd, A., Wellman, B., & Takhteyev, Y. (2011). Imagining Twitter as an imagined community. *American Behavioral Scientist*, *55*, 1294–1318. https://doi.org/10.1177/0002764211409378

Guegan, J., Buisine, S., Mantelet, F., Maranzana, N., & Segonds, F. (2016). Avatar-mediated creativity: When embodying inventors makes engineers more creative. *Computers in Human Behavior*, *61*, 165–175.

Guegan, J., Moliner, P., & Buisine, S. (2015). Why are online games so self-involving: A social identity analysis of massively multiplayer online role-playing games. *European Journal of Social Psychology*, *45*, 349–355. https://doi.org/10.1002/ejsp.2103

Haimson, O. L., & Hoffmann, A. L. (2016). Constructing and enforcing "authentic" identity online: Facebook, real names, and non-normative identities. *First Monday*, *21*(6). https://doi.org/10.5210/fm.v21i6.6791

Hall, C., Chown, E., & Nascimento, F. (2021). A critical, analytical framework for the digital machine. *Interdisciplinary Science Reviews*, *46*, 458–476. https://doi.org/10.1080/03080188.2020.1865659

Hancock, J. T., & Dunham P. J. (2001). Impression formation in computer mediated communication revisited: An analysis of the breadth and intensity of impressions. *Communication Research*, *28*, 325–347.

Harris, R., Dance, G. J. X., & Debelius, D. (2018, July 13). The Twitter purge: How many followers Trump, Nicki Minaj and others lost. The New York Times. https://www.nytimes.com/interactive/2018/07/13/technology/twitter-purge-fake-followers.html

Harris, T. E., & Sherblom, J. C. (2018). *Small group and team communication* (reprinted 5th ed.). Waveland Press.

Hawkins, I., Saleem, M., Gibson, B., & Bushman, B. J. (2021). Extensions of the Proteus effect on intergroup aggression in the real world. *Psychology of Popular Media*, *10*, 478–487. https://doi.org/10.1037/ppm0000307

Hayes, J. L., Britt, B. C., Applequist, J., Ramirez Jr., A., & Hill, J. (2020). Leveraging textual paralanguage and consumer–brand relationships for more relatable online brand communication: A social presence approach. *Journal of Interactive Advertising*, *20*, 17–30. https://doi.org/10.1080/15252019.2019.1691093

Hayes, R. A., & Carr, C. T. (2015). Does being social matter? Effects of enabled commenting on credibility and brand attitude in social media. *Journal of Promotion Management*, *21*, 371–390. https://doi.org/10.1080/10496491.2015.1039178

Hecht, M. L. (1993). 2002—a research odyssey: Toward the development of a communication theory of identity. *Communication Monographs*, *60*, 76–82.

Heeter, C. (1992). Being there: The subjective experience of presence. *Presence*, *1*(2), 262–271.

Herring, S. C., & Martinson, A. (2004). Assessing gender authenticity in computer-mediated language use: Evidence from an identity game. *Journal of Language and Social Psychology*, *23*, 424–446. https://doi.org/10.1177/0261927X04269586

Hoffmann, C. P., Lutz, C., & Ranzini, G. (2016). Privacy cynicism: A new approach to the privacy paradox. *Cyberpsychology: Journal of Psychosocial Research on Cyberspace*, *10*(7). https://doi.org/10.5817/CP2016-4-7

Hogan, B. (2010). The presentation of self in the age of social media: Distinguishing performances and exhibitions online. *Bulletin of Science, Technology & Society*, *30*, 377–386. https://doi.org/10.1177/0270467610385893

Houtman, E., Makos, A., & Meacock, H. L. (2014). The intersection of social presence and impression management in online learning environments. *E-Learning and Digital Media*, *11*, 419–430.

Hsu, C., Lin, J. C., & Miao, Y. (2020). Why are people loyal to live stream channels? The perspectives of uses and gratifications and media richness theories. *Cyberpsychology, Behavior, and Social Networking*, *23*(5), 351–356. https://doi.org/10.1089/cyber.2019.0547

Huang, C. (2022). A meta-analysis of the problematic social media use and mental health. *International Journal of Social Psychiatry*, *68*(1), 12–33. https://doi.org/10.1177/0020764020978434

Ingold, T. (2018). Back to the future with the theory of affordances. *HAU: Journal of Ethnographic Theory*, *8*, 39–44. https://doi.org/10.1086/698358

Ishii, K., Lyons, M. M., & Carr, S. A. (2019). Revisiting media richness theory for today and future. *Human Behavior and Emerging Technologies*, *1*, 124–131. https://doi.org/10.1002/hbe2.138

Jackson, S. J., Bailey, M., & Foucault Welles, B. (2020). *#Hashtag activism: Networks of race and gender justice*. The MIT Press.

Jaidka, K., Zhou, A., Lelkes, Y., Egelhofer, J., & Lecheler, S. (2021). Beyond anonymity: Network affordances, under deindividuation, improve social media discussion quality. *Journal of Computer-Mediated Communication*, *27*(1). https://doi.org/10.1093/jcmc/zmab019

James, W. (1918). *The principles of psychology*. Dover Publications. First published 1890

James, W. (1948). *Psychology*. Fine Editions.

Jiang, J. A., Fiesler, C., & Brubaker, J. R. (2018). "The perfect one": Understanding communication practices and challenges with animated GIFs. *Proceedings of the ACM on Human-Computer Interaction*, *2*, 80. https://doi.org/10.1145/3274349

Jiang, L. C., Bazarova, N. N., & Hancock, J. T. (2011). The disclosure–intimacy link in computer-mediated communication: An attributional extension of the hyperpersonal model. *Human Communication Research*, *37*, 58–77.

Jiménez, A. G., Orenes, P. B., & Puente, S. N. (2010). An approach to the concept of a virtual border: identities and communication spaces. *Revista Latina de Comunucacion Social*, 214–221. https://web.archive.org/web/20170921222505/http://www.revistalatinacs.org/10/art2/894_Madrid/RLCS_art894EN.pdf

Jin, S. A. (2011). "I feel present. Therefore, I experience flow": A structural equation modeling approach to flow and presence in video games. *Journal of Broadcasting & Electronic Media*, *55*(1), 114–136.

Jo, W., Jang, S. H., & Shin, E. K. (2023). Stage distinctive communication networks of the online breast cancer community. *Scientific Reports*, *13*(1726). https://doi.org/10.1038/s41598-023-28892-7

Johnson, B. K., & Rosenbaum, J. E. (2023). Sharing brands on social media: The roles of behavioural commitment and modality in identity shift. *International Journal of Consumer Studies*, *47*(3), 995–1010. https://doi.org/10.1111/ijcs.12880

Johnson, B. K., & Van Der Heide, B. (2015). Can sharing affect liking? Online taste performances, feedback, and subsequent media preferences. *Computers in Human Behavior*, *46*, 181–190. https://doi.org/10.1016/j.chb.2015.01.018

Joinson, A. N. (2001). Self-disclosure in computer-mediated communication: The role of self-awareness and visual anonymity. *European Journal of Social Psychology*, *31*, 177–192.

Jones, Q. (1997). Virtual-communities, virtual settlements & cyber-archaeology: A theoretical outline. *Journal of Computer-Mediated Communication*, *3*(3). https://doi.org/10.1111/j.1083-6101.1997.tb00075.x

Jordan, J. W. (2005). A virtual death and a real dilemma: Identity, trust, and community in cyberspace. *Southern Communication Journal*, *70*(3), 200–218.

Jung, E., & Hecht, M. L. (2004). Elaborating the communication theory of identity: Identity gaps and communication outcomes. *Communication Quarterly*, *52*, 265–283.

Jung, E., & Hecht, M. L. (2008). Identity gaps and level of depression among Korean immigrants. *Health Communication*, *23*(4), 313–325.

Kang, S. H., & Watt, J. (2013). The impact of avatar realism and anonymity on effective communication via mobile devices. *Computers in Human Behavior*, *29*, 1169–1181. https://doi.org/10.1016/j.chb.2012.10.010

Karimi, F., Ramenzoni, V. C., & Holme, P. (2014). Structural differences between open and direct communication in an online community. *Physica A: Statistical Mechanics and Its Applications*, *414*, 263–273.

Karl, K. A., Peluchette, J. V., & Aghakhan, N. (2022). Virtual work meetings during the COVID-19 pandemic: The good, bad, and ugly. *Small Group Research*, *53*, 343–365. https://doi.org/10.1177/10464964211015286

Kear, K., Chetwynd, F., & Jefferis, H. (2014). Social presence in online learning communities: The role of personal profiles. *Research in Learning Technology*, *22*, 1–15. http://doi.org/10.3402/rlt.v22.19710

Kellerman, K., & Reynolds, R. (1990). When ignorance is bliss. The role of motivation to reduce uncertainty in uncertainty reduction theory. *Human Communication Research*, *17*(1), 5–75.

Khati, A., Wickersham, J. A., Rosen, A. O., Luces, J. R. B., Copenhaver, N., Jeri-Wahrhaftig, A., Halim, M. A. A., Azwa, I., Gautam, K., Ooi, K. H., & Shrestha, R. (2022). Ethical issues in the use of smartphone apps for HIV prevention in Malaysia: Focus group study with men who have sex with men. *Journal of Medical Internet Research, JMIR Formative Research*, *6*, e42939. https://doi.org/10.2196/42939

Kim, H., Chung, M., Rhee, E. S., & Kim, Y. (2022). Is it reciprocating or self-serving? Understanding coping strategies for postpartum depression in an online community for Korean mothers. *Health Care for Women International*, *43*(12), 1464–1481. https://doi.org/10.1080/07399332.2022.2037604

Kim, J., Kim, J., & Park, H. S. (2016). Model comparison in group decision making: Effects of the visual cue conditions on social identification process and compensatory nonconformity process. *Communication Research*, *43*, 159–179. https://doi.org/10.1177/0093650213509666

Klein, O., Spears, R., & Reicher, S. (2007). Social identity performance: extending the strategic side of SIDE. *Personality and Social Psychology Review*, *11*, 28–45. https://doi.org/10.1177/1088868306294588

Kock, N. (2004). The psychobiological model: Towards a new theory of computer-mediated communication based on Darwinian evolution. *Organization Science*, *15*, 327–348.

Kock, N. (2005). Media richness or media naturalness? The evolution of our biological communication apparatus and its influence on our behavior toward e-communication tools. *IEEE Transactions on Professional Communication*, *48*, 117–130.

Kock, N., Carmona, J., & Moqbel, M. (2015). Media naturalness and compensatory adaptation: Counterintuitive effects on correct rejections of deceitful contract clauses. *IEEE Transactions on Professional Communication*, *58*, 381–395.

Kock, N., Verville, J., & Garza, V. (2007). Media naturalness and online learning: Findings supporting both the significant and no-significant-difference perspectives. *Decision Sciences Journal of Innovative Education*, *5*, 333–355.

Kocur, M., Kloss, M., Schwind, V., Wolff, C., & Henze, N. (2020). Flexing muscles in virtual reality: Effects of avatars' muscular appearance on physical performance. *Proceedings of the Annual Symposium on Computer-Human Interaction in Play*, 193–205. https://doi.org/10.1145/3410404.3414261

Koh, J., & Kim, Y. G. (2004). Sense of virtual community: A conceptual framework and empirical validation. *International Journal of Electronic Commerce*, *8*, 75–93.

Koles, B., & Nagy, P. (2012). Who is portrayed in Second Life: Dr. Jekyll or Mr. Hyde? The extent of congruence between real life and virtual identity. *Journal of Virtual Worlds Research*, *5*(1). https://journals.tdl.org/jvwr/index.php/jvwr/article/view/2150

Komito, L. (2011). Social media and migration: Virtual community 2.0. *Journal of the American Society for Information Science and Technology*, *62*, 1075–1086. https://doi.org/10.1002/asi.21517

Konrad, A., Herring, S. C., & Choi, D. (2020). Sticker and emoji use in Facebook Messenger: Implications for graphicon change. *Journal of Computer-Mediated Communication*, *25*, 217–235. https://doi.org/10.1093/jcmc/zmaa003

Korostelina, K. (2014). Intergroup identity insults: A social identity theory perspective. *Identity*, *14*, 214–229. https://doi.org/10.1080/15283488.2014.921170

Korzenny, F. (1978). A theory of electronic propinquity: Mediated communications in organizations. *Communication Research*, *5*, 3–24.

Korzenny, F., & Bauer, C. (1981). Testing the theory of electronic propinquity. *Communication Research*, *8*, 479–498.

Kowalski, R. M., Limber, S. P., & McCord, A. (2019). A developmental approach to cyberbullying: Prevalence and protective factors. *Aggression and Violent Behavior*, *45*, 20–32. https://doi.org/10.1016/j.avb.2018.02.009

Latour, B. (1994). On technical mediation. *Common Knowledge*, *3*(2), 29–64.

Latour, B. (2005). *Reassembling the social: An introduction to actor-network theory*. Oxford University Press.

Latour, B. (2011). Networks, societies, spheres: Reflections of an actor-network theorist. *International Journal of Communication*, *5*, 796–810.

Lauring, J. (2008). Rethinking social identity theory in international encounters: Language use as a negotiated object for identity making. *International Journal of Cross Cultural Management*, *8*, 343–359.

Law, J. (2009). Actor network theory and material semiotics. In B. S. Turner (Ed.), *The new Blackwell companion to social theory* (pp. 141–158). Blackwell.

Lea, M., & Spears, R. (1991). Computer-mediated communication, deindividuation, and group decision-making. *International Journal of Man Machine Studies*, *34*, 283–301. https://doi.org/10.1016/0020-7373(91)90045-9

Lee, D. K. L., & Borah, P. (2020). Self-presentation on Instagram and friendship development among young adults: A moderated mediation model of media richness, perceived functionality, and openness. *Computers in Human Behavior*, *103*, 57–66. https://doi.org/10.1016/j.chb.2019.09.017

Lee, E. (2020). Authenticity model of (mass-oriented) computer-mediated communication: Conceptual explorations and testable propositions. *Journal of Computer-Mediated Communication*, *25*, 60–73. https://doi.org/10.1093/jcmc/zmz025

Lee, J. J., & Lee, J. (2023). #StopAsianHate on TikTok: Asian/American women's space-making for spearheading counter-narratives and forming an ad hoc Asian community. *Social Media + Society*, 1–11. https://doi.org/10.1177/20563051231157598

Lee, J. R., Nass, C., & Bailenson, J. N. (2014). Does the mask govern the mind? Effects of arbitrary gender representation on quantitative task performance in avatar-represented virtual groups. *Cyberpsychology, Behavior, and Social Networking*, *17*, 248–254.

Lee, K. M. (2004). Presence, explicated. *Communication Theory, 14,* 27–50.

Lengel, R. H., & Daft, R. L. (1988). The selection of communication media as an executive skill. *Executive, 2,* 225–232.

Leonard, L. G., Sherblom, J. C., Withers, L. A., & Smith, J. S. (2015). Training effective virtual teams: Presence, identity, communication openness, and conversational interactivity. *Connexions: International Professional Communication Journal, 3,* 11–45.

Leonardi, P. M. (2011). When flexible routines meet flexible technologies: Affordance, constraint, and the imbrication of human and material agencies. *MIS Quarterly, 35,* 147–167.

Leonardi, P. M. (2013). When does technology use enable network change in organizations? A comparative study of feature use and shared affordances. *MIS Quarterly, 37,* 749–775.

Leonardi, P. M., Huysman, M., & Steinfield, C. (2013). Enterprise social media: Definition, history, and prospects for the study of social technologies in organizations. *Journal of Computer-Mediated Communication, 19,* 1–19.

Li, H. (2004). Virtual community studies: A literature review, synthesis and research agenda. *Americas Conference on Information Systems 2004 Proceedings, 324.* aisel.aisnet.org/amcis2004/324

Li, S., Chang, Y. Y., & Chiou, W. (2017). Things online social networking can take away: Reminders of social networking sites undermine the desirability of offline socializing and pleasures. *Scandinavian Journal of Psychology, 58,* 179–184.

Li, S., & Zhang, G. (2021). Intergroup communication in online forums: The effect of group identification on online support provision. *Communication Research, 48,* 874–894. https://doi.org/10.1177/009365021 8807041

Licoppe, C. (2004). "Connected" presence: The emergence of a new repertoire for managing social relationships in a changing communication technoscape. *Environment and Planning D: Society and Space, 22,* 135–156.

Licoppe, C., & Smoreda, Z. (2005). Are social networks technologically embedded? How networks are changing today with changes in communication technology. *Social Networks, 27*(4), 317–335.

Lim, S. S. Vadrevu, S., Chan, Y. H., & Basnyat, I. (2012). Facework on Facebook: The online publicness of juvenile delinquents and youths-at-risk. *Journal of Broadcasting & Electronic Media, 56,* 346–361. https://doi.org/10.1080/08838151.2012.705198

Lin, J. T., & Wu, D. (2021). Exercising with embodied young avatars: How young vs. older avatars in virtual reality affect perceived exertion and physical activity among male and female elderly individuals. *Frontiers in Psychology, 12.* https://doi.org/10.3389/fpsyg.2021.693545

Lin, J. T., Wu, D., & Yang, J. (2021). Exercising with a six pack in virtual reality: Examining the Proteus effect of avatar body shape and sex on self-efficacy for core-muscle exercise, self-concept of body shape, and actual physical activity. *Frontiers in Psychology, 12.* https://doi.org/10.3389/fpsyg.2021.693543

Lin, N. (1999). Building a network theory of social capital. *Connections, 22,* 28–51.

Lindholm, C. (2013). The rise of expressive authenticity. *Anthropological Quarterly, 86,* 361–395.

Littlepage, G. E., Hollingshead, A. B., Drake, L. R., & Littlepage, A. M. (2008). Transactive memory and performance in teams: Specificity, communication, ability differences, and work allocation. *Group Dynamics: Theory, Research, and Practice, 12,* 223–241.

Liu, M., Wong, A., Pudipeddi, R. Hou, B., Wang, D., & Hsieh, G. (2018). ReactionBot: Exploring the effects of expression-triggered emoji in text messages. *Proceedings of the ACM on Human-Computer Interaction, 2,* 110. https://doi.org/10.1145/3274379

Lohmann, R. C. (2013). *The two-sided face of teen catfishing.* Psychology Today. www.psychologytoday.com/us/blog/teen-angst/201304/the-two-sided-face-teen-catfishing

Lombard, M., & Ditton, T. (1997). At the heart of it all: The concept of presence. *Journal of Computer-Mediated Communication, 3*(2). https://doi.org/10.1111/j.1083-6101.1997.tb00072.x

Lombardo, T. J. (1987). *The reciprocity of perceiver and environment.* Erlbaum.

Luangrath, A. W., Peck, J., & Barger, V. A. (2017). Textual paralanguage and its implications for marketing communications. *Journal of Consumer Psychology, 27,* 98–107.

Madianou, M. (2016). Ambient co-presence: Transnational family practices in polymedia environments. *Global Networks: A Journal of Transnational Affairs, 16*(2), 183–201. https://doi.org/10.1111/glob.12105

Majchrzak A., Faraj, S., Kane, G. C., & Azad, B. (2013). The contradictory influence of social media affordances on online communal knowledge sharing. *Journal of Computer-Mediated Communication*, *19*, 38–55.

Marciano, L., Schulz, P. J., & Camerini, A. (2020). Cyberbullying perpetration and victimization in youth: A meta-analysis of longitudinal studies. Journal of Computer-Mediated Communication, 25, 163–181. https://doi.org/10.1093/jcmc/zmz031

Martindale, C. (1981). *Cognition and consciousness*. Dorsey.

Marwick, A. E., & boyd, d. (2011a). I tweet honestly, I tweet passionately: Twitter users, context collapse, and the imagined audience. *New Media & Society*, *13*, 114–133. https://doi.org/10.1177/1461444810365313

Marwick, A. E., & boyd, d. (2011b). To see and be seen: Celebrity practice on Twitter. *Convergence: The International Journal of Research into New Media Technologies*, *17*, 139–158. https://doi.org/10.1177/1354856510394539

Marwick, A. E., & boyd, d. (2014). Networked privacy: How teenagers negotiate context in social media. *New Media & Society*, *16*, 1051–1067. https://doi.org/10.1177/1461444814543995

Marwick, A., Fontaine, C., boyd, d. (2017). "Nobody sees it, nobody gets mad": Social media, privacy, and personal responsibility among low-SES youth. Social Media + Society, 1–14. https://doi.org/10.1177/2056305117710455

Mazgaj, M., d'Amato, A., Elson, J., & Derrick, D. (2021). Exploring the effects of real-time hologram communication on social presence, novelty, and affect. *Proceedings of the 54th Hawaii International Conference on System Sciences.* https://doi.org/10.24251/HICSS.2021.056

McEwan, B. (2021). Modality switching to modality weaving: Updating theoretical perspectives for expanding media affordances. *Annals of the International Communication Association*, *45*, 1–19. https://doi.org/10.1080/23808985.2021.1880958

McGrath, J. E., & Hollingshead, A. B. (1994). *Groups interacting with technology*. SAGE.

McMillan, D. W. (1996). Sense of community. *Journal of Community Psychology*, *24*, 315–325.

McVeigh-Schultz J., & Baym, N. K. (2015). Thinking of you: Vernacular affordance in the context of the microsocial relationship app, couple. *Social Media + Society*, 1–13.

Mead, G. H. (1962). *Mind, self, and society*. University of Chicago Press. First published 1934

Meier, A., Gilbert, A., Börner, S., & Possler, D. (2020). Instagram inspiration: How upward comparison on social network sites can contribute to well-being. *Journal of Communication*, *70*, 721–743. https://doi.org/10.1093/joc/jqaa025

Meier, A., & Johnson, B. K. (2022). Social comparison and envy on social media: A critical review. *Current Opinion in Psychology*, *45*(101302), 1–6. https://doi.org/10.1016/j.copsyc.2022.101302

Meier, E. P., & Gray, J. (2014). Facebook photo activity associated with body image disturbance in adolescent girls. *Cyberpsychology, Behavior, and Social Networking*, *17*, 199–206. https://doi.org/10.1089/cyber.2013.0305

Meng, J., & Dai, Y. (2021). Emotional support from AI chatbots: Should a supportive partner self-disclose or not? *Journal of Computer-Mediated Communication*, *26*, 207–222. https://doi.org/10.1093/jcmc/zmab005

Metzger, M. J., Flanagin, A. J., & Medders, R. B. (2010). Social and heuristic approaches to credibility evaluation online. *Journal of Communication*, *60*, 413–439. https://doi.org/10.1111/j.1460-2466.2010.01488.x

Milton, A., Ajmani, L., DeVito, M. A., & Chancellor, S. (2023). "I see me here": Mental health content, community, and algorithmic curation on TikTok. *Proceedings of the 2023 CHI Conference on Human Factors in Computing Systems*, *480*, 1–17. https://doi.org/10.1145/3544548.3581489

Minsky, M. (1980). Telepresence. *Omni*, pp. 45–51. web.media.mit.edu/~minsky/papers/Telepresence.html

Mosley, M. A., Lancaster, M., Parker, M. L., & Campbell, K. (2020). Adult attachment and online dating deception: A theory modernized. *Sexual and Relationship Therapy*, *35*, 227–243. https://doi.org/10.1080/14681994.2020.1714577

Muir, K., Joinson, A., Cotterill, R., & Dewdney, N. (2017). Linguistic style accommodation shapes impression formation and rapport in computer-mediated communication. *Journal of Language and Social Psychology*, *36*, 525–548. https://doi.org/10.1177/0261927X17701327

Nagy, P., & Koles, B. (2014a). "My Avatar and her beloved possession": Characteristics of attachment to virtual objects. *Psychology and Marketing*, *31*, 1122–1135. https://doi.org/10.1002/mar.20759

Nagy, P., & Koles, B. (2014b). The digital transformation of human identity: Towards a conceptual model of virtual identity in virtual worlds. *Convergence: The International Journal of Research into New Media Technologies, 20*, 276–292. https://doi.org/10.1177/1354856514531532

Navarro, J., Peña, J., Cebolla, A., & Baños, R. (2022). Can avatar appearance influence physical activity? User-avatar similarity and Proteus effects on cardiac frequency and step counts. *Health Communication, 37*, 222–229. https://doi.org/10.1080/10410236.2020.1834194

Nimmo, R. (2011). Actor-network theory and methodology: Social research in a more-than-human world. *Methodological Innovations Online, 6*, 108–119. https://doi.org/10.4256/mio.2011.010

Oetzel, J. G., & Ting-Toomey, S. (2003). Face concerns in interpersonal conflict: A cross-cultural empirical test of the face negotiation theory. *Communication Research, 30*, 599–624. https://doi.org/10.1177/0093650203257841

Oh, C. S., Bailenson, J. N., & Welch, G. F. (2018). A systematic review of social presence: Definitions, antecedents, and implications. *Frontiers in Robotics and AI, 5*, 114. https://doi.org/10.3389/frobt.2018.00114

Oldenburg, R. (1991). *The great good place*. Paragon.

Orgad, S. (2005). *Storytelling online: Talking breast cancer on the internet*. Peter Lang.

O'Sullivan, P. B., Hunt, S. K., & Lippert, L. R. (2004). Mediated immediacy a language of affiliation in a technological age. *Journal of Language and Social Psychology, 23*, 464–490.

Öztok, M., & Kehrwald, B. A. (2017). Social presence reconsidered: moving beyond, going back, or killing social presence. *Distance Education, 38*, 259–266. https://doi.org/10.1080/01587919.2017.1322456

Palen, L., & Dourish, P. (2003). Unpacking "privacy" for a networked world. *CHI 2003: New Horizons, 5*(1). 129–138.

Pang, A., Shin, W., Lew, Z. & Walther, J. B. (2018). Building relationships through dialogic communication: Organizations, stakeholders, and computer-mediated communication. *Journal of Marketing Communications, 24*, 68–82. https://doi.org/10.1080/13527266.2016.1269019

Pantumsinchai, P. (2018). Armchair detectives and the social construction of falsehoods: An actor-network approach. *Information, Communication & Society, 21*, 761–778. https://doi.org/10.1080/1369118X.2018.1428654

Papacharissi, Z. (2011). Conclusion: A networked self. In Z. Papacharissi (Ed.), *A networked self: Identity, community, and culture on social network site*s (pp. 304–218). Routledge.

Park, E. K., & Sundar, S. S. (2015). Can synchronicity and visual modality enhance social presence in mobile messaging? *Computers in Human Behavior, 45*, 121–128. http://doi.org/10.1016/j.chb.2014.12.001

Park, Y. W., & Lee, A. R. (2019). The moderating role of communication contexts: How do media synchronicity and behavioral characteristics of mobile messenger applications affect social intimacy and fatigue? *Computers in Human Behavior, 97*, 179–192. https://doi.org/10.1016/j.chb.2019.03.020

Parks, M. R. (2017). Embracing the challenges and opportunities of mixed-media relationships. *Human Communication Research, 43*, 505–517. https://doi.org/10.1111/hcre.12125

Pearce, K. E., & Malhotra, P. (2022). Inaccuracies and Izzat: Channel affordances for the consideration of face in misinformation correction. *Journal of Computer-Mediated Communication, 27*. https://doi.org/10.1093/jcmc/zmac004

Peña, J., Khan, S., & Alexopoulos, C. (2016). I am what I see: How avatar and opponent agent body size affects physical activity among men playing exergames. *Journal of Computer-Mediated Communication, 21*, 195–209. https://doi.org/10.1111/jcc4.12151

Petersen, A., Schermuly, A., & Anderson, A. (2020). Feeling less alone online: Patients' ambivalent engagements with digital media. *Sociology of Health & Illness, 42*, 1441–1455. https://doi.org/10.1111/1467-9566.13117

Petronio, S. (2010). Communication privacy management theory: What do we know about family privacy regulation? *Journal of Family Theory & Review, 2*, 175–196. https://doi.org/10.1111/j.1756-2589.2010.00052.x

Pew Research Center. (2022, September 20). *Social media and news fact sheet*. https://www.pewresearch.org/journalism/fact-sheet/social-media-and-news-fact-sheet/

Pihlaja, B. (2020). Inventing others in digital written communication: Intercultural encounters on the U.S.-Mexico border. *Written Communication, 37*, 245–280. https://doi.org/10.1177/0741088319899908

Plant, R. (2004). Online communities. *Technology in Society, 26*, 51–65.

Postmes, T., & Spears, R. (2002). Behavior online: Does anonymous computer communication reduce gender inequality? *Personality and Social Psychology Bulletin, 28*, 1073–1083.

Postmes, T., Spears, R., & Lea, M. (1998). Breaching or building social boundaries: SIDE effects of computer-mediated communication. *Communication Research, 25*, 689–715.

Presti, D. E. (2016). *Foundational concepts in neuroscience*. Norton.

Quan-Haase, A., Wang, H., Wellman, B., & Zhang, R. (2018). Weaving family connections on and offline: The turn to networked individualism. In B. B. Neves & C. Casimiro (Eds.), *Connecting families? Information & communication technologies in a life course perspective* (pp. 59–80). Policy Press.

Rahman, N. A. A. (2017). Electronic propinquity in the hospital management system among ICT integrated hospitals in Malaysia. *Malaysian Journal of Communication, 33*, 125–139.

Rainie, L., & Wellman, B. (2019). The internet in daily life: The turn to networked individualism. In M Graham, W. H. Dutton, & M. Castells (Eds.), *Society and the internet: How networks of information and communication are changing our lives* (pp. 27–42). Oxford University Press. https://doi.org/10.1093/oso/9780198843498.003.0002

Rains, S. A., Kenski, K., Coe, K., & Harwood, J. (2017). Incivility and political identity on the internet: Intergroup factors as predictors of incivility in discussions of news online. *Journal of Computer-Mediated Communication, 22*, 163–178. https://do.org/10.1111/jcc4.12191

Ramirez, A., & Burgoon, J. K. (2004). The effect of interactivity on initial interactions: The influence of information valence and modality and information richness on computer mediated interaction. *Communication Monographs, 71*, 422–447.

Ramirez, A., Dimmick, J., Feaster, J., & Lin, S. (2008). Revisiting interpersonal media competition: The gratification

Ramirez, A., Walther, J. B., Burgoon, J. K., & Sunnafrank, M. (2002). Information-seeking strategies, uncertainty, and computer-mediated communication: Toward a conceptual model. *Human Communication Research, 28*(2), 213–228.

Rao, V. (2008, February 25). *Ambient presence and virtual social capital*. Ribbon Farm. https://www.ribbonfarm.com/2008/02/25/ambient-presence-and-virtual-social-capital

Ratan, R., Beyea, D., Li, B. J., & Graciano, L. (2020). Avatar characteristics induce users' behavioral conformity with small-to-medium effect sizes: A meta-analysis of the Proteus effect. *Media Psychology, 23*, 651–675. https://doi.org/10.1080/15213269.2019.1623698

Ratan, R., & Dawson, M. (2016). When Mii is me: A psychophysiological examination of avatar self-relevance. *Communication Research, 43*(8), 1065–1093. https://doi.org/10.1177/0093650215570652

Ratan, R. A., & Hasler, B. (2009, November 12). *Self- presence standardized: Introducing the self-presence questionnaire*. Paper presented at the 10th Annual International Workshop on Presence, Los Angeles, California, United States.

Reade, J. (2020). Keeping it raw on the 'Gram: Authenticity, relatability and digital intimacy in fitness cultures on Instagram. *New Media & Society, 22*(3), 1–19. https://doi.org/10.1177/1461444819891699

Reinhard, R., Shah, K. G., Faust-Christmann, C. A., & Lachmann, T. (2020). Acting your avatar's age: Effects of virtual reality avatar embodiment on real life walking speed, *Media Psychology, 23*, 293–315. https://doi.org/10.1080/15213269.2019.1598435

Reints, R. E., & Wickelgren, B. F. (2019). From texting to tangible: When online communicators meet offline. *Intercultural Communication Studies, 28*(2), 153–172.

Rogers, P., & Lea, M. (2005). Social presence in distributed group environments: The role of social identity. *Behavior and Information Technology, 24*(2), 151–158.

Rosenbaum, J. E. (2018). *Constructing digital cultures: Tweets, trends, race, and gender*. Lexington.

Ruesch, J., & Bateson, G. (1968). *Communication*. Norton.

Rui, J. R. (2018). Source-target relationship and information specificity: Applying warranting theory to online information credibility assessment and impression formation. *Social Science Computer Review, 36*, 331–348. https://doi.org/10.1177/0894439317717196

Salisbury, M., & Pooley, J. D. (2017). The #nofilter self: The contest for authenticity among social networking sites, 2002–2016. *The Social Sciences, 6*, 1–24. https://doi.org/10.3390/socsci6010010

Saran, I., Fink, G., & McConnell, M. (2018). How does anonymous online peer communication affect prevention behavior? Evidence from a laboratory experiment. PLoS ONE, 13, e0207679. DOI: 10.1371/journal.pone.0207679

Sashi, C. M. (2021). Digital communication, value co-creation and customer engagement in business networks: A conceptual matrix and propositions. *European Journal of Marketing*, 55, 1643–1663. https://doi.org/10.1108/EJM-01-2020-0023

Sassenberg, K., & Boos, M. (2003). Attitude change in computer-mediated communication: Effects of anonymity and category norms. *Group Processes & Intergroup Relations*, 6, 405–422.

Schlenker, B. R., Dlugolecki, D. W., & Doherty, K. (1994). The impact of self-presentations on self-appraisals and behavior: The power of public commitment. *Personality and Social Psychology Bulletin*, 20(1), 20–33. https://doi.org/10.1177/0146167294201002

Schreurs, L., Meier, A. & Vandenbosch, L. (2022). Exposure to the positivity bias and adolescents' differential longitudinal links with social comparison, inspiration and envy depending on social media literacy. *Current Psychology*, 42, 28221–28241. https://doi.org/10.1007/s12144-022-03893-3

Schrock, A. R. (2015). Communicative affordances of social media: Portability, availability, locatability, and multimediality. *International Journal of Communication*, 9, 1229–1246.

Schroeder, R. (2005). Being there together and the future of connected presence. *Presence*, 339–344.

Seiter, C. R., & Brophy, N. S. (2021). Social support and aggressive communication on social network sites during the COVID-19 pandemic. *Health Communication*, 37(10), 1295–1304. https://doi.org/10.1080/10410236.2021.1886399

Senge, P., Scharmer, C. O., Jaworski, J., & Flowers, B. S. (2004). *Presence*. Random House.

Sherblom, J. C. (2010). The computer-mediated communication (CMC) classroom: A challenge of medium, presence, interaction, identity, and relationship. *Communication Education*, 59(4), 497–523.

Sherblom, J. C., Withers, L. A., & Leonard, L. G. (2009, February, 15). *Interpersonal uncertainty reduction in Second Life* [Paper presentation]. Western States Communication Association convention, Phoenix, AZ, United States.

Sherblom, J. C., Withers, L. A., Leonard, L. G., & Smith, J. S. (2018). Virtual team communication norms: Modeling the mediating effects of relational trust, presence, and identity on conversational interactivity, openness, and satisfaction. In K. Lakkaraju, G. Sukthankar, & R. T. Wigand (Eds.), *Social interactions in virtual worlds* (pp. 103–129). Cambridge: Cambridge University Press.

Short, J., Williams, E., & Christie, B. (1976). *The social psychology of telecommunications*. Wiley.

Shpeer, M., & Howe, W. T. (2020). Socialization, face negotiation, identity, and the United States military. *International Journal of Communication*, 14, 726–744. https://ijoc.org/index.php/ijoc/article/view/11885/2951

Simmons, M., & Lee, J. S. (2020). Catfishing: A look into online dating and impersonation. In G. Meiselwitz (Ed.), *Social computing and social media design, ethics, user behavior, and social network analysis* (pp. 349–358). Springer Nature.

Slater, M., & Wilbur, S. (1997). A framework for immersive virtual environments (FIVE): Speculations on the role of presence in virtual environments. *Presence*, 6(6), 603–616.

Smith, E. B., Brands, R. A., Brashears, M. E., & Kleinbaum, A. M. (2020). Social networks and cognition. *Annual Review of Sociology*, 46, 159–174. https://doi.org/10.1146/annurev-soc-121919-054736

Smith, E. B., Menon, T., & Thompson, L. (2012). Status differences in the cognitive activation of social networks. *Organization Science*, 23, 67–82. https://doi.org/10.1287/orsc.1100.0643

Son, J., Lee, H. K., Jin, S., Lee, J. (2019). Content features of tweets for effective communication during disasters: A media synchronicity theory perspective. *International Journal of Information Management*, 45, 56–68. https://doi.org/10.1016/j.ijinfomgt.2018.10.012

Song, F. W. (2009). *Virtual communities: Bowling alone, online together*. Peter Lang.

Spears, R., Lea, M., Corneliussen, R. A., Postmes, T., & Haar, W. T. (2002). Computer-mediated communication as a channel for social resistance: The strategic side of SIDE. *Small Group Research*, 33, 555–574. https://doi.org/10.1177/104649602237170

Spears, R., Lea M., & Lee S. (1990). De-individuation and group polarization in computer-mediated communication. *British Journal of Social Psychology*, 29, 121–134.

Spears, R., Lea, M., Postmes, T., & Wolbert, A. (2014). A SIDE look at computer-mediated communication: Power and the gender divide. In Z. Birchmeier, B. Dietz-Uhler, & G. Stasser (Eds.). *Strategic uses of social technology: An interactive perspective of social psychology* (pp. 16–39). Cambridge University Press.

Spitzberg, B. H. (2006). Preliminary development of a model and measure of computer-mediated communication (CMC) competence. *Journal of Computer–Mediated Communication, 11*, 629–666.

Stavropoulos, V., Pontes, H. M., Gomez, R., Schivinski, B., & Griffiths, M. (2020). Proteus effect profiles: How do they relate with disordered gaming behaviours? *Psychiatric Quarterly, 91*, 615–628. https://doi.org/10.1007/s11126-020-09727-4

Stavropoulos, V., Rennie, J., Morcos, M., Gomez, R., & Griffiths, M. D. (2021). Understanding the relationship between the Proteus effect, immersion, and gender among *World of Warcraft* players: An empirical survey study. *Behavior and Information Technology, 40*(8), 821–836. https://doi.org/10.1080/0144929X.2020.1729240

Street, R. L., & Giles, H. (1982). Speech accommodation theory: A social cognitive approach to language and speech behavior. In M. E. Roloff & C. R. Berger (Eds.), *Social cognition and communication* (pp. 193–226). SAGE.

Sun, N., Rau, P. P., & Ma, L. (2014). Understanding lurkers in online communities: A literature review. *Computers in Human Behavior, 38*, 110–117.

Tanis M., & Postmes, T. (2003). Social cues and impression formation in CMC. *Journal of Communication, 4*, 676–693.

Thai, H., Davis, C. G., Mahboob, W., Perry, S., Adams, A., & Goldfield, G. S. (2023). Reducing social media use improves appearance and weight esteem in youth with emotional distress. *Psychology of Popular Media*, 1–8. https://doi.org/10.1037/ppm0000460

Tice, D. M. (1992). Self-concept change and self-presentation: The looking glass self is also a magnifying glass. *Journal of Personality and Social Psychology, 63*(3), 435–451. https://doi.org/10.1037/0022-3514.63.3.435

Tidwell, L. C., & Walther, J. B. (2002). Computer-mediated communication effects on disclosure, impressions, and interpersonal evaluations: Getting to know one another a bit at a time. *Human Communication Research, 28*, 317–348.

Tiggemann, M., & Zaccardo, M. (2015). "Exercise to be fit, not skinny": The effect of fitspiration imagery on women's body image. *Body Image, 15*, 61–67. https://doi.org/10.1016/j.bodyim.2015.06.003

Toma, C. L., & Hancock, J. T. (2010). Looks and lies: The role of physical attractiveness in online dating self-presentation and deception. *Communication Research, 37*(3), 335–351.

Torro, O., Pirkkalainen, H., & Li, H. (2022). Media synchronicity in organizational social exchange. *Information Technology & People, 35*, 162–180. https://do.org/10.1108/ITP-06-2020-0384

Treem, J. W., & Leonardi. P. M. (2013). Social media use in organizations: Exploring the affordances of visibility, editability, persistence, and association. *Annals of the International Communication Association, 36*, 143–189. https://doi.org/10.1080/23808985.2013.11679130

Treem, J. W., Leonardi, P. M., & van den Hooff, B. (2020). Computer-mediated communication in the age of communication visibility. *Journal of Computer-Mediated Communication, 25*, 44–59.

Trepte, S. (2021). The social media privacy model: Privacy and communication in the light of social media affordances. *Communication Theory, 31*, 549–570. https://doi.org/10.1093/ct/qtz035

Trevisan, F. (2020). "Do you want to be a well-informed citizen or do you want to be sane?" Social media, disability, mental health, and political marginality. *Social Media + Society*, 1–11. https://doi.org/10.1177/2056305120913909

Tseng, C.-H., & Wei, L.-F. (2020). The efficiency of mobile media richness across different stages of online consumer behavior. *International Journal of Information Management, 50*, 353–364. https://doi.org/10.1016/j.ijinfomgt.2019.08.010

Tseng, F., Cheng, T. C. E., Li, K., & Teng, C. (2017). How does media richness contribute to customer loyalty to mobile instant messaging? *Internet Research, 27*, 520–537. https://doi.org/10.1108/IntR-06-2016-0181

Turnage, A. (2016). Electronic discourse, agency, and organizational change at Enron Corporation. *Western Journal of Communication, 80*, 204–219. https://doi.org/10.1080/10570314.2015.1075062

Turner, J. W., & Foss, S. K. (2018). Options for the construction of attentional social presence in a digitally enhanced multicommunicative environment. *Communication Theory, 28*, 22–45. https://doi.org/10.1093/ct/qty002

U.S. Surgeon General. (2023a). *Our epidemic of loneliness and isolation: The U.S. Surgeon General advisory on the healing effects of social connection and community.* https://www.hhs.gov/sites/default/files/surgeon-general-social-connection-advisory.pdf

U.S. Surgeon General. (2023b). *Social media and youth mental health.* https://www.hhs.gov/surgeongeneral/priorities/youth-mental-health/social-media/index.html

Utz, S. (2002). Social information processing in MUDs: The development of friendships in virtual worlds. *Journal of Online Behavior, 1*(1), 1–23.

Vallverdù, J., & Trovato, G. (2016). Emotional affordances for human–robot interaction. *Adaptive Behavior, 24*(5), 1–15.

Van der Heide, B., Schumaker, E. M., Peterson, A. M., & Jones, E. B. (2012). The Proteus effect in dyadic communication: Examining the effect of avatar appearance in computer-mediated dyadic interaction. *Communication Research, 40,* 838–860.

Verhulst, A., Normand, J., Lombart, C., Sugimoto, M., & Moreau, G. (2018). Influence of being embodied in an obese virtual body on shopping behavior and products perception in VR. *Frontiers in Robotics and AI, 5*(113). https://doi.org/10.3389/frobt.2018.00113

Vicari, S. (2021). Is it all about storytelling? Living and learning hereditary cancer on Twitter. *New Media & Society, 23*(8), 2385–2408. https://doi.org/10.1177/1461444820926632

Vogel, E. A., Rose, J. P., Roberts, L. R., & Eckles, K. (2014). Social comparison, social media, and self-esteem. *Psychology of Popular Media Culture, 3,* 206–222. https://doi.org/10.1037/ppm0000047

Wadley, G., Vetere, F., Kulik, L., Hopkins, L., & Green, J. (2013). Mobile ambient presence. *Proceedings of the 25th Australian Computer-Human Interaction Conference: Augmentation, Application, Innovation, Collaboration,* 167–170. https://dl.acm.org/citation.cfm?id=2541080

Walther, J. B. (1992). Interpersonal effects in computer-mediated interaction: A relational perspective. *Communication Research, 19*(1), 52–90.

Walther, J. B. (1996). Computer-mediated communication: Impersonal, interpersonal, and hyperpersonal interaction. *Communication Research, 23,* 3–43.

Walther, J. B. (2009). Theories, boundaries, and all of the above. *Journal of Computer-Mediated Communication, 14,* 748–752.

Walther, J. B. (2010). Computer-mediated communication. In C. R. Berger, M. E. Roloff, & D. R. Roskos-Ewoldsen (Eds.), *The handbook of communication science.* (2nd ed., pp. 489–505). SAGE.

Walther, J. B., & Bazarova, N. N. (2008). Validation and application of electronic propinquity theory to computer-mediated communication in groups. *Communication Research, 35*(5), 622–645.

Walther, J. B., & Bunz, U. (2005). The rules of virtual groups: Trust, liking, and performance in computer-mediated communication. *Journal of Communication, 55*(4), 828–846.

Walther, J. B., & D'Addario, K. P. (2001). The impacts of emoticons on message interpretation in computer-mediated communication. *Social Science Computer Review, 19,* 324–347.

Walther, J. B., Lew, Z., Edwards, A. L., & Quick, J. (2022). The effect of social approval on perceptions following social media message sharing applied to fake news. *Journal of Communication, 72*(6), 661–674. https://doi.org/10.1093/joc/jqac033

Walther, J. B., Liang, Y. J., DeAndrea, D. C., Tong, S. T., Carr, C. T., Sppottswood, E. L., & Amichai-Hamburger, Y. (2011). The effect of feedback on identity shift in computer-mediated communication. *Media Psychology, 14,* 1–26. https://doi.org/10.1080/15213269.2010.547832

Walther, J. B., Loh, T., & Granka, L. (2005). Let me count the ways. The interchange of verbal and nonverbal cues in computer-mediated and face-to-face affinity. *Journal of Language and Social Psychology, 24*(1), 36–65. https://doi.org/10.1177/0261927X04273036

Walther, J. B., & Parks, M. R. (2002). Cues filtered out, cues filtered in: Computer-mediated communication and relationships. In M. L. Knapp & J. A. Daly (Eds.), *Handbook of interpersonal communication* (3rd ed., pp. 529–563). SAGE.

Walther, J. B., & Whitty, M. T. (2021). Language, psychology, and new new media: The hyperpersonal model of mediated communication at twenty-five years. *Journal of Language and Social Psychology, 40*(1), 120–135.

Watzlawick, P., Bavelas, J. B., & Jackson, D. D. (1967). *Pragmatics of human communication.* Norton.

Wellman, B. (2001). Physical place and cyberplace: The rise of personalized networking. *International Journal of Urban and Regional Research, 25*, 227–252.

Wellman, B., Quan-Haase, A., Boase, J., Wenhong, C., Hampton, K., Díaz, I., & Miyata, K. (2003). The social affordances of the internet for networked individualism. *Journal of Computer-Mediated Communication, 8*(3). https://doi.org/10.1111/j.1083-6101.2003.tb00216.x

Wells, T. M., & Dennis, A. R. (2016). To email or not to email: The impact of media on psychophysiological responses and emotional content in utilitarian and romantic communication. *Computers in Human Behavior, 54*, 1–9. https://doi.org/10.1016/j.chb.2015.07.036

Westerman, D., Spence, P.R., & Lin, X. (2015). Telepresence and exemplification in health messages: The relationships among spatial and social presence and exemplars and exemplification effects. *Communication Reports, 28*(2), 92–102. https://doi.org/10.1080/08934215.2014.971838

Wilding, R. (2006). "Virtual" intimacies? Families communicating across transnational contexts. *Global Networks, 6*, 125–142.

Willson, M. A. (2006). *Technically together: Rethinking community within techno-society*. Peter Lang.

Woehler, M., Floyd, T. M., Shah, N., Marineau, J. E., Sung, W., Grosser, T. J., Fagan, J., & Labianca, G. (2021). Turnover during a corporate merger: How workplace network change influences staying. *Journal of Applied Psychology, 106*(12), 1939–1949. https://doi.org/10.1037/apl0000864

Wombacher, K. A., Harris, C. J., Bucker, M.M., Frisby, B., & Limperos, A. M. (2017). The effects of computer-mediated anxiety on student perceptions of instructor behaviors, perceived learning, and quiz performance. *Communication Education, 66*(3), 299–312. http://doi.org/10.1080/03634523.2016.1221511

Wood, J. V. (1996). What is social comparison and how should we study it? *Personality and Social Psychology Bulletin, 22*, 520–537. https://doi.org/10.1177/0146167296225009

Xiao, H., Zhang, Z., & Zhang, L. (2021). An investigation on information quality, media richness, and social media fatigue during the disruptions of COVID-19 pandemic. *Current Psychology, 42*, 2488–2499.

Yang, M. (2020). Painful conversations: Therapeutic chatbots and public capacities. *Communication and the Public, 5*, 35–44. https://doi.org/10.1177/2057047320950636

Yang, S.-Y., Wang, Y.-C., Lee, Y.-C., Lin, Y.-L., Hsieh, P.-L., & Lin, P.-H. (2022). Does smartphone addiction, social media addiction and/or internet game addiction affect adolescents' interpersonal interactions? *Healthcare, 10*, 963. https://doi.org/10.3390/healthcare10050963

Yee, N., & Bailenson, J. N. (2007). The Proteus effect: The effect of transformed self-representation on behavior. *Human Communication Research, 33*, 271–290.

Yee, N., Bailenson, J. N., & Ducheneaut, N. (2009). The Proteus effect: Implications of transformed digital self-representation on online and offline behavior. *Communication Research, 36*, 285–312.

Young, N. L., Kuss, D. J., Griffiths, M. D., & Howard, C. J. (2017). Passive Facebook use, Facebook addiction, and associations with escapism: An experimental vignette study. *Computers in Human Behavior, 71*, 24–31. http://dx.doi.org/10.1016/j.chb.2017.01.039

Zhong, Q., & Frey, S. (2022). Institutional similarity drives cultural similarity among online communities. *Scientific Reports, 12*(18982). https://doi.org/10.1038/s41598-022-23223-8

Index

Milton Keynes UK
Ingram Content Group UK Ltd.
UKHW051222210524
442742UK00012B/7